NATION & CITIZEN

IN THE

DOMINICAN REPUBLIC,

1880–1916

NATION & CITIZEN

IN THE

DOMINICAN REPUBLIC,

1880–1916

Teresita Martínez-Vergne

The University of North Carolina Press

CHAPEL HILL

© 2005 The University of North Carolina Press
All rights reserved
Designed by Rebecca Gimenez
Set in Monotype Baskerville
by Keystone Typesetting, Inc.
Manufactured in the United States of America

Publication of this work was supported by a
grant from Macalester College.

The paper in this book meets the guidelines
for permanence and durability of the Committee
on Production Guidelines for Book Longevity of
the Council on Library Resources.

Library of Congress Cataloging-in-Publication Data
Martínez Vergne, Teresita.
Nation and citizen in the Dominican Republic,
1880–1916 / by Teresita Martínez-Vergne.
p. cm.   Includes bibliographical references and index.
ISBN 0-8078-2976-5 (cloth: alk. paper)
ISBN 0-8078-5636-3 (pbk.: alk. paper)
1. Nationalism—Dominican Republic—History.
2. Dominican Republic—Intellectual life.
3. Dominican Republic—Politics and government—1844–1930.
4. National characteristics, Dominican.
5. Citizenship—Dominican Republic.
I. Title.
F1938.4.M338 2005   972.93′04—dc22
2005005928

cloth * 09 08 07 06 05   5 4 3 2 1

paper * 09 08 07 06 05   5 4 3 2 1

CONTENTS

ILLUSTRATIONS

TABLES

PREFACE

H istorians of nationalism, traditional and postmodern, will recognize the questions that drive this book. Among other things, I am
interested in examining the process by which Dominican intellectuals at the turn of the twentieth century forged a common sense of purpose
that befitted what they felt were new circumstances—hence their conviction
that the time was ripe for sweeping change. This line of inquiry follows a long
succession of theoretical explorations on the rise of nation-states and on the
development of a sense of nationhood in the age of modernity. For the Latin
American case specifically, scholars have asked: How did elites embrace the
masses as part of the nation they set out to construct, once independence was
achieved and the former colonies became states in their own right? In the
Dominican Republic, this query becomes complicated by the fact that the
state was formally inaugurated in 1844 with independence from Haiti, and
yet political leaders compromised the island's sovereignty repeatedly by inviting foreign powers to rule over the country until 1865. Moreover, elites did
not engage in deliberate nation-building until much later—perhaps 1879,
with the ascent of the *Azul* (Blue) brand of Liberalism to power, or as late as
1899, with the death of President Ulises Heureaux. The shaping of collective
notions of national identity, then, involved the recasting of metropolitan
representations of colonial (and postcolonial) Dominicans and the creation
of useful self-images on the part of the country's elite late in the course of
state formation.[1]

A number of assumptions underlie the statements above, and I must
clarify my take on the processes scholars of nationalism have identified as
central. It goes without saying that I am concerned with the socially constructed aspects of national identity—with the function of men of letters in
the forging of a sense of nationhood, with the collaborations of men of state,
and with those actions of their "inferiors" that contributed to this process.

Emphasizing as I do the subjective nature of nationalism, I see it also as an ongoing practice, one in which powerful (because educated) actors project an inevitably self-serving discourse meant to manipulate their subordinate (and illiterate) associates, who are themselves deploying their own notions of participation and fairness through daily interactions. As did Florencia Mallon when she enhanced our understanding of hegemony as both process and result,[2] I privilege the negotiated aspects of nation-building, as shaped by forces both internal to the Dominican Republic and outside the national territory.[3] In denying that any one actor had primacy in this eminently fluid context, I am also looking at the "articulations that support and fracture the nation," at the several locations from which historical players sought to constitute the national community.[4] The working out of the "invention" that is Dominicanness, then, is for my purposes predicated on the material context in which human beings interacted and thus straddles the ideological plane that elites presumably inhabited and the lived experience that supposedly solely fueled the behavior of their lesser neighbors. In this book, nationalism is invented, always underway, both verbal and physical, and definitely political.[5]

A secondary premise in this book is that the construction of the nation takes place at many levels, some—most—of which I only make a passing reference to. One such context that seems central to the Dominican case in the early twentieth century is the relationship between the Dominican Republic and the United States, between the political leadership of both countries, and between the ideologues of each. Having adopted Mallon's notion of the process of nation-building in Latin America as a "struggle over citizenship and liberty" to gain "nationalism and democracy," the looming presence of North American political and ideological interests in the region has to be taken into account. If, internally, states have erected a political edifice that they deploy as natural to dominate their citizens, the same process, I believe, was taking place internationally in this period as the United States installed in the Caribbean its own ideas of democratic government and citizen participation with the weight of universal principles. This is not to say that the United States imposed wholesale its vision of participatory politics and free market capitalism on the Dominican Republic. As is true of the state-level workings of hegemony, what gets elevated as a common project exists through coercion and consent, and negotiation and contention were part and parcel of the process of national anticolonial affirmation for Dominicans.[6]

Dominican historiography has generally treated the development of national consciousness as a spontaneous process, activated in the heart of a community bound by territory, language, and culture; fixed in time and place; and hegemonic in its outcome. Several scholars have set out to determine precisely when and how Dominican national identity was formed. They have come up with numerous dates or historical moments and an even greater variety of events that promoted, until it was achieved, a sense of "*lo dominicano*" (that which is Dominican). For these authors, the sources of Dominicanness tended to be heroic occurrences in which the best of the national character was exposed and subsequently permeated the whole of society. In one familiar account, the sequence of events is strictly chronological. In the early nineteenth century, residents of the eastern part of the island disassociated themselves from the revolting slaves of the west and gravitated toward "civilized" Europe (France, and when possible, Spain). Rejecting annexation and finding that independence was a viable option, Dominicans turned their backs on Spain after 1865. Threatened by the United States in the early 1900s, a virulent nationalism, with renewed Hispanic roots, dominated the first half of the twentieth century.[7]

Another current of thought has fixated on the geographical origins of Dominicanness. The leading candidate for the birthplace of the national character is the rich agricultural north, the Cibao, the prosperous land of moderate-sized tobacco holdings, owned by established families of Spanish descent, who were the mainstay of Liberal politics. Although José Joaquín Hungría Morell favors the inclusion of the capital, Santo Domingo, as a player in the process, interpretations that highlight the affluence, the whiteness, and the nonimmigrant origins of the inhabitants of Santiago and the surrounding countryside have to this day held more sway in popular conceptions of what is truly Dominican. A recent addition to the "geographical location" variety of a sense of nationalism has been Lauren Derby's work, which pinpoints the Dominico-Haitian border as the cradle of national identity, "the site where power relations on the island have been measured throughout the centuries." In her provocative article on the changing concept of *raza* (in its common usage, as nation) in the early twentieth century, Derby recounts the story of how Haitians became "foreigners" who threatened the Dominican nation precisely at the time dictator Rafael Leonidas Trujillo was beginning to include border Dominicans in the body politic.[8]

A sizable group of writers leans toward broader cultural interpretations of the phenomenon, even if only at the theoretical level. They define "the nation" as a collectivity, attached to a particular geographic area, with common blood ties, values, beliefs, history, and goals. Oftentimes implicit in this interpretation is the notion, both current and attributed to previous generations, that Dominicans acquired a sense of self as a function of the proximity of Haiti, its racial, cultural, and national "other" for the entire nineteenth century.[9] A sense of nationhood that was based, as these explanations suggest, on intrinsic traits that either emerged at crucial points in time, were a function of geography, or simply evolved through accidents of time and place appears permanent and unchanging. In these broadly defined conceptions, national identity is constructed as an organic occurrence, prompted by popular events or reinforced by everyday practice and firmly in place. In this scheme, the initial sources of existing notions of *lo dominicano* are rarely questioned, and the functions of current conceptualizations remain unchallenged.

There is a practical reason for this elaborate, and seemingly anti-intellectual, search for the roots of Dominican national identity. Trujillo, the darkest political figure in Dominican history, and his minions were responsible in the 1930s for the most brilliant exposition of the essence of Dominicanness. Based as it was on a fabled Hispanic heritage and on a jingoistic rejection of Haitians, and deployed by Trujillo's own intelligentsia, this brand of national consciousness succeeded in incorporating the generality of the population in a common discourse of progress and therefore installing Trujillo as the founder of the Dominican nation.[10] Progressive intellectuals, outraged by what they viewed as a flagrant rewriting of the past for Trujillo's benefit, set out after his assassination to set the record straight for posterity. Marxists endeavored to discover traces of a national bourgeoisie in the early twentieth century that, if not willing to mobilize the common folk for a more equitable future, was capable of standing up to the United States, whose increasingly overbearing presence in Dominican economic, financial, and political affairs threatened Dominican sovereignty.[11] More recently, writers have focused on the role of the intelligentsia at the turn of the last century in building the discursive apparatus of nationalism.[12] As did others in the past, including Trujillo's ideologues, these authors constructed a national history that traced the development of Dominicanness through a series of momentous circumstances that shaped it until complete. In their writings, the process appears inevitable, and the historical actors that participated in key events play their parts as required. Perhaps unaware that they themselves had an agenda as they, too, constructed history, Dominican scholars since the 1960s have also created a notion of nationalism as instinctive (not artificial), disinterested (not for direct political application), generalized (not limited to a specific group), and static (unchanging).

Two very recent contributions to the conversation about nationalism, modernity, and citizenship come from outside the Dominican Republic. Richard Lee Turits and Pedro San Miguel have each revisited the Trujillato with fresh eyes in search of both the discursive and the material bases for the dictator's longevity in power. The inclusion of the peasantry in the polis and in the discourse of progress, both conclude, explains Trujillo's long-lasting political appeal. The "poetic" national project of the early twentieth century received a "political injection" in the 1930s, and so, according to these authors, the largest component of the Dominican population that remained outside the formal political apparatus was brought into the fold—"domesticated," to use a word now part of the Dominicanist lexicon. According to these authors, it was Trujillo who succeeded in inserting the final piece into the national puzzle: the incorporation of the peasantry into the political life of the country.[13]

Contrary to the foregoing, I argue in this book that a generation of men actively shaped Dominican turn-of-the-century nationalism by launching a comprehensive and forward-looking discourse, which they hoped would capture the imagination of the population as a whole at a critical juncture of Dominican political, economic, and social life. This intellectual elite, I maintain, found little inspiration in the events that punctuated the country's past—the so-called Haitian domination, the flirtations with European states with a view to protectorate status, the return to the Spanish fold, the constant civil strife after the restoration of the republic—and concentrated instead on outlining a brilliant future, based on the far-reaching changes they promoted. Their definition of what constituted the nation was, moreover, inclusive, which is not to say that men of letters embraced indiscriminately the West Indian and Haitian migrants, the working class, and the bourgeois women, who made up the country's lesser inhabitants. On the contrary, these communities were to be incorporated into the national project, first textually and then practically, once their loyalties were reorganized, their minds educated, and their behavior made to conform.[14]

I concur with Dominican historians in the significance of the "common people" (el pueblo llano) in shaping the national discourse and in forging their own variants of political and cultural processes, but the conclusions I reach might appear unconventional by Dominican standards. I give proof in this book for a popular basis for nationalism, which I call in this manifestation "citizenship" and which I locate in the cities. It was urban centers that contained the combination of cultural accoutrements (the schools, the newspapers, the economic opportunities) and human material (some of it from the much-maligned countryside) necessary for "civilization" (read "citizenship"). Independently of the existence of deliberate efforts to incorporate or co-opt their interests by higher-ups, I submit, the urban underclasses persistently acted to preserve their well-being in the face of official or peer attempts, deliberate or unintentional, to limit their activity—these were nothing if not exercises in participatory politics, rooted in an as yet un-developed notion of entitlement. Ultimately, in viewing Dominican identity as a mutable (therefore inclusive) fellowship of values (and not an exclusive community of descent, based on fixed, distinguishing qualities, such as language, culture, and history), I deviate from the more common understanding of Dominicanness. I am studying here elite and popular struggles to gain ground within the power structure in a particular time and space, and not quintessential traits that endure unspoiled in the ageless Dominican character or impositions from above that determined the shape of the future.[15]

Other elements in my analysis deserve explanation. I refer to the architects of the national project variously as an "intellectual elite," "political thinkers," "*letrados*" or "men of letters," "the intelligentsia," and other labels that seem to correspond to the processes under scrutiny. In all cases, I want to evoke the image of a self-proclaimed intellectual leadership, legitimated almost entirely by their possession of knowledge, and intent on contributing to the task of nation-building through their written and oral interventions on current debates.[16] Likewise, I use the terms "subaltern," "the underclasses," "the urban working class," "the popular classes," the elite's "inferiors," and similar ones for those groups that were denied citizen status, in the sense that they were excluded from participation in political and social intercourse and also were considered incapable of contributing to the national project.[17] The state apparatus, the third player in the construction of a modern national image, appears variously in the guise of the municipal authorities, the town council, the police, or the republican guard; that is, any position from which flowed the official discourse of law and order. This book comes back time and again to situations in which these groups colluded with each other, co-opted one or several of the other players, and interacted directly or in passing to forge what we could call a common sense of purpose.

The binding notion of the future as the effort of today's citizens did not originate in the early twentieth century nor with Trujillo's henchmen. Neither was it the creation of more recent scholarship, which, in deploying a glorious representation of the national self, concealed the hand of a new generation of men and women of letters in it. Rather, I believe, it is a work permanently in progress, fashioned by various social forces at different times in Dominican history and in the writing of that history. Whether it calls upon fictional memories or insists on a total makeover, imports alien ideas or works at the grass roots, imposes or negotiates, it is a process that is ongoing and susceptible to human action.

In reconstructing this undertaking by elite and subaltern in turn-of-the-century Santo Domingo, I thus embrace the task of the historian, as understood by Gail Hershatter. She holds that "reaching for the past is an interactive process that constitutes even as it purports to retrieve." Recovering subaltern subjectivity, I am aware, is a form of political work. So is critiquing liberal, bourgeois, and modern conceptualizations of knowledge and projects as well as elite representations of the subaltern, as I try to do here. I am hoping that my work, as Ileana Rodríguez proposes in the introduction to *The Latin American Subaltern Studies Reader*, will offer "new ways of approaching some of the riddles created by the incapacity of bourgeois culture to think about its own conditions of discursive production."[18]

I AM PROUD TO HAVE completed this book with inspiration from myriad sources—paper, electronic, and human. I have been collecting information and processing it since 1996, when I first spent a semester's leave in the Dominican Republic. At that time and in subsequent visits, I had the good fortune of getting to know, to a greater or lesser degree, people whose knowledge, friendship, and assistance I am grateful for. Among them are José Leopoldo Artiles, Roberto Cassá and Angeles Calzada, Raymundo González and Córdula Ammann, Benita Hernández Alcalá, Eddy Jaquez, Nilda Lebrón Montas, Mu-Kien Adriana Sang, Cyrus Veeser and Lilian Bobea, and Selma Zapata. During all of these years, people in the Twin Cities saw me through good and bad times. I found my colleagues at Macalester College supportive, and my neighbors and friends patient, and vice versa. Mahmoud El-Kati, Rhonda Gonzales, David Itzkowitz, Herta Pitman, Peter Rachleff, Emily and Norman Rosenberg, Paul Solon, Yue-Him Tam, and Peter Weisensel encouraged me in the Department of History. Outside that secure perimeter, Miggie Cramblitt, Val Evje and Gerald Barnes, Donna Fehrenbach, Ruthann Godellei and Craig Upright, Sherry Gray and David Blaney, Lois and Jeff Knutson, Wendy Malinsky, Anna Meigs, Ramón Rentas, Maddie Sachs and William Weisert, Mary Ann Sachs and Bob, Pia Sass and Kris Lockhart, Jan Serie, and Jim and Anita Von Geldern offered encouragement, good laughs, and perspective. David Sisk, Mike Nelson, and Mark Lewis were always there for me when my computer misbehaved. And I always felt supported by Provost Dan Hornbach, whose integrity and hard work I value highly. Several students carried out top-quality work for me as this book came together. I appreciate the efforts of Shaina Aber, Sheeba Jacobs, Danielle Maestretti, Anna Meyer, Ironelly Mora, Raphael Simono, Inés Tófalo, and Kate Villarreal. One of the two anonymous readers selected by UNC Press to review my book manuscript went above and beyond the call of duty—to him goes my gratitude and admiration.

I spent my sabbatical at the National Humanities Center and in wonderful Carrboro, North Carolina, in academic year 2002–2003. Here, Barbara and Rob Anderson, Kathryn Burns, Karen Carroll, Sherman Cochran, Bob Connor, Teresa Chapa, Betsy Dain, Ginger Frost, Linda and Maddie Haake, Grace Hale, Susan Hirsch, Lloyd Kramer, Elaine Maisner, Kent Mullikin, Joanne Rappaport, Eliza Robertson, Paula Sanders, Moshe Sluhovsky and Jim Green, Erin Smith, Faith Smith, Helen Solterer, Griet Vankeerberghen and Tom Beghin, Oscar and August, and Lois Whittington critiqued my work, went out with me for coffee or walks, danced with me, shared stories about their work, commiserated over U.S. foreign policy, and generally listened and kept me company. Here and in other research locations, I have relied on the efficient services of library and archival staffs—at the DeWitt Wallace Library at Macalester, the Sala Dominicana at the general library of the Universidad Autónoma de Santo Domingo (UASD), the Biblioteca Nacional, the Archivo General de la Nación, and the Hispanic Division at the Library of Congress. Among the people whose help I took advantage of in these repositories were Aaron Albertson, Julio Enrique del Campo Castillo, Alfonso Ferreras, Adalgiza, Beth Hillemann, and Amy Puryear. I should also thank the American Philosophical Society, the National Endowment for the Humanities, and Macalester College for several summers' worth of research and a sabbatical leave dedicated to writing. Anyone who has written a book knows how much goes into it—it really is the collective effort of many people and institutions, and I have been fortunate to count on all of the above.

There is another category of people, who cannot be sorted out by locale, or type of assistance rendered, or professional or personal support. For the most part, the people who follow supported me from a distance, in ways they cannot imagine, sometimes simply by being there at the right time. They are Idsa Alegría, Nigel and Ellie Bolland, Arturo José García and Tere Palou, Roberto García and Astrid Martínez, Mercedes Goyco, Franklin Knight, Peggy McLeod, Gonzalo Martínez-Lázaro, Noel Martínez-Vergne, Marina I. Martínez-Vergne and Thomas Stepka, Gonzalo Martínez-García, Chris O'Brien, Lourdes Rojas, Hildy Teegen, and Gloria Vergne and Rafael Rivero.

Two thousand four was a year of loss for me. My father, Gonzalo Martínez-Lázaro, and a good friend, Maddie Sachs, passed away in the first half of the year. I was fortunate to recover another good friend I was afraid I had lost, Pia Sass, as the year closed. I dedicate this book to Papi, Maddie, Pia, and, as always, to my daughter, Irene, who is my support and joy.

NATION & CITIZEN

IN THE

DOMINICAN REPUBLIC,

1880–1916

INTRODUCTION

Intellectuals and the Formation of

the National Character

In the last years of the nineteenth century, the Dominican Republic
brimmed with hopes for political, social, and economic renovation. The
economic growth that political stability had stimulated, beginning in
1879, especially evident in the nascent sugar industry, inspired many to imagine a brighter future for the island. Dominicans of all walks of life, who had
no choice but to concede that the hated dictator Ulises Heureaux was partly
responsible for the country's modernization, knew from experience that
there were alternatives to the repression and venality that characterized his
rule. Lilís, as the president was popularly known, was assassinated in 1899,
making way for a core of highly committed political thinkers to promote
their agenda. Already they had mapped out the blueprint for the island's
progress and had professed their allegiance to modern agricultural techniques, secular education, and political participation as the cornerstones of
the new nation. Espousing Liberal principles like their precursors in the last
twenty years, these advocates of reform endeavored to develop the notion of
hardworking, peaceful, voting citizens as the key to the future. Progress, as
they envisioned it, was the concerted effort of a political and intellectual elite,
with regulated input from common people.[1]

Neither the transformation experienced nor the ideology of progress was
exempt from conflict. Sugar had brought, along with economic prosperity,
the dispossession of peasants in some areas, the importation of workers from
the West Indies, foreign investment, and other changes about which even the
proponents of modernization were uneasy. The chance to redefine the political framework of the state was also compromised by the growing role of the

United States in Caribbean internal affairs and its overpowering influence in Dominican fiscal policy. As I will argue in this chapter and the next, the ideology of progress and its practical application, the development of a list of traits that collectively defined the national character, were colored by these circumstances. As a result, the Dominican intellectual elite was careful to subsume and render neutral the thorny issues of race, class, and gender in their inventory of attributes necessary to renovate the country.[2]

MEN OF LETTERS

The self-proclaimed intellectual leadership that emerged in the Dominican Republic at the turn of the last century tried to follow the steps Angel Rama masterfully described for Mexico and Argentina in his seminal work, *The Lettered City*. In these countries, as in most of Latin America, the enlightened notion that an intellectual elite was best suited to run the country took root at independence. Along with the wholesale adoption of the most current social, economic, and political doctrines, this idea required major transformations in the material and ideological outlook of the former Spanish American colonies. A more accessible educational system and the widespread circulation of the printed word, nineteenth-century reformers believed, would set the stage for the appearance of the "total" intellectual, whose legitimacy rested on his knowledge alone (and not on wealth or family connections). Indeed, as reading publics increased, so too did the possibility of political dialogue and consequently of supporting oneself from written work, independent of government sinecures. Auspiciously, newspapers proliferated in the cities, even as most of the population remained illiterate, and "the philosophical development of a political opposition" was apparently becoming a reality. By the end of the nineteenth century, according to Rama, the class of men who had earlier combined wealth, political clout, and a university education to influence the course of events relied solely on their claim to higher learning to opine, direct, criticize, and propose.[3]

Regardless of whether this process was as seamless in the more developed countries of Latin America as Rama would have us believe, it was certainly a more conflicted affair in the Dominican Republic. Despite the aspirations of the local intellectual elite, the Dominican experience fits better Julio Ramos's "*desencuentros*" (run-ins) scheme for plotting the activities of intellectuals in Latin America. Ramos correctly characterizes the region as unevenly modernized, so that the divorce of intellectual activity from economic life or political happenings was difficult at best, chimerical in most cases. Intellectuals in the Dominican Republic were not "continuously in control of written expression," to use Ramos's words, despite their best efforts. They continued to rely on government appointments and do so even today, not only because their livelihood was "precarious" but also because the state was, after all, the medium through which some of their ideas could become a reality.[4]

This does not mean, however, that the island's educated elite did not see itself as what Nicola Miller calls an "intelligentsia" and adopted as a mission the development of a common sense of nationhood. Like its counterparts in the American continent, the intellectual class of the Dominican Republic believed itself to be especially capable of providing the theoretical under-pinnings for a new social and economic order and felt compelled to set the standards for political conduct. As did Liberal governments all over Latin America, Dominican administrations began to treat universal secular schooling as a priority in the development contest. The political use of language would no longer be the prerogative only of those who could afford to attend private schools or learn from tutors, but of all those who could read the paper and so engage in political discourse. A contemporary, José Ramón López, called this phenomenon "corporatist elitism" to highlight both the collective aspects of the "civilizing" activity and the superior standpoint that legitimated it. The creation of "languages-of-power," which acquired status by association that was ultimately politicized, occurred in the Dominican Republic at the end of this period, just as other circumstances intimated the promise of change.[5]

Dominican literati utilized several media to disseminate knowledge, de-bate issues, and also amuse themselves. Beginning in the 1880s, a normal school as well as public primary and secondary schools for boys and girls emphasized the value of scientific, secular education, from which cohorts of young men and women, notably Salomé Ureña de Henríquez and her stu-dents, benefited. The advantages of associating with like-minded individuals had been recognized since the founding of the first sugar mills, and cultural, charitable, mutual-aid, religious, commercial, and sporting societies existed in Santo Domingo, the capital, and San Pedro de Macorís, a booming sugar town, throughout this period. Literary clubs organized "cultural evenings" in which local or visiting artists presented their work for discussion.[6] The estab-lishment of newspapers and the publication of magazines presumably di-rected at a general readership interested in politics, the economy, literature, and social events created additional avenues for the circulation of ideas of national import. At the turn of the century, a plethora of publications—*Nuevo Réjimen, Renacimiento, El Eco de la Opinión, Mireya* (in San Pedro de Macorís), alongside the old-timer *El Listín Diario*—circulated in the capital and the larger cities. The editors of these publications, men such as José Ricardo

Roques, Raúl Abreu, Manuel Flores Cabrera (a Venezuelan political exile), Francisco Gregorio Billini, and Rafael Justino Castillo, and one woman, Petronila Angélica Gómez, were prominent figures in social circles and, in some cases, in public affairs as well. In many instances, the same men who wrote reasoned editorials on the suitability of alternative political and economic arrangements for the emerging state also published moving fiction and poetry whose literary value was insignificant.[7] As was the case in the United States and Western Europe, the Dominican journalistic establishment became the instrument of the educated and the civic-minded to express their ideas, to influence others, and to entertain.[8]

The men who jump-started the conversation regarding the country's potential and so engaged in an ambitious exercise in self-reflection belonged to a growing class of families, which can be dubbed "middle class," insofar as the priority of the parents was their children's schooling, whether they had the economic resources or made every sacrifice to achieve that goal. In either case, the young men (and a few women) who became the intellectual cream of the Dominican Republic obtained a privileged education, in some cases advanced or professional degrees, which both facilitated their entry into the old-time elite circles that combined wealth, politics, and status and legitimated their voices in such spheres of influence. Out of this cadre of new professionals rose men of letters who were not distinguished gentlemen who read for leisure, but who were committed instead to writing on behalf of the majority of the population, increasingly called "the masses."[9]

Eugenio María de Hostos (1839–1903), the Puerto Rican sage who inspired an entire generation of Dominican thinkers in the 1880s and beyond, received a liberal education in San Juan and Bilbao and a law degree in Madrid. He studied and traveled in the United States, France, and Chile before settling in Santo Domingo in 1875. He advanced many progressive causes (the rights of workers, equal educational opportunities for women, the abolition of slavery) but dedicated his life to the dream of an Antillean confederation, free from Spain. To this end, he wrote extensively, spoke publicly, and founded schools, newspapers, and literary societies.

Francisco Henríquez y Carvajal (1859–1935) came from a well-to-do family and studied medicine in Paris after working closely with Hostos in setting up primary schools for boys and girls. He was outspoken against the Heureaux dictatorship and so left the country, later returning to become president shortly before the U.S. invasion in 1916. His brother Federico (1848–1952), another Hostos "collaborator" (they refused to be called disciples), participated both in the literary scene and in political circles. Among the posts he held were director of the normal school, rector of the university, member of

Congress, and president of the Supreme Court. He was a good friend of José Martí, the Cuban nationalist, and was offered the presidency of the Dominican Republic during one of the impasses prior to the U.S. occupation.

Francisco Moscoso Puello (1885–1959), a physician and educator, wrote a seminal novel about the working class in the sugar industry and serialized his "Cartas a Evelina" (Letters to Evelina), identifying in them for his presumably European bride-to-be the qualities and flaws of the Dominican Republic and its people. Emiliano Tejera (1841–1923) was instrumental in establishing the Instituto Profesional in 1866 but is better known for his role as minister of foreign affairs during Ramón Cáceres's tenure as president (1905–11), when the Dominican Republic permitted the United States to set up a receivership general to collect customs duties for the purposes of foreign debt repayment. Tejera wrote extensively about the formation of the Dominican character vis-à-vis the despised Haitians. Pedro Francisco Bonó (1828–1906) hailed from a rural middle-class northern family and served as a local judge in his home jurisdiction. Whereas he embraced many of the tenets of Liberalism and got involved in national politics, he evokes more often notions of civic integrity and selfless patriotism, especially as the author of sociological tracts in defense of the Dominican small landholder and in opposition to reckless modernization.

Américo Lugo (1870–1952) was trained as a lawyer and wrote from this perspective about the duties of government toward the people it represents, the illegitimacy of the U.S. intervention, and the capacity of Dominicans to govern themselves. Federico García Godoy (1857–1924) combined, as many of these men did, fiction writing with a current political agenda. He wrote historical novels as well as newspaper articles, both of which sought to bring to light contemporary issues that merited public discussion. José Ramón López (1866–1922) might be the only one in the group who did not have a university education, as he had to work as a child to put himself through primary and secondary school. He was outspoken in newspapers and journals against Heureaux and had to leave the country from 1885 to 1887. In the early twentieth century, he entered public service, holding the posts of principal of the normal school, director of statistics, and senator, during which time he published treatises on the problem of political violence and the condition of the peasantry. These three men—Lugo, García Godoy, and López—much more so than the others, stand out for their pessimism when dissecting the potential of the country and its people for overcoming the obstacles to progress.

Given their class backgrounds and their social contacts, one would assume that the Dominican intelligentsia spoke for the interests of a modernizing bourgeoisie and promoted its cause before the state. This would have been the case in industrialized European countries at the time and earlier too. But the Dominican Republic, along with what Antonio Gramsci called the peripheral states of Europe, could not count on an organized bourgeois class whose interests the intellectual elite could respond to, because no such class existed. Rather, as Gramsci described the situation, the modern state had come from above and depended on foreign capital supported by a strong military, a construction not unlike the Dominican reality. It had been only recently that the island's economy had produced a sustained output, and this—in the form of an agricultural export, sugar—was controlled by foreigners. The national bourgeoisie-to-be, if it could have been tapped at all, resided in the northern tobacco lands, whose residents had supported the Liberal governments earlier in the century. But it had never coalesced so as to have a coherent program of reforms or agenda for action. Dominican intellectuals, then, had no social base from which to act, no civil society to mobilize or in whose stead to exist in "productive tension" with the state.[10]

The Dominican intelligentsia's relationship with the state is in other ways less than precise. Although the integrity of their labor depended on their autonomy from the state, they continued to depend on the government for "employment," in the sense that it was their function to critique it, either from within or at the margins. Several of the writers listed above accepted positions within administrations, and they did so in a particularly tumultuous period during which, presumably, they should not have risked compromising their ideals. The decision to collaborate made perfect sense, if one considers the context. The Liberal interventionist state was, after all, the sine qua non of the modernist project—it was the responsibility of the apparatus of government to correct the imbalances that the invisible hand inevitably produced. Intuitively, maybe, Dominican intellectuals perceived the state as a political actor with whom they shared goals, and they promptly surmised that the inchoate bourgeoisie had little to offer by way of ideas or economic support. They might have been correct in their assessment but ignored the dangers of becoming the co-opted supporters or ritual opponents of a strong state. Thus, the notion of an independent thinker, an impartial social critic by virtue of his isolation—Gramsci's "traditional" intellectual—was a fiction. As if having no social base were not bad enough, Dominican intellectuals could easily become "the accomplices of the ruling group in the battle of hegemony."[11]

MEN OF SOCIAL ACTION

Unknowingly assisting the state in manipulating the citizenry, colluding with it to legitimize their social status, out of touch with social groups they should have spoken for, promoting the interests of a narrow band of self-seeking entrepreneurs—however they operated or whatever they thought they were achieving, Dominican intellectuals were of one mind regarding the philosophical tenets of their labor: they were Liberals, rational men, positivists. The Liberal agenda in Latin America repeated itself, with some local variations, across the continent and throughout the nineteenth century. The earliest manifestations of this modernizing trend were free trade, limited democracy, and their corollaries—secular education, administrative rationalization, infrastructure investment, and the more elusive nationalism, civic responsibility, individual liberties, property rights, and the like.[12] The Dominican Republic had already experienced a version of the practical application of these ideals on its own soil, with the *Azul* (Blue) administrations of Gregorio Luperón (1879–80), Father Fernando A. Meriño (1880–82), Francisco Gregorio Billini and Alejandro Woss y Gil (1884–86), and Heureaux himself (1882–84, 1887–99).[13]

Hostos was the figure around whom these principles and their proponents converged, a stalwart defender of the most radical social transformations Dominicans had yet to come across. During the presidency of Luperón and Horacio Vásquez's stint in the executive (1899–1903, first as vice president and then as president), Hostos single-handedly laid the foundations for the public school system, advocating a positivist education, one free from the strictures of Catholicism and committed to scientific methods. With the motto "*civilización o muerte*" (civilization or death), he stressed the importance of hard work, that is, of economic pursuits grounded on scientific study—a connection he and his followers continued to make throughout this period. Like others at the time, Hostos was suspiciously watchful of developments in the nascent sugar industry; his preferred developmental strategy was diversified agriculture, in medium-sized private holdings, worked by immigrant families acquainted with modern cultivation methods, under government auspices, and with state financial support. To that end, he proposed a number of bills to Congress, which were heatedly debated in the press as well, a practice consistent with Hostos's own conviction regarding the benefits of informed discussions.[14]

As did Hostos, Bonó advanced from early on the notion that many and diverse newspapers would serve to promulgate opinions regarding current rulers, existing or potential government programs, and other issues of importance for the general public. He blamed bad government for the backwardness of the country and, pinning his hopes on the integrity of political processes, advocated respect for minority voices on the part of the powerful. Placing his trust in the peasantry, he was convinced that, once the rural population was educated, they could rightly participate in the political life of the country. He believed that the heart of the citizenry lay in the countryside and worried that divesting peasants of their communal lands, a position slightly at odds with the sacred Liberal principle of private property, was nothing short of eradicating the basis of nationhood.[15]

These men and others like them were almost fanatical advocates of education and employment as fundamental to the regeneration of society. They also exhibited the characteristic Liberal enthusiasm for the potential of humankind. One writer captured the general outlook of the moment in a sentence intended to challenge Dominicans to rise to the occasion: "[It] is unfortunately true, very true, that when societies abandon the noble exercise of their rights, substituting them with the enervating resignation of serfs, and with the clumsy negligence of savages, they lose the habit and the duty, of cultured and civilized societies, of looking after their great interests and of imposing their legitimate will on the uncurbed appetites of recklessness and blind ignorance."[16] Conceivably, Dominicans were not among this group and, using reverse logic, were intellectually prepared and eager to work together for a propitious future.

THE ECONOMIC BASE

Economically, there was also much to be hopeful for, due to the success of the sugar industry in generating wealth, both for the treasury and for the population as a whole. Production for export rose sharply from 1880 to 1916 (see Table 1), and investments in sugar reached $11 million (pesos, not dollars) as early as 1893. The first mills were established between 1879 and 1882, under the sponsorship of Liberal governments intent on taking advantage of the tumult caused in Cuba by the Ten Years' War. From that time onward, the vagaries of the market and the island's own paucity of resources resulted in unpredictable ups and downs, until the industry stabilized in the 1890s. The drop in prices in 1884 resulted in bankruptcy for several mills, but those that survived modernized and spread the risks by contracting with cane growers rather than taking on the cultivation and manufacturing aspects of production themselves. With the low wages that sugar mills offered (fifty centavos a day) in the early days and the availability of land at that time, there was not much incentive for Dominican peasants to abandon their land and work in the sugar fields. Their demands to be paid by the job, in fact, were countered with a vigorous program of importation of workers from the nearby British-owned islands, beginning in the 1880s. By 1893, with wages between two and three pesos per *tarea* (a unit of land equivalent to .16 acre), Dominican

TABLE I
Sugar Exports from the Dominican Republic
(in tons), 1880–1916

1880	7,000
1890	24,352
1905	48,169
1913	86,892
1916	144,911

SOURCE: Roberto Cassá, *Historia social y económica de la República Dominicana*, vol. 2 (Santo Domingo: Editora Alfa y Omega, 1992), 136.

peasants went in and out of sugar production irregularly to obtain cash. British West Indian workers, known derisively as *cocolos*, made up the majority of the labor force, especially during the harvest. Technological advances, mainly to save on labor costs, characterized the industry, and foreign capitalists, mostly Americans, increasingly invested in the Dominican Republic. Other signs of progress—such as railroads, the telegraph, electric lighting, and the like—accompanied or closely followed sugar. Without a doubt, the cane industry altered the relationship between land, labor, and capital and set the stage for further economic growth.[17]

These transformations, however, could not reverse overnight the downward trend that had marked Dominican fiscal policy both during the Heureaux presidency and in the turbulent years following it. In order to keep his modernization program afloat, Heureaux borrowed nationally, first from the northern tobacco producers and then from the southern sugar planters, and abroad from various European creditors, the most important of which was the Westendorp Company, based in Amsterdam. Unable to pay back old loans, he borrowed from new sources, until he was forced in 1893 to allow a number of American individuals and companies, associated as the San Domingo Improvement Company, to administer the European debt. As was the case with the Westendorp firm, "*la Improvement*," as Dominicans referred to the company, had control over the customshouse and in addition monopolized steamship service from New York to Santo Domingo and had enormous investments in the sugar industry. Lilís, having encumbered the country's finances beyond the point of recovery, tried to conceal the muddle by printing worthless paper money, which was rejected by the population. By 1897, the treasury was bankrupt, which did not prevent the president from ransacking its vaults for personal gain.[18]

The men that followed Lilís in office inherited an untenable situation that could hardly have been turned around. A feeble attempt to dislodge the Improvement Company from customs collection, and so repay European creditors directly, met with forceful opposition not just from the company but more important, from the U.S. government, which sought sole control of access to the Panama Canal area and thus feared that European lenders would collect what was owed them by force of arms.[19] By 1904, the Dominican government agreed to buy from the Improvement Company its numerous properties in the country, including the Ferrocarril Central (Central Railroad), from Santiago to Puerto Plata, for $4.5 million and to submit to the advice of a U.S. financial agent, without whose approval the island's treasury could not disburse any funds. In 1905, the direction of U.S. intervention became irreversible—the U.S. government took charge of all obligations of the Dominican Republic and collected customs duties, 45 percent of which would go to the Dominican treasury and 55 percent to pay creditors and customs personnel. The Dominican government could not alter its tariff structure nor enter into obligations without approval from the president of the United States. Although this agreement was not officially approved by the U.S. Senate nor satisfactory to the Dominican Republic or its creditors, it was honored until 1907, when the Dominico-American convention ratified its stipulations, basically making the Dominican Republic a U.S. protectorate. The only change to the fiscal status of the country as a receivership was that the debt was reduced to $17 million through negotiations with creditors and was paid by a U.S. bank, from which the Dominican Republic borrowed $20 million for debt repayment and public works.

The recent fiscal and financial history of the Dominican treasury left much to be desired. The country had given up more and more of its autonomy, first to a number of foreign creditors and then solely to the U.S. government. Sugar, although bringing much-needed revenues and the promise of renewed economic activity, came with strings attached in terms of both labor and capital. Still, precisely because private and public U.S. funds revitalized the Dominican economy, the expectation throughout all these years remained that the country would stand up on its own again.

POLITICAL ASPIRATIONS

The assassination of the reviled Heureaux made possible a political aperture that the Dominican intellectual class had been endeavoring to bring about for decades. Lilís was a Liberal positivist with authoritarian tendencies, not unlike his Mexican counterpart, Porfirio Díaz. He opened the country to foreign investment, showered upon his supporters concessions and public posts, and modernized agriculture. In the manner of the more ruthless strongmen that he epitomized, he also persecuted his enemies, traded the island's sovereignty for momentary financial gains, and made use of public monies as if they were personal funds. Although his administration was responsible for the installation of the sugar industry on Dominican soil and for the development of a local commercial sector, his elevation of person-alized local and regional strongman rule and his tenacious suppression of other viable power bases virtually eliminated the prospect of participatory politics. With his death, however, the Liga de Ciudadanos (Citizens' League) was founded with the objective of "inciting patriotism, civilization, civic commitment, and representative democracy." The more humane version of Liberalism, resolutely respectful of private property, committed to economic development, and intent on rationalizing political processes, would enter the political arena, as Lilís had promised upon his initial accession to power and the intelligentsia had clamored for ever since.[20]

The period that immediately followed Heureaux's assassination did not conform to these auspicious plans. Soon after his demise and after a brief period of political stability, Dominican politics erupted again into personalis-tic strife. Historians have characterized this period quite negatively. Valentina Peguero finds that the period's most prominent feature was "the alternation of provisional and constitutional governments, that follow[ed] each other in the midst of brusque and sudden changes." Ernesto Sagás believes the coun-try "fell back into a vicious circle of *caudillismo*, political instability, and economic indebtedness." Roberto Cassá, dismissing the possibility of bour-geois democracy, is even more pessimistic: "In truth, the alternatives were articulated [as] caudillista disorder or [Lilisista] tyranny." By reintroducing the specter of caudillismo to the Dominican political continuum, these au-thors are emphasizing the apparent lack of ideological content of the two parties that vied for power from 1899 to 1916, with a brief respite during Ramón Cáceres's tenure as president (1905–11). Conceivably, Horacio Vás-quez, Juan Isidro Jimenes, Desiderio Arias, Alejandro Woss y Gil, Carlos Mo-rales Languasco, and others acquired their following because of "their fame, the[ir] social rank, the[ir] regional origin, and their personal attributes."[21]

Without denying the political uncertainty that seventeen rulers in as many years can and did produce, it seems unfair to suggest that these men had no political program to offer the country and that their supporters were after nothing but the spoils of power. Undoubtedly, there was a lot of the latter— the wrangle over the administration of the Ferrocarril Central in 1913 is only one of a number of disputes over moneymaking enterprises or office-holding among opposing party associates.[22] And perhaps the factions were, in fact,

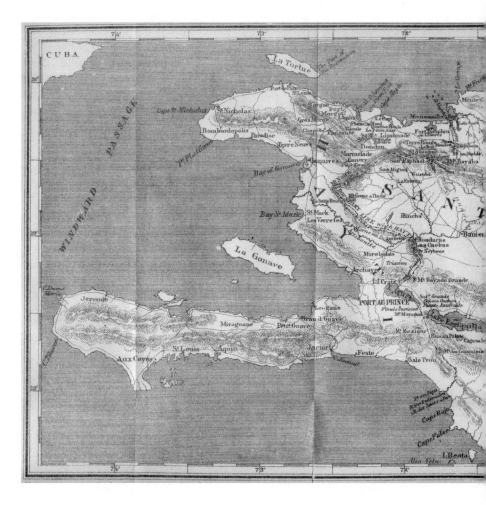

Map of the Dominican Republic, 1873. (Samuel Hazard, *Santo Domingo, Past and Present; with a Glance at Hayti* [New York: Harper & Brothers, 1873].)

virtually indistinguishable as their leaders tried equally forcefully and unsuccessfully to keep the United States at bay, to stabilize the country politically in the midst of civil war, and to launch economic reforms with an empty treasury and without full control over financial policy. But to reduce the practice of politics to popular appeal, or worse yet, to greed, says very little about the reasons why people took up arms and died to put their candidate in power. The continuous political discourse that men of letters engaged in during this period strongly indicates that ideology was the moving force behind many of the actions that together marked these years as chaotic and

disorganized. Far from being apolitical, I aver, Dominicans were in fact forging, with words and with arms, the future of the country.

THE IDEOLOGY OF PROGRESS

Socially, economically, and politically, Dominicans were ready for change, or so the intelligentsia assumed. The blueprint for development, on the island as in the rest of Latin America, rested on the notion that citizens could coalesce around a universal definition of progress. Agreement was impera-

TOP LEFT: Eugenio María de Hostos. (Enrique Deschamps, *La República Dominicana: Directorio y guía general* [Santiago de los Caballeros: Vda. de J. Cunill, Barcelona, n.d., ca. 1906–11], 156.) TOP RIGHT: Américo Lugo. (Archivo General de la Nación, Indice Fototeca, Colección Luis Mañón, *Blanco y Negro* [19 Oct. 1913].) BOTTOM LEFT: Emiliano Tejera. (Archivo General de la Nación, Indice Foto 12 [6], José G. García, A–Z, p. 1-21, photo 254.) BOTTOM RIGHT: José Ramón López. (Unidentified magazine page in Archivo General de la Nación.)

tive (and assumed) over the pivotal role of private property, the necessity of participatory democracy, and the capacity of individuals to contribute to the welfare of the country. The writings of the intelligentsia duly recognized the tension caused by the coexistence of *terrenos comuneros* (communal lands) and a capitalistic sugar industry. Newspaper editors, political essayists, and educators clamored for responsible government, attentive to popular needs and open to more than hegemonic interests. In the social sphere, some of these men insisted that respect for the common folk and state-sponsored education were essential in the construction of a cohesive Dominican nation. Some of the proponents of progress advocated the immigration of white settlers in family units, whose function was both to populate and make productive the vast expanses that remained unoccupied and to strengthen through miscegenation the "*raza criolla*" (Creole race), a term that underscored the national at the expense of the racial—the European and African mix that characterizes Dominicans, much to their dismay.[23] Although there were differences of opinion regarding the country's endowment and the appropriate strategy for development, turn-of-the-century intellectuals agreed that education, employment, democratic government, national sovereignty, freedom of the press, and private property held the promise of progress for the nation-in-the-making.

The task ahead, then, consisted of forming citizens where the very notions of social responsibility, economic justice, and political participation had been systematically suppressed. In this sense, the national project was both forward-looking and inclusive. Political thinkers refused to dwell on the past and issued ahead a plethora of prescriptions and proposed methods of application to propel the necessary changes. They were equally intent on producing a national community of interests based on a shared set of values to which everyone would subscribe—conceivably, the citizenry's commitment to progress. In the race for a functional nationalism, for a working definition of citizenship that embraced the entire Dominican population and projected their needs and aspirations to a higher plane, strategically political objectives prevailed over historically divisive racial, ethnic, class, or gender factors—at least for the intelligentsia.[24]

Rodolfo Domingo Cambiaso reinforced this shift in direction in his brief pamphlet on history writing, *Bosquejo sobre la historia* (1913). In it, he appeals to young people, the current keepers of the materials that their descendants will use to write the history of the country. The responsibility of "the present generation," he asserts, is to safeguard the historical record so that the next cohort, "*already* educated, conscious, impartial, will be able to relate to posterity really how the Dominican Republic was formed [*se hizo*], how great

[were] the struggles [*qué de luchas*], the injustices, and the vicissitudes that had to be endured so that it could become a Nation" (emphasis mine). In a modern concatenation of progress, fatherland, history, national heroes, and common people, he beseeched his readership:

> Engrave [the following words] in your memory, so that you will con-
> stantly have [them] in the eyes of the soul: "That all peoples undergo
> vicissitudes, some more than others, and that even at the edge of the
> abyss, apostles rise who teach a redemptive doctrine than cannot fade
> even though the preacher is crucified. The march of progress, there-
> fore, is inevitable, a fact that no one can ever disrupt. The important
> [thing] is to know how to appreciate those who want to lift the Father-
> land. . . . Because of that, now, full of faith and hope in the future, I
> conclude thinking: 'That a small group of young people, well inten-
> tioned and conscious, proposed to reform the country, and to them
> [we] owe the redemption of the People, who were capable of establish-
> ing the dignity of the Fatherland' " [*i a ellos se le debe la redención del
> Pueblo, que supo establecer la grandeza de la Patria*].

Nothing short of an "invented tradition," the history Cambiaso proposed would be written by men of letters, who would work with the historical symbols purposefully gathered for their use by their equally educated and politically committed predecessors, themselves the proponents of national progress and the servants of the fatherland.[25]

The discourse of progress collected the binding tenets of European Liber-alism and tried to apply them to the Dominican context. Finding the state of affairs on the island wanting, the intelligentsia hurried to prescribe formulas to facilitate the process of modernization, part and parcel of which were the activation of the citizenry and the rehabilitation of the economy. To rebuild the country, Dominican men of letters realized, the hardworking, peaceful, and committed citizens who would be its building blocks had yet to be formed. The architects of the national project, then, included in their plans the controlled inclusion of groups that had only recently been recognized as part of the polity and suspended judgment regarding their full incorporation into Dominican society. At no point did Dominican intellectuals, even those who were wary of modernization, consider rethinking existing social hier-archies, nor did they draw inspiration from the Dominican Republic's tur-bulent past. The intelligentsia deployed their schemes for progress with the assurance that education confers and constructed citizenship with the au-thority that political savvy facilitates.[26]

The architects of the ideology of progress, in their efforts to mold the country's first modern citizens, then, embarked on a more ambitious journey—the formation of the nation. Writings on Dominican nationalism have generally strung together a number of words and phrases and have used some interchangeably to describe aspects of the same process—the conception of national identity, the development of nationhood, the birth of the nation, the growth of patriotic sentiments, the ascendancy of a distinct cultural and ethnic community, a Dominican consciousness, racial solidarity, the national soul, Dominicanness, shared values, "*lo nacional*" (that which is national), linguistic ties, national unification, and so on. The reason for this semantic diversity is the emphasis that historians and sociologists (and also psychologists and anthropologists) have placed on lived experience (economic or political events that motivated people to coalesce); on the coincidence of place, language, culture, ethnicity, or race that some believe bind people together; or on the capacity of the state to manipulate either collective memory or future prospects so that a social group builds its desire to cooperate around a common past or around an unfolding destiny. Scholars, then, notwithstanding the influence that they reputedly can exert on our understanding of the factors and circumstances that link people politically, disagree widely with respect to the correct weight given each.

Dominican historians from the late nineteenth century onward have dedicated much effort to determining when and how a sense of nationalism developed. Manuel Arturo Peña Batlle and Pedro Troncoso Sánchez placed the moment as far back as the "*devastaciones*" of 1605, when the inhabitants of the northern part of the island rebelled against metropolitan instructions to evacuate the area to reduce contraband with the French. Hugo Tolentino Dipp, basing himself like Juan Pablo Duarte, the "father of the republic," on the factors that held common people together—language, territory, economy, and psychology—conferred nationhood on Dominicans at the time of their independence from Haiti (1844). The same was true for Carlos Dobal, who added, only to dismiss, the element of race; according to him, "black Spaniards" (Dominicans) fought against the French first, then against the Haitians, and out of these battles emerged the Dominican nation, which, bound by virtue, transcended color. As might be expected, Pedro Francisco Bonó was wedded to the juridical apparatus and dated the nation to the creation of the constitutional state. Pedro Henríquez Ureña emphasized a longer intellectual process that occurred throughout the nineteenth century among literate groups and the bourgeoisie, who professed the island's sovereignty as they fought for independence from Haiti and rejected foreign rule and its proponents. Roberto Cassá and Genaro Rodríguez examined a variety of elements from the sixteenth century onward to conclude that "in the nineteenth century, the emergence of the nation was conditioned by the leading role of the people in the struggle for self-determination." Frank Moya Pons placed the realization on the part of Dominicans that they were a nation in 1865, after the war to restore the republic to island statesmen, when Dominicans finally recognized, to paraphrase Moya Pons, that they were not Spanish, or French, or Haitian. Américo Lugo, one of the masterminds of the national project himself, negated the capacity of Dominicans to form a nation up until the early twentieth century but reversed himself promptly when the United States invaded in 1916. The list of scholars and their positions is extensive.[27]

The modern debate on the timing and the factors of Dominicanness, although seemingly an innocent intellectual pastime, was from the outset, as mentioned in the preface, a pointed political response to the discourse on nationhood deployed by the ideologues of the dictatorship of Rafael Leonidas Trujillo. Claiming itself responsible for restoring the material and cultural well-being of the country after the U.S. occupation, the Trujillo regime produced a version of Dominicanness that set the eastern part of the island apart from its neighbor. Joaquín Balaguer and Manuel Arturo Peña Batlle, Trujillo's deputies, gave the authoritarian state coherence by weaving an elaborate "official nationalist" tale of the development of nationalism, based on the cultural differences between Haitians and Dominicans. Vis-à-vis the historically fierce enemy and the more recent pathetic exploited worker, and for the benefit of their former imperial master, Dominicans declared themselves white (not black), Hispanic (not African), and Catholic (not Vodou practitioners). It was important for Trujillo to deploy a nationalist discourse that exalted Dominicans at the expense of Haitians. Claiming cultural (read "racial") superiority over his neighbors to the west facilitated his manipulation of Haitians as a cheap labor force; it also allowed him to more closely approximate Western notions of political order, economic organization, and social balance. Although many accepted, even embraced, this construction and still do today, others, respected scholars for the most part, have sought to qualify it, if not to debunk it.[28]

It is not my intention to directly engage Dominican scholars and statesmen on the details of the source of a sense of nationhood. Rather, I seek to understand how the intellectual and political elite in the early twentieth century constructed the nation, which they approached, I believe, in typical

Liberal fashion, as "a broad vision for organizing society, a project for collective identity based on the premise of citizenship—available to all, with individual membership beginning from the assumption of legal equality."[29] The mechanism they used to create a sense of belonging, I maintain, was not a shared past, but rather a common destiny. The Dominican past, in fact, might not have been "usable," as Louis Pérez points out for the Cuban case, in the sense that it could hardly inspire people to come together with a collective sense of purpose.[30] If anything, recalling the island's history would only prove advantageous if it served to change the people's "anachronistic way of being in the century of constant evolution and limitless progress," the twentieth century.[31] Political writers, as pointed out, chose not to revisit the past but rather to dwell on the advantages of a change in outlook. Shortly after Heureaux's assassination, for example, good citizens were judged by their active stance in favor of the fatherland. "Those who are interested in the future of the fatherland must work out of their space. The ones who write, the ones who work in factories, the ones who till the soil, must work, [and] not allow [themselves to be influenced] by those who want to lead them away from their labors. And when the moment comes to defend the fatherland from foreigners, then they must give their lives. But in the meantime, there's work to do."[32] A more comprehensive list of citizen duties (including honoring the "usable" past) constituted the formula for nationalism as Dominicans in 1913 celebrated the Restoration:

> [S]etting in the befitting place of honor the great men who dismantled the yoke of colonialism; taking a dignified and discerning attitude as an independent state; not thrashing with [our] feet what we make with [our] hands and have conceived in the heart; worshipping reverently our historical artifacts as a memory of our past and stimulating the development of our private and public wealth, without alien [notions] of any kind, wanting to fit in our milieus what is not ours nor [is] appropriate, we will create a NATIONALISM or we will recover it, because if at any time we had it [we have to] confess, with our contrite soul, that we have been gradually losing it, and the expansionist tentacles of the Northern octopus, acting as protector of its younger sisters, will end up sucking, if we do not thwart him in time, the last drop of blood of our dignity and our honor.[33]

Anti-imperialism, disguised as love of the fatherland above all else or brazenly forged out of anti-American sentiment, was a powerful force in defining the future of the country, as is evident from the statement above. Beginning with suspicions that the San Domingo Improvement Company was acquiring the foreign debt that the Dominican Republic owed a number of European creditors, Dominicans pointed to the "unsaintly intention of North Americans," about whom one writer commented, "once they clench [their fist], they don't let go." U.S. actions in Puerto Rico, Cuba, Nicaragua, and Panama alarmed some, but not others. As late as 1907, when the Dominico-American convention was signed, turning over customs collections and the management of debt service to the United States, Emiliano Tejera, minister of foreign relations, asserted that critics of the convention were wrong in thinking that the Dominican Republic was losing autonomy. Just the opposite, he argued; the island was protecting itself from continued indebtedness to other countries. Still, the weighty presence of the "American colossus" must have clued in Dominican intellectuals to the importance of "perform[ing] their capacity for civilization," to use Ada Ferrer's apt phrase for Cuba's parallel process of achieving status as a nation. As was true for many countries occupied by the United States in the early years of the twentieth century, the Dominican Republic had to prove itself worthy of joining the ranks of civilized and modern nations without U.S. assistance—or become vulnerable to intervention. As occurred in Cuba, it must not have been lost on the ruling and enlightened classes that American intervention depended on whether or not they conformed to the formula for progress, which was, after all, shared with the United States.[34]

THE NATIONAL CHARACTER

Dominican men of letters and men of state, then, were of one mind when it came to identifying the characteristics that the country needed to develop if it were to modernize. These "domestic virtues," as Miriam Fernández Sosa calls them, grew out of a local blueprint for progress that associated civilization, education, culture, and moral worth.[35] Not surprisingly, given material circumstances and the espousal of Liberal principles, these men ultimately grounded economic and social advances in the rational cultivation of food crops and some export products by Dominican males—either the owners of small tracts of land or the industrious peasants already partially dispossessed by commercial agriculture.

The intellectual and political class who imagined the island's future did not include urban residents—merchants and workers alike—among the Dominicans who produced for the country. References to women were aesthetic (they were like flowers; they cultivated beautiful gardens) or reproductive (land, like women, was fertile; the motherland, a woman, sought the welfare of her progeny).[36] Sugar workers from nearby islands, and especially from

Haiti, were suspect insofar as it was believed they introduced diseases, consorted with Dominicans (especially women), and took their wages home after the harvest. Journalists and essayists, then, either embraced immigrants, women, and urban wage workers as contributors to the process of national development in predetermined roles or suspected their ability to participate in building a common sense of purpose.

Interestingly, although the composite ideal Dominican was based in the countryside, there was no rural archetype, as existed in Cuba (the *guajiro*) or Puerto Rico (the *jíbaro*), that represented the nation, but rather a set of characteristics that conceivably qualified the common person as fit to contribute to the national project. The most important of these probably was, and still is, color. Dominicans, as other Hispanic-descent peoples of Latin America, had internalized the value of whiteness and had even cultivated it vis-à-vis their neighbor, Haiti. To accentuate this tendency, scientific racism had introduced the notion that progress and modernity depended on the appropriate racial mix.[37] Given these circumstances, it was incumbent upon the intelligentsia to claim nationhood on the basis of racial unity by subsuming blackness into the discourse and by erasing it through white immigration. Regardless of the actual racial composition of the population, the ideal Dominican was imagined to be of indeterminate race (the identifier was never mentioned), but undoubtedly conceived as more white than black, as befit the heir to the country's future. Ironically, the more common racial mix in the Dominican Republic became popularly known as "*indio*," not because of any attachment to or admiration for the indigenous past, but rather strictly as a way of minimizing the black contribution to the national configuration.

The second important attribute of Dominicanness in this period, as it has remained, was its affinity with Europe and, logically, with Spain, the former colonial master. Although Hostos denigrated Spain's actions as a colonial power, most writers in this period saw the need to connect to familiar attitudes and friendly nations. On Spain's four-hundredth anniversary in the Antilles, one author proposed putting behind "four hundred years of civilized life and, with short interruptions, four hundred years of cruel and heartless suffering."[38] The disagreement with Spain regarding the location of Columbus's remains (Havana or Santo Domingo) is another example of the desire to establish a spiritual connection with the cultural matriarch of the region and the source, after all, of many recent immigrants. In a critique of *Alma dominicana*, a novel by Federico García Godoy, in which the protagonist, a young and uneducated peasant, takes up arms against Spain and dies fighting for the independence of the Dominican Republic, the reviewer made clear that the author's intention was not to discredit Spaniards, because, he asserted, the ties between the two nations became only tighter with time. *Renacimiento* lauded the creation of a Centro Español in San Pedro de Macorís as contributing to the development of a national culture—intellectual and business rapprochement with the mother country was an admirable goal. This desire for figurative proximity to its European roots could be explained by the increasing need to set the Dominican Republic off from the orbit of influence of the United States through language or culture, as Puerto Rico was trying to do, or to align with the "Latin American race threatened by North American expansionism" on the basis of "the harmony in customs, the form of government, . . . the unity of religion, [and] practices and vices that necessarily tend to unify [the region] under the same ideal."[39]

The third set of desired traits in the new citizens could be labeled "love of country." For the fatherland, men died, worked hard, loved their children, were moral in their transactions, acted rationally for the welfare of their communities, and more. In one short story, the seed of liberty, although having fallen in loving soil, cannot germinate until the blood of a soldier, who had been fighting for the ideals of freedom and the law, flows into the seedbed.[40] Dominicans had also to work hard, which they did in the fields, whether as peasants or hired hands. Schools would provide the opportunity for the general populace to become educated, and as such, more productive. With all this in place, only the right conditions had to exist in order for the exercise in citizenship and nationalism to begin.

Two significant conundrums flow out of this discussion. One is the realization that the national attributes are, in fact, a wish list that veils some very objective uncertainties. The other is the economy by which subalterns were to insert themselves practically into these ideological constructs.[41] With respect to the first, it is impossible to learn with any assurance how contemporaries reconciled the traits that defined the national character, whose source seems to be the ageless countryside, and the milieu in which these qualities would be developed, the modern city. Without a doubt, stringing together transparent honesty, love of work, intelligence, capacity to produce, political acumen, moral integrity, and the like was an effort to identify qualities essential to Dominicanness that responded to the anxieties of government authorities and the bourgeoisie, with whom the intelligentsia socialized, regarding a number of circumstances that marred the Dominican future. Rural areas were, after all, the recruiting ground for insurrections against the government, and writers identified the practice of indiscriminate conscription on the part of caudillos and of military service with the expectation of obtaining government posts as evidence of the backward state of political development. Still, it was a commonplace to find romantic references to rural practices or peasant ways when the subject was the generic "*el domini-cano*" (the Dominican man, person, people), although the realities of the countryside were the thorn in the side of progressive thinkers. Certain historians have identified the dichotomy between the country and the city denounced by some contemporary writers as the running thread of Dominican twentieth-century history.[42] I have chosen, instead, to point out the contradiction between the elite's low opinion of the political performance of peasants and its projection of a lofty future for the country based on their capacity for work as representative of the nation.

In addition, it is pertinent to highlight the sublimation of these perceived differences, which is another way of looking at contemporary writings on the construction of nationality, in the context of the labor unrest that marked the sugar-producing areas in this period. In Costa Rica, racial-national solidarity was used to dilute class cohesion—black West Indian workers were made the outsiders against ladino Costa Rican managers and workers. In Puerto Rico, a similar phenomenon occurred, and the *jíbaro*, an innocuous white peasant figure, was created to assuage the fears of the national sugar aristocracy. In Guatemala, the national archetype became an urban artisan, to compensate for proletarianization in coffee plantations. A similar case could be drawn for the Dominican Republic, whose sugar-producing areas since the early days had experienced worker agitation, presented then and still understood as anti-immigrant sentiment. Although no idiosyncratic figure arose that encapsulated all the national virtues or represented any one of them, it is certainly the case that the dedication to work and the love of land that the intellectual elite focused on as a national asset assuaged any fears of the restless rural laborer.[43]

Likewise, the racelessness that was characteristic of the Dominican ideal type, if one can use a shortcut for the list of national traits, pointed to insecurities regarding the racial makeup of the country. Knowing full well that the legacy of Africa flowed in their blood, Dominicans declared themselves superior, by virtue of their color, to the West Indian and Haitian immigrants who crossed their borders. Undoubtedly aware of the reasoning behind the eugenics movement as it had traveled to Latin America, the Dominican intelligentsia followed the imperative of developing a national identity that resembled that of European nations. Unable to claim whiteness, they settled for directing attention to the racial mix that marked the population and playing down issues of race in political discourse. Their faith in the redeeming value of education served to multiply in their minds the chances for the hybrid population to regenerate and make good on their economic potential, despite their heterogeneous origins.[44]

Two other traits—the implicit maleness of the national character, and its propensity for Western ways—were also a function of the uneasy circumstances in which the country found itself vis-à-vis the overwhelming presence of the United States in the area. As I will elaborate in chapter 4, nationalist writers have commonly portrayed foreign penetration qua violation of territory in sexual terms. To properly protect the virtue of the homeland, then, virility was of the utmost importance. Identification with the Spanish mother country can be easily explained, at least on the cultural plane, by the threat that the United States posed in the region. Although the North American neighbor was much admired for its economic system and its political stability, Dominicans knew it was perfectly within its power and will to impose by force its notions of economic well-being and political security in the area. As a result, identification with civilized Spain, and disassociation from savage Haiti, were in order.

The second quandary is easier to navigate. Regardless of how deliberately the Dominican intelligentsia set out to impose their will, the people to whom they directed their efforts had their own ideas about how they would insert themselves into the national story. By "buying into" the discourse of nationalism, internalizing it, appropriating its language for their own purposes, or injecting their own values and thus transforming it, they molded it to their specifications.[45] Because notions of political activism without citizens, or without people who think of themselves as such, are absurd, this book will revisit the roles of the intelligentsia, the state, and the people of early twentieth-century Santo Domingo and San Pedro de Macorís in conceptualizing the nation and writing its history.

CHAPTER ONE

The National Project

The resolute desire to "modernize" captured the minds and hearts of Dominican intellectuals at the turn of the century much as it did all of Latin America. In tandem with developments on the continent, the Dominican discourse of progress portrayed the country's social, economic, and political trajectory in negative terms and yet hypothesized a favorable aftermath. Its grounding in the universal doctrines of European Liberalism provided for the ideology of progress a sense of common purpose that would be forged out of the joint will of government and civil society. The national project, though, was fraught with contradictions, which historians can easily identify with hindsight. At the time, however, the thrust to modernize was powerful enough to reconcile the disparities in goals and methods that only a few contemporaries could point to.

PESSIMISM AND THE NATIONAL CHARACTER

Contrary to the impression given in the last chapter through the enthusiastic listing of the qualities innate to Dominicans, island intellectuals had serious misgivings about the country's social capital. "Dominicans" (those fictional archetypes of the "national character"), the intelligentsia proclaimed, were given to gambling, women, and alcohol. They were careless with their finances and generally spent more than they earned. Ranchers neglected their cattle, as did parents their children. The population in general displayed an atavistic propensity to abandon the tasks that were most significant to their well-being and remained apathetic to the political life of the country. It was "not easy to remove the farmer from his work to take him to the book, nor to convert the idler into a hardworking man by way of an education that he will not seek nor apply"—it was impracticable, in fact, and the only solution the minister of justice and public education could think of was training young people in agricultural tasks as part of the school curriculum. In the words of Américo Lugo, the most biting critic of the national character:

> Let's not harbor any illusions about the moral worth of the Dominican people. Moral worth reaches always the limit of intellectual capacity, and our intellectual capacity is almost nil. An immense majority of citizens who do not know how to read nor write, for whom there are no real needs, but impulses and passions; barbarians, in short, who do not recognize any law other than instinct; any right other than force; any home other than a hovel; any family other than females [to party with; *más familia que la hembra del fandango*]; any schools other than the cock-pit; a minority, a fleeting minority; who knows how to read and write, and [who knows] about duties and rights, among which stand out, it is true, figures that are worth [all the riches in the] world, such is the Dominican people, semisavage on the one hand, enlightened on the other, in general apathetic, bellicose, cruel, and uninterested.[1]

These negative images of the country and its people, rightfully dubbed "pessimism" by twentieth-century scholars, alarmed the elite for two reasons. On the one hand, there was the fear that, just as the country was taking off, the impression of Dominicans abroad was precisely that of a backward people, whose political stability and economic promise were chimerical. This concern pervaded official and public discourse on the island's capacity for modernization in the last decades of the nineteenth century and the first decades of the twentieth, when the state sought capital investment from abroad as well as immigrants to both work the land and establish agricultural enterprises. The second reason for anxiety was the related and very real fear that Dominicans, or the Dominican Republic, was really not a properly constituted country and so was an illegitimate actor on the world stage. Lugo put it as bluntly as only he was capable of:

> Out of history's careful lessons, we can deduce that the Dominican people are not constituted as a nation. It is certainly a spiritual community united by language, customs, and other ties; but its lack of culture does not allow it the political development necessary for a people to become a nation . . . The Dominican State reflects what it can, the fluctuating will of the popular masses; in no way a public will, which does not exist here. The Dominican people are not a nation because they have no consciousness of the community that they con-

stitute, because their political activity is not sufficiently far-reaching. Not being a nation, the State that aspires to represent it is not a real State.[2]

If Dominican intellectuals worried about the impression they gave abroad, high government officials had every reason to suspect the underhanded compliments foreign travelers paid the country and its people. Otto Schoenrich, U.S. special commissioner in charge of assessing the Dominican Republic's financial solvency in 1905, described Dominicans as robust and vigorous, but somewhat lazy, because the climate, nature, and the political situation encouraged them to postpone tasks. Culturally, he considered them Spanish, although, he remarked, the racial mix had produced a very dark population. He observed that patriotism and liberty were the two ideals in whose names Dominicans committed the most noble and the most perverse acts. Schoenrich believed that the men were womanizers and gamblers, while the women were virtuous, and he placed the out-of-wedlock birthrate at 60 percent. Ten years later, an analyst of the island's tourism potential portrayed Dominicans as "simple and good-natured people"—moderate in their drinking habits, honest, intelligent, hardworking, and happy. He predicted a bright future for the country, once its inhabitants laid down their arms and picked up instead agricultural tools. Later in the period, a Protestant evangelist depicted Dominicans as hospitable, pleasant, cosmopolitan (in their attitudes to race and nationality), hardworking, and fun-loving. He believed they would have achieved more had nature not been so prodigal. Compared to Haiti, which remained under U.S. scrutiny at all times during this period, the Dominican Republic shone for its hard work and organization, "a state of affairs certainly unexpected in a republic governed by a black man [Heureaux]." At the end of this period, foreigners' opinions of Dominicans were more or less the same as at the beginning—helpful, respectful, obliging, "a simple group, instinctive and innocuous, that preferred to live with indifference forgetting the duties and responsibilities of life." These foreigners' assessments of the general population were indeed condescending, but more dangerously, they implicitly measured Dominican achievement against American standards, already very familiar to the political and social elites, and pitted the eastern part of the island against its poorer neighbor to the west as the potential recipient of American favor.[3]

Other writers found qualities in the Dominican people that they praised wildly, but they remained equivocal or qualified their statements to the point of retracting them. José Ramón López, whose claim to fame remains his doomsday forecast of the country's inadequacies due to poor nutrition, declared that native peasants worked twice as hard as foreign laborers, despite being malnourished. Similarly, a newspaper columnist proclaimed Dominican "moral, political, and social superiority over the sectarians of Vodou [Haitians], and . . . equally superior standing, compared to them, . . . among civilized nations." Pedro Francisco Bonó himself considered Dominicans, as individuals, to be "brave, bold, . . . generous, hospitable, simple, hardworking, intelligent, enterprising." But collectively—he qualified his statement— "Dominican society does not have the cohesion that is indispensable for a human aggregate that seeks to be definitively independent, [to be the] absolute master of its destinies." Dominicans, then, demonstrated satisfactory progress only as hard (and not necessarily good) workers, when compared to Haitians (the Dominican Republic's most despicable enemy), and as individuals whose accomplishments were personal.[4]

Various theories circulated that explained, but never justified, the negative traits Dominican intellectuals and foreign visitors identified in the general population. The first blamed an unfortunate racial mix between low-class Spaniards and savage Africans for the tragic result: a disparate collection of individuals, of mixed race, incapable of self-regulation, highly susceptible to influence from above, and hardly worth the appellative "nation."[5]

Another explanation, frequently overlapping with the first, pointed to three hundred years of colonialism as the cause of the Dominican population's deficiencies. The legacy of colonial rule—total domination by the imperial power and its representatives, pervasive economic dependence, and generalized use of force—continued to afflict the country. Even López, more given to natural explanations than social ones, agreed with this interpretation: "The monopoly of a few is a solvent for social ideas. The privilege of the few, based on abusive practices, destroys society."[6]

Other thinkers presented a third theory for the insufficiencies of the Dominican people—a gentle climate, a fertile soil, poor nutrition, scarce resources, and inadequate education were responsible for the political limitations of individual citizens. López was convinced that hunger, and the mental and physical inertia it caused, directly affected national wealth, and in combination with civil unrest, diminished population and morality. This occurred not only in the countryside, to which most of his pamphlet appears dedicated, but in the cities as well, where degeneration was mostly psychological. An influential analyst listed as problematic several facts: there was no information about the geography and geology of the island, its people, and natural resources; the roads and ports were in poor condition; and there was a high rate of illiteracy. A short story recounted the tragic destiny of Reducindo Nicolás, who was born, not coincidentally the same year as the republic, in 1844. He became an orphan at two and was able nevertheless to grow up strong. His field was the best in the area, much to the chagrin of his neighbors, who were "lazy, loafers, most of them eaten up by black envy" (clearly, Haitians). Boredom, "or perhaps destiny," led him to war, and the hands that could have been tilling fields now carried a rifle. The ease with which Dominican existence almost constructed itself without any human effort was to blame for what intellectuals identified as the population's political and economic deficiencies, for their propensity for war and aversion to work. The end result of genetic material, circumstance, and fate, however imagined, left much to be desired.[7]

Although it may be transparent to us that these explanations, especially the attempt to treat acquired characteristics as inherited traits, were terribly flawed, writers at the time mixed and matched elements of each in order to give meaning to their reality. López blamed race and the environment for the Dominican people's violent nature, carelessness, indolence, and distrust of others—despite finding workers generally "cheerful, hardworking, serious, and resistant." Another example of the tendency to attribute negative traits to nature, nurture, and fortune is Francisco Henríquez y Carvajal's zealous outburst at the turn of the portentous century:

> Do you expect a people that has lived in an atmosphere of public immorality and injustice, that is tainted with vices, with fundamental errors, that knows no other governmental practices than those which have been able to persist in this land, those [pertaining to] tyranny; that is always agitated by subversive ideas against the instituted governmental order, whether good or bad, it matters little; do you expect such a people, that lacks absolutely any practical tradition or education, turns overnight, rising from the night of horrors, wrecked, ragged, hungry, with wan and haggard visage, to the delicious morning of an unexpected awakening, to become, we repeat, an adult people, robust and healthy, full of moral vigor, with just ideas, with noble purposes, with political and social habits that permit it to produce in this new kind of life the same accomplishments as those countries, who like Switzerland, England, and the United States of America, not only needed centuries to get there, but also counted on ethnic elements evidently superior because of a preparation and a slow and natural adaptation to the geographic and international milieu?[8]

Interestingly, racial inferiority, abuse by the colonizer, and lack of resources made the process of decline of the Dominican people understandable but did not excuse them from inaction.

The Liberal intelligentsia was obviously in a bind. The entire edifice of the country's prosperity lay in the capacity of its people to coalesce around a common sense of purpose. The "people," however, seemed to have no inclination to rise to the occasion. This was dangerous, not only because states were judged by the quality of their institutions, which would be upheld, after all, by civil society, but also because the Dominican Republic had a history of seeing these insufficiencies jeopardize its sovereignty. The memory of the Haitian occupation, glorious as its denouement was, and subsequent attempts to obtain the protection of European powers against Haiti weighed down on the Dominican psyche. That other countries discounted the Dominican Republic as a contender in the economic race was merely a source of embarrassment; more serious for Liberals might have been compromising another of their cherished ideals: the participation of the majority in the political life of the country.

ECONOMIC OBSTACLES TO PROGRESS

Another source of worry for the Dominican intelligentsia lay in the economic sphere. Here the spokesmen for progress also found the country lacking, as agricultural pursuits had not replaced cattle raising, the scientific method did not yet prevail over traditional farming practices, and private property had not asserted itself as the dominant form of landholding. Given that the cane industry had held the promise of modernizing the country's economy in the early 1880s—through wage work, the use of technology, capital investment, and the like—most concerns about the island's future revolved around sugar and were expressed in reference to it, although the more generic term "agriculture" was used instead. In the eloquent words of one of the proponents of this vision, "[the] love for land is the same one that patriotism engenders; that's how agriculture is at one and the same time the source of prosperity and a way of maintaining peace among the people."[9]

Two issues worried economic commentators: *crianza libre* (free-range livestock raising) and *terrenos comuneros* (communal lands). *Crianza libre* posed an insurmountable obstacle to agriculture, reformers believed, because the threat of animals roaming and destroying fields by feeding and stepping on crops inhibited farmers from investing in their property to improve production. Cattle and especially pigs wandering about towns and cities were also a problem, not only because of cleanliness but also, remarkably, because of aesthetic considerations. But laws requiring cattle ranchers to erect fences if they lived within a certain radius (twelve kilometers) of plantings or of urban areas were revoked over and over again until 1906.

Another related issue was production techniques: even cattle that were properly fenced in and raised for consumption left much to be desired—countless articles denounced insufficient nutrition, careless breeding, and sloppy record keeping. A solution presented itself in the raising of goats, ideal to some on many counts: they could be raised in very dry areas where agriculture was not feasible; and they could be bred so that they produced more milk, meaning that cheese and butter did not have to be imported. But, to complicate the mix and give it a political twist, a leading figure explained that, because political violence continued to be the rule in the countryside, the incompatibility of animal husbandry and agriculture had never really become an issue. *Crianza libre*, in short, was "the base and nourishment of idleness, the beginning and the end of disturbances in the countryside." Needless to say, it had to be eliminated.[10]

Communal lands were a problem insofar as their existence conflicted with notions of private individual property that were privileged by Liberals. *Terrenos comuneros* were owned collectively by a group of individuals who could sell their share of the property or bequeath it to a family member or friend. This system of landholding developed in the east, where population density was low and lent itself to the operations of lumberers and cattle ranchers, who had no need for exclusive access points or use of watering facilities. Agriculturists, of course, needed the assurance that private property carried with it, especially at resale time, when the improvements they had made to their property would raise the price of their particular piece. But not everyone was convinced of the automatic benefits of individual property ownership. Hostos, for one, was very suspicious of giant private corporations in the sugar industry. Bonó would dramatically declare that the dislocation of peasant landholders to make way for private ownership of land was tantamount to stripping citizens of their rights. Nevertheless, reformers pushed for a land register, but it was not until 1922, during the American occupation, that lands were surveyed and demarcated.[11]

There were other reasons for the country's backwardness. A unanimous lament on the part of economic commentators was the terrible state of the roads. An essentially agricultural country, the author of a pamphlet entitled *Vías de comunicación* argued, needed reliable transportation and modern highways. Two small railways served the tobacco industry by connecting Moca and Santiago with Puerto Plata, and La Vega and San Francisco de Macorís with the port of Sánchez. The sugar industry was gradually meeting its own transportation needs through the use of locomotives and wagons, but people who wanted to travel from one part of the island to another had to endure overland travel through intractable paths and hope for dry weather. Francisco J. Peynado, future secretary of state and architect of the 1922 agreement to withdraw U.S. troops, vehemently linked material advances to moral worth:

> The lack of highways shames and humiliates us in such a way that we would almost die from hunger, if the steamships that anchor in our port did not bring the rice, the beans, the oils, the beef and the potatoes, the garlic and the onions, that daily we consume with the greatest indifference, without thinking that by buying these articles of first necessity from abroad, we are cultivating our own reputation as loafers and we become spokespeople of our own discredit and our own disgrace![12]

A string of other economic obstacles to progress troubled the Dominican intelligentsia. Journalists who reported on the advances of local enterprises were well aware of the fragility of capital investment and its impact on the general outlook of industry. In a glowing account of entrepreneurial perseverance in the face of adversity, *El Eco de la Opinión* praised the efforts of the New Jersey and Santo Domingo Brewing Company, whose representative sailed to Cuba in search of the materials necessary to reconstruct a collapsed wall. The purpose of the piece was to highlight the success of the brewery—an unusual event that "would call, as is natural, the attention of other capitalists who will come to this land, that lacks everything, and will protect it with new industries and great works." As this quote suggests, the spirit of association, one of the pillars of capitalism, was in fact intimately related to the investment of capital. The Sociedad Agrícola Dominicana (Dominican Agricultural Society) was founded in 1880 to

> become the great center of activity that would propel and develop the wealth of the country in large scale: become involved in leveling obstacles, solving the economic problems of the locality by means of [spreading] information in the press and [sending] requests to the Government and to Congress; promote the establishment of a greater number of sugar estates; make way for hardworking immigration; set up agricultural expositions for the stimulus of all those who are dedicated to working in the fields; and, in every way that the country and circumstances permit, guarantee and consolidate the interests of the respectable guild of landowners.[13]

The Liberal economic agenda suffused the Dominican national project and pointed to some practical, if not conceptual, deficiencies. Economic modernization required the adoption of the principle of private property and scientific approaches to the production process. The spirit of association, a mainstay of market capitalism in the absence of direct state support, was also necessary if private interests were going to flourish. The quandary remained, however, the external nature of investment and, as related in chapter 3, of labor, a circumstance that effectively took the "national" out of the project at hand. Moreover, the mixed results that could obtain from a regime of private property and modern agriculture on the rural masses had already been witnessed—the dream of economic prosperity and political stability was, after all, grounded on flesh-and-blood individuals.

POLITICAL CONCERNS

The political realities that had been lived in recent years brought some sense of alarm into the vision of the future. A number of concerns dominated the conversation in this period: the rule of men had prevailed over the rule of law; the government served only for personal gain; public service remained an alien concept; and there were no vehicles in place to convey differences of opinion. Political modernization required much more than standing up to the colonial master or to the invading neighbor; it demanded a political maturity that only the establishment of civil institutions could authenticate.

The failure of the rule of law was all too recent for Dominicans to ignore. Magazines founded immediately after the death of Lilís lamented that he had stayed in power as long as he did by simply violating the constitution and keeping the country ignorant so as to ensure its total subjection.[14] In this respect, Heureaux was not different from other politicians—"The greatest national weakness [was] the irrepressible desire for perpetuity in the highest public [position of] power."[15] Rafael J. Castillo, the editor of *Nuevo Réjimen*, challenged its readership to find a glimmer of hope:

> Mention just one instance [of governmental rule] in the past, aside from a few provisional governments, that has not disrespected the constitution, that has not committed arbitrary acts, that has not misappropriated the nation's funds, that has not perverted the administration of justice, that has not cared more about maintaining itself [in power] at all costs, than about honestly putting into practice the principles of free government, that has not preferred to keep the people ignorant of their rights and duties rather than contributed to educate it for the exercise of the former and the fulfillment of the latter.[16]

These negative influences, one author bemoaned, had made people think liberty was a privilege (not a right) granted them by their ruler, who constantly undermined it. The solution was for Dominicans to turn their back on individualistic, personalistic appeals and to become "civilist," that is, defenders of everyone's rights, which the author believed was the only way to have one's own rights respected. Rather than worry about international forces that might impose their will on their weaker neighbors, one writer suggested, Dominicans should be alert against "interior imperialism," an equally fearsome enemy, if only because of the rapidity of its actions. Conversely, peace, insofar as it came from the rule of law (and not the rule of force), guaranteed "citizenship," "civilization," "nationhood."[17]

In the hands of an all-powerful executive, then, the purpose of government had turned to rewarding the winner's followers with public office and other material benefits. Parties appeared to be organized for that purpose, to promote the interests of their leadership and to favor those who had distinguished themselves for their loyalty.[18] In words now famous because they have been so often quoted, Francisco Moscoso Puello called the government a mutual-aid society, which offered all kinds of services at predetermined interest rates. The budget he referred to as "the great table [for] the national banquet, [where] we all expect to have a place setting."[19] Similarly, another writer likened the government to a tree whose fruit defied the laws of physics, because they did not fall down so other trees would grow from the seeds. Instead, some fruit held onto the tree so tightly that neither rain nor storm could shake them off. Other fruit "fell" upward, going to the higher branches. There were a few, though, that would fall down, but that was because they were rotten.[20] A well-known poet composed some verses to denounce the abuses of the powerful, who always took advantage of their inferiors to pursue the easiest path:

> . . . person of high rank
> who likes mangoes a great deal
> because it is a pleasant fruit.
> But to climb the tree
> and find himself stuck in the knots
> and in infinite tight spots
> since this is so dangerous
> he finds it more delightful
> to grab the low mangoes.[21]

Similarly, in one short story from a series on war, the author highlighted the unequal power differential that often brought about unfair consequences. Tiburcio, a soldier who had not distinguished himself either by his physique or his intellect, played a lead role in a battle in which the general in command had blundered. The latter receives the recognition due Tiburcio, and meanwhile the soldier's leg is amputated. Dominicans knew what domination was, Bonó fatefully stated, because there was no counterweight that lightened the despotism of the party in power, which established itself through cruelty and injustice to pursue the advantage of its members. In an effort to rectify the situation, *Nuevo Réjimen* flatly stated that it would attack with equal force those who in the past had governed the country to promote their interests and those who continued to defend the power of the executive. Still, in a short story published many years later, after the United States had invaded the island, the author found himself reinforcing the importance for Dominicans of the authority of law over the will of the executive. In it, Julius Caesar, the Roman emperor, defends the practice of assuming innocence until proof of guilt is given, even at the risk of having criminals walk the streets. In a very convoluted way, too complicated to relate here, Caesar convinces his challenger that brute force (against criminals, against his opponent) achieves very little without the power of logic, of law.[22]

Compounding this situation was the absence of a tradition of public service that could guide the performance of government appointees or employees. The dismal situation was due, some believed, to inexperience in public administration, which resulted in reckless spending and in the limited generation of income and of desirable outcomes. There was also plain abuse of authority, notoriously among the *alcaldes pedáneos* (village mayors), who earned no salaries and felt at liberty to require levies, labor, and services (including sexual favors) from the inhabitants of their jurisdiction. A change in regime, the clever proponent of the tree simile mentioned above opined, would not improve matters—it was no different from a family moving into a new home. The family has to clear the new house of old items, including cats, which persistently attempt to stay put, infiltrating the home even through the pipes. Such were ministerial employees, who did anything to remain in their posts and continue to "gnaw at" the budget. (This detail and other circumstances suggest the animals in question are really rats, but the author is careful to always use the word "cats.") The law, as it existed, punished petty crime more severely than it did threats to peace, to the independence of the country, and to life and property, another writer remarked. For the author, the latter were more serious offenses because discerning people, some of them political figures, had deliberately committed them with full awareness of the consequences.[23]

Finally, political essayists complained that there was no effective means to channel differences of opinion. Francisco Henríquez y Carvajal, a prominent political figure, placed the Dominican Republic in the same category as other Latin American countries whose citizens believed that there was no change possible except through violent means. Politics on the island, they would concur, was a matter of personal (not public) interest and was conducted with "passion," a code word for disorder and violence. Arms had become the first resort to express opposition, common wisdom asserted, since the wars of independence; Dominicans were so used to fighting Haitians that they continued to do the same to resolve domestic differences. The words of Heureaux in 1888, at the start of his second term in office, would prove foreboding: "You will always see me acting as the standard-bearer of general confraternity. And I will state and I believe that only a well-balanced political eclecticism, in which there is room for all colors [read "parties"], will avert calamitous days for the fatherland." Heureaux did not deliver on the promise, and a writer would demand, shortly after the president's death, action that corresponded to the pledge to end "personalism, favoritism, the politics of [financial] speculation, the marketing of public office, and delving into the national treasury."[24]

The description above of the political situation the self-appointed spokesmen of the Dominican population sought to rectify fits the European Liberal agenda of individual rights and representative democracy to a tee. A body of law encapsulated in the constitution, to which every citizen was bound; government for the majority of the population and not only for the few in power; a civil service committed to serving people and not the executive who had appointed them; and the possibility of institutionalizing citizens' input—these ideas floated and took root in Great Britain first and traveled to the Caribbean and Latin America by way of France.[25] The constitution of 1908, in fact, confirmed statesmen's continued efforts to incorporate these principles into the supreme law of the land. The already Liberal constitutions of 1865 and 1875, and the modifications that followed (1881, 1887, 1896, 1907)— virtually indistinguishable, but reissued simply because there was no provision for amendments—were altered, this time with a marked propinquity for French Liberal thought.[26] The division of powers was redrawn, making the executive more dependent than before on the legislative branch, which was itself strengthened by making Congress unicameral. Universal male suffrage remained in place for electors, who had the responsibility of choosing the members of Congress and of selecting a replacement in case the president died, resigned, or was incapacitated (since the post of vice president was abolished). The Supreme Court had the authority to annul laws, acting in this capacity as a check on the legislative branch. All that was left to do was to make this complicated apparatus work—no small feat, indeed.[27]

The schemes of the late nineteenth-century advocates of progress rested on the regeneration of the common person. At a time when the Latin American republics sought to claim their autonomy, this time vis-à-vis the United States, it was essential that they prove their capacity to conform to Western ideals. From the perspective of reformers, the rehabilitation of Dominican society would be achieved through public education, productive employment, and the exercise of individual liberties—a triad that generated its own diversity of opinion, even controversy.

The public education system launched by Liberal governments since the 1870s was the product of positivism as put into practice by Hostos, the highly influential ultra-Liberal thinker. Hostos and his followers had turned their back on Spain's scholastic tradition, labeling it "intolerant, inquisitorial, fanatic, and superstitious,"[28] and embraced a practical (positivist) education, based on the observation of phenomena, the knowledge from which could be directly applied to advances in the material world.[29] When so enlightened, positivists argued, societies would progress and become truly free: "The new school would produce in a few years a radical change in the temperament of Dominican society, and the little republic, deserving only of annexation or of pacification by a bloody and whorish oligarchy, would be transformed into a nation in which work and knowledge would be worth more than conceit and hypocrisy, and government by the people, for the people, would be a constitutional reality."[30] The new school, moreover, promised to be an antidote to U.S. intervention: "The only [thing with which] we can successfully counter North American imperialism (with the exception of a profound and wretched misery that makes us undesirable) is a civilization of our own, daughter of our personal effort, that neutralizes any pretext for intervention in the name of humanity."[31] The battle cry "civilization or death" pervaded the discourse of progress disseminated by political cliques and high-minded reformers, to be picked up at the local government level and by the press.[32]

The opponents of positivist schooling organized an ad hominem campaign directed at the method's secular character and, one surmises, at the heavy-handed intervention of the state on the intellectual formation of youth, including, apparently, sex education. One defender of Hostos's work, in denying the allegations of one of his accusers, suggested the antagonist had said that Hostos's normal school was a school without God and that it undermined the authority of parents by telling children that they existed only because of a moment of fleeting pleasure on the part of their parents. In response, this disciple (they called themselves so) declared that nobody at the school was forced to profess any particular faith, and that Hostos himself was a family man. An earlier enthusiast, in fact, had not been bothered at all by the influence of teachers on the children. He recounted that children learned a great deal and had fun. When they went home, they would tell their mothers what they had learned, and their mothers would relay the news to their fathers. Teachers, he emphasized, were recognized for being almost as important as parents. Lugo himself turned the argument on its head with his characteristic command of language: Hostos's efforts, he explained, were directed at founding schools that took God into account, precisely because they sought to bring light, respect, liberty, and understanding; and in their search for knowledge, freedom, and good judgment, Hostos's schools inevitably respected children, mothers, and priests. Not surprisingly, another writer ridiculed Antonio Alfau, whom he suspected was responsible for the malicious attack on Hostos, by making fun of some grammatical mistakes or infelicities of language he had noticed in the article. The defense of "truth," along with the power of the word, were not only the byproducts of positivist education but also the weapons their advocates used against its detractors.[33]

The second column upon which the edifice of the future rested was gainful employment. This particular conversation was as much about hard work and its products as about idleness and its results. As was to be expected, laws existed to encourage men to find useful occupations. Idleness was "the source of all vices, and . . . those who had no fixed residence, means of subsistence, or a regular job [did] not fulfill the duties society imposed and continuously injure[d] it."[34] Vagrants, in fact, were defined loosely and could include, apart from those who had no steady income or land for subsistence crops, alcoholics, young men who abandoned the path chosen by their parents "thus disrespecting and disobeying them," and married men who "without an evident motive, mistreat their wife, abandon their family and live from outings to amusements, and do not constantly work."[35] In a transparently didactic small treatise on morals, the author captured the sense of accomplishment deliberate work was expected to produce:

It is not fortune, but labor, that makes men. Fortune—says an American author—is always waiting for something to present itself; work, with a penetrating gaze and a firm will, always bears fruit. Fortune lies in bed and waits for the mailman to bring news of an inheritance; work wakes up at six, with an active pen or resounding hammer, [and] establishes the basis of welfare and wealth. Fortune complains, work whistles. Fortune relies on chances; work on character. Fortune slides [downward] to please itself; work struggles upward, and aspires toward independence.[36]

"Blessed be the power of work," one columnist exclaimed, "which uplifts people; and turns them from poor and miserable into rich and respectable!"[37]

Finally, there was some disagreement over how well-positioned the country was to take advantage of the individual liberties, leading among them freedom of the press and of association, that Liberals considered essential for a prosperous future. The success and effectiveness of the print media in maintaining a respectful tone, reporting objectively, and advancing the general interest were under contention. Some writers held that freedom of the press was in an "embryonic stage," so that any kind of verbal exchange was welcome. Another position avowed that, independently of the underhanded ways in which an honorable person might be attacked in print, the truth would prevail. (It is telling that this account of the triumph of good over evil came in the shape of a short story, in which a rich man decides to cultivate a piece of fallow land. He hires a gardener to no avail, because his neighbors trash the property with kitchen wastes and excrement. The garden, of course, grows and achieves outstanding beauty—to prove to the simplest minds that nothing can deter what is bound for greatness.) The most pessimistic believed that powerful interests, which were working against the general welfare, controlled the press and distorted the truth. All agreed that the function of journalism was to elevate the country: "It is an august mission, that of the journalist, if upon becoming the spokesperson of goodness, he clamors for [the rule of] law, dashes against injustice and rebukes abuse, and making the newspaper the chair, the lectern, or school, he teaches, preaches, and moralizes. When he fulfills his mission thus, then he will rise above the common level and will turn into a priest, teacher, legislator." The revival of the free press was associated with the new generation, with liberty, with integrity, and with the fatherland.[38]

Similarly, freedom of association was "the foundation of material and intellectual progress in societies" across the globe and a prerequisite of liberty. In characteristic fashion, the political repercussions of free association were not lost on the intelligentsia. Two positions were in place. One held the "marriage of commerce and [free] enterprise with politics" as indissoluble. The other encouraged private initiative (free association) precisely because neither central government nor local municipality was expected to contribute to material progress. In either case, the strength of numbers encouraged Liberals to embrace "meetings" (the English word was used) where particular projects were proposed and general causes advanced.[39]

Regaining their composure (and losing it again in the next round), Dominican intellectuals struggled to put a positive spin on the task they faced. Despite the dire prospects, Liberal thinkers took hope in the promise of education and employment and imagined the impact of these stimuli on the life of the country. Although there were differences of opinion regarding methods and actual practices, social critics agreed that some redirecting of productive energies was in order. As one writer put it:

> We have the obligation of instating peace, of compelling the multitudes [to take up] the rough and ennobling struggles of labor, of extinguishing in our souls the self-serving egotisms, [and] political rivalries; we have to work for the general good and [social] order, we have to exhaust our powerful energies in work, to enrich and make great and respectable our peoples; we have to train our aptitudes so that they will render the good fruit they should give naturally.[40]

SUGAR'S PROMISE AND ASSOCIATED MISGIVINGS

Like the island's social capabilities, the economic fate of the country was also a subject of avid discussion, and again sugar was at the center of the debate. Public figures praised or criticized the industry on a number of counts, especially its role in the transformation of the country's economic landscape. Sugar manufacturing, inarguably suspect due to the absorption of the peasantry by latifundia and the introduction of workers from nearby islands, operated also with imported capital from foreign entrepreneurs. Writers debated the degree to which the government should respond to its needs, including the proactive stance it took toward immigration. The application of scientific methods, naturally at the forefront of deliberations about the course of progress, was also a topic among economic commentators.

Journalists, politicians, and sugar planters argued the pros and cons of the cane industry. The press generally supported the sugar economy and advocated on its behalf. Newspapers, notable among them *El Eco de la Opinión*, regularly published accounts of sugar's contribution to the treasury and to the economic vibrancy of the country. From the perspective of this journal, the benefits were many. Sugar had transformed San Pedro de Macorís, a sleepy fishing village in the southeast, into a busy port town where progress, work, and capital had made their mark—the gun, the symbol of lawless politics, had been replaced by the plow. It had encouraged the formation of associations that promoted the scientific cultivation of crops and mounted expositions of methods and products. Although one writer warned against the dangers of monoculture, and another hoped that scientific knowledge would "liberate . . . farmers from the yoke of speculation which overwhelmed them," the verdict repeatedly favored sugar over other agricultural enterprises.[41]

Throughout this period, newspapers collected and published universal dictums that connected farming with political stability, exalted the productivity of the soil, praised the work of farmers, and celebrated the material benefits of agriculture. The sugar sector, along with commerce and industry, "brought . . . after material progress, the light that would illuminate the road to civilization and culture." Prosperity in the rural areas, in fact, was expected to reduce the propensity for political violence; more than one writer pointed to the recruitment practices of disaffected politicians among idle rural residents. In the first years of the boom, a writer expressed it this way: "Economic revolutions are winning [in number] over political revolutions here, and the seed that is trusted to the fertility of the soil apparently kills the lowly ambition that can engender ignoble aspirations in the spirit of our men. Agriculture is and will be the savior of this country, which is essentially agricultural, and cane represents the large-scale regeneration of all that constitutes the base of happiness in this country." Twelve years later, only the wording had changed: "The importance of our commerce and even the state of our culture as a civilized people is due to the sugar industry; the love of peace, the political prudence and the respect toward constituted government, that have always characterized this small, but important portion of the republic, has as its solid base the aforementioned industry."[42]

Writers worried at the same time about the survival of the peasantry as a self-sufficient and potentially prosperous class in the face of the advance of sugar. Even today, historians are divided on whether or not proletarianization actually occurred in the period between 1880 and 1916, and if it did, where. Apparently, continued access to land and the availability of foreign laborers sheltered many Dominican peasants from selling their labor as their only means of subsistence. Some did, however, abandon or sell their *conucos* (small tracts of cultivated land), attracted by high wages and the rising price of land, after the initial vacillations of the industry. According to Roberto Cassá, the single region in the country where this occurred was the quadrilateral formed by Santo Domingo in the west, La Romana in the east, and Higüey, Hato Mayor, and El Seybo, to the north of La Romana, going from east to west, as far as San Pedro de Macorís, but not reaching Santo Domingo. Dispossessed farmers could have inserted themselves successfully in the sugar economy, but it is more likely, given the seasonal nature of production and the influx of immigrants, that they looked for wage work, which they came to solely depend on for food and housing, more often than they were actually employed. Others managed to remain attached to land, supplementing local production with cash obtained from wage work in export crop production or even road building and urban work. In hindsight, it is clear that, where it located itself with monopolistic force, sugar destroyed local crop cultivation, cattle ranching, and production by peasants. The existence of pockets of valiant resistance and even healthy adaptation to the presence of these business giants, which is evident to us now, was unimaginable for contemporaries, and they rightly feared the consequences of such a powerful economic force on the rural population.[43]

Hostos, the defender of small property holding, took up the cause that Bonó had already advocated fervently. He pointed to the sugar industry's origins in slavery, its need to control vast expanses of territory, and its questionable profit margins to cast doubt on the wisdom of embracing it as the centerpiece of the country's projected path. Internal migration on the part of dispossessed farmers and the temporary abandonment of local crop production on the part of semi-proletarianized peasants had resulted in food shortages and steep prices for staples. Wages did not match the cost of living, some warned, a situation that would be a deterrent to immigration, but more important, according to two sources, was a public order problem, "as it help[ed] debase the population [*degenerar la raza*] and so weaken[ed] the capacity of the people to exercise morality, to [engage in] good politics and to produce." The predominance of foreigners as providers of capital and labor raised doubts as to the long-term benefits of the industry and its trickle-down capacity. Contemporaries might not have stated the issues as boldly as Bruce Calder—in his opinion, sugar made the Dominican Republic dependent on the world market, drove food production down, impoverished peasants, reduced the internal market, and concentrated political and economic power— but they endeavored to take into account its negative aspects, with a view to offsetting them.[44]

The government supported the industry in a number of ways and was at least attentive to the opinions of its spokespersons, if not downright proactive in its policies. Taking the viewpoint of the planters, government officials and intellectuals alike remarked on the "unavailability of labor" during the crisis and blamed underpopulation and the demeaning of manual work by a history of slavery as responsible. It was a literary commonplace to group together violence and economic insecurity with their antithesis, liberty, peace, education, and employment. The words of the president of the 1908 Congress capture the logic: "[Agriculture] makes possible . . . the commercial relations of countries and awakens in society the love of work, so much more fruitful in [terms of material] goods when through it one secures the definitive establishment of the reign of peace, the wellspring that safeguards the progress of nations." In the early 1880s, Liberal administrations openly referred to sugar as the source of wealth for the island and privileged it with special treatment, such as sponsoring the formation of scientific committees, exempting it from taxes, lowering export duties, and raising tariffs. Sugar stood for modernization, for the triumph of human ingenuity over nature, for civilization: "Exchanging animal power, slow and ancient, which should only be evoked in the canvas of our artists, [in favor of] steam and electricity, the magicians who, like the griffin of the fable, swallow distances, we will be taking over that omnipotent lady, our advocate called civilization." It was not unusual for journals to lobby on behalf of the industry—*El Eco de la Opinión*, ever the supporter of sugar, advocated that the government exonerate from export duties for a fixed number of years the additional product of estates that were committed to increasing production.[45]

In addition, the municipal government took into account, perhaps too readily, the needs of planters, as channeled both through the press and through government circuits. William Bass, the owner of Consuelo, the largest mill until 1920, felt comfortable suggesting to the town council that by paying "some sum" he could be exempted from closing the factory on Sundays, holidays, and days of national mourning, as required by law. Juan Serrallés, owner of Ingenio Puerto Rico, questioned the charging of a toll to cross the river with food for workers, since—he asserted—he was using his own boat, and the tax was not charged to anyone else. He included in his statement a passionate plea for the government to facilitate, rather than impede, the development of agriculture, by which he meant sugar cultivation, "so that capital, which gives it life, will feel secure and encourage new capital to establish . . . new industries." When two planters disagreed about the way one constructed a railway so that it affected the other's property, the aggrieved party wrote to the town council and to his opponent expressing his position, while the other simply invited the town council to the inauguration of the line. *Nuevo Réjimen*, the watchdog of corrupt politics, found some of these actions suspicious and once accused Salvador Ross, co-owner of Ingenio Santa Fe with Alexander Bass, William's father, of attempting to bribe deputies to the Congress. The article stated that Ross wrote a letter to Bass, suggesting a dollar figure to be distributed among the legislators—the purpose of which was not explicit. The courting of possible supporters extended to the press: Bass invited an *El Eco de la Opinión* journalist for lunch, a tour, and a late afternoon cocktail. Reading an issue of *Consuelo News*, William's "little newspaper," the journalist praised him as a "Cyclops who forges light by hammering in the anvil of dignifying work."[46]

Another piece of the progress puzzle over which there was some discussion was the establishment of scientific methods of cultivation and manufacturing. Most everyone agreed that a successful agricultural program required the establishment of schools for the exchange of scientifically obtained information on crops and methods. The situation was critical in 1901—international prices had been going down; internal markets suffered from low quality either because of deliberate fraud or because of ignorance; and production costs were going up for some products, namely sugar. "Agriculture is not, as most people think, a gross and empirical art that only relies on practice and routine. If it does not yet belong in the group of exact sciences, it is making advances on the road that leads to that position and is, at least, a scientific art that encompasses varied knowledge, based on rules and doctrines that have been tested and have been recognized [as] useful." To that effect, proposals to institute agricultural classes, agronomic schools, agricultural associations, and so on were common throughout this period. As early as 1880, the government legislated into existence agricultural committees in every municipality "to form the register of national assets and the general census of all administrative units, to promote expositions, compile [Dominican] agricultural legislation, and intervene in favor of immigrants," but there is no evidence that any were actually established.[47]

Although there was no disagreement over the benefits of information-gathering mechanisms, some doubted the wisdom of the methods proposed. Agricultural schools, in fact, were not slated only for serving the purposes of agriculture,

> but as a great means of public education appropriate to forming the character of the students, to infuse in them the purest morality, to transmit habits of discipline and order, to prepare them for studies in the most advanced sphere, and to train them in the most accurate use of each other's faculties, teaching the rich the most correct direction of their properties and the poor a safer and honorable way of acquiring a satisfactory position, being useful to themselves and their fellow citizens.[48]

Others ridiculed these objectives obliquely:

> We have had, and have, and never will be in need of, very enlightened men; but we have not had, nor do we have, and we need badly men

who know how to make the land produce. . . . It is gratuitous to talk at every opportunity of the inexhaustible fertility of our fields, of the great material wealth that our soil holds. . . . More than a school . . . [we need] a field for demonstration. Our peasants are almost all illiterate, and it is necessary to teach them through [their] eyes.[49]

Despite these discrepancies, most would celebrate the power of learning. Having dismissed the lack of resources, the absence of cooperation on the part of the commercial class, and the lack of initiative on the part of the government as insignificant in the formula for progress, one journalist ardently suggested: "Good management in economic affairs lies in [the maxim] KNOWLEDGE IS POWER [in English]: to desire is to be able to. Let everyone be governed by that notion, and we will see who it is that triumphs in the end in all spheres of social and economic activity."[50]

Part of the plan for reform included diversifying production, introducing European immigrants, and supporting farmers in other ways. The idea of producing a variety of crops, including products for local consumption to develop internal markets, was driven home by the drop in the price of sugar in 1884. After that, every so often, writers revisited the feasibility of a number of crops: ramie, bananas, cocoa, coffee, tobacco, rice, beans, tamarinds, figs, avocados, and others. The hope was that drops in market price, when they occurred, would be distributed among a number of products, and that at any given time some of the products would be in high demand and so bring high profits. In addition, writers advocated a deliberate marketing strategy, leaning on consuls to conduct consumer research and make contacts to introduce Dominican products to foreign markets. Several advocates of European immigration argued that they could form colonies that would serve as models of scientific agriculture. Railways, paved roads, and credit unions would make the Dominican Republic more attractive to immigrants. In addition, the country would be in a better position to grow economically if it took a definitive stance on the persistence of *terrenos comuneros* amid the push for private property, and if it could reconcile production for foreign markets with small-scale cultivation for subsistence and limited regional markets.[51]

The variety of opinion regarding the preferred economic path allowed a forceful discussion of important issues about the development of the country. Bonó, Hostos, and López feared blanket modernization based on sugar and its concomitant proletarianization as cane fields multiplied and increased their production for export. Journalists praised the efforts of planters in collectively advocating modern production methods and sharing scientific information and encouraged them to spread the word to other foreigners who might want to make similar investments. At the same time, immigration schemes, as discussed in chapter 3, were not devoid of conflict. Still, the words of President Cáceres to Congress in 1908 captured the mood that prevailed in this period:

> I do not make any other promise but that I will sow every day with sincere faith the good seed. We Dominicans must, for every drop of blood spilled in the fratricidal struggles [of the past], give the earth two of sweat; only work offers us a dignified and prosperous life appropriate to free men. Fulfilling the duty of exploiting the riches that our indifference has preserved inactive and spilling them around the world, we will lay [the foundation for] the progress and the glory of the fatherland.[52]

POLITICAL IMAGININGS

A vigorous conversation about the Dominican Republic's political potential matched the difference of opinion that marked the discourse on the country's economic future. Among the political concepts that were the object of thoughtful consideration in the Dominican Republic at this time were the centuries-old sovereignty of the people, decentralization, and individual rights. Ideology paved the way for practical solutions so that good ideas would conceivably become everyday realities.

The input of the general public into the decision-making process became an essential component of the notion of legitimate government in this period. Several authors highlighted the difference between "the people" and "the government," sometimes referred to as "the state." For example, a column in *Renacimiento* established the distinction between a type of sovereignty that resided in the constituted authorities and was synonymous with power, and the sovereignty of law, which resided in the people and was a divine right that only God could withdraw. There was general consensus that the interests of government had in the past been synonymous with the benefits those in power wanted to obtain from their tenure. Under such circumstances, the welfare of the people was constantly at stake—under Heureaux, literally pillaged by his protégés. For Bonó, there was no question that citizens had repeatedly endeavored to achieve progress, and governments had placed obstacles to it. But imminent as the exercise of political liberties was, one writer proposed, the inevitable path for the country was an indiscriminate mix of high-level and popular objectives. As he put it, "our unavoidable mission is to work with [those who are] good, to fight for the welfare of our fatherland, and our work will be much more effective, more meritorious, more noble, and more honorable the more [government] and people are fused."[53] Francisco Henríquez y Carvajal and Américo Lugo went so far as to declare that rebellions (as opposed to revolts) were justified insofar as they opposed the violation of fundamental rights and were "a sign of the virility of a people." How that circumstance was defined depended, of course, on the writer. Henríquez y Carvajal himself, in his defense of President Juan Isidro Jimenes, objected to "revolutionaries" (those who could express themselves only through armed revolt), "doctrinaire theorists" (who, with the best of intentions, misread situations in an exaggerated way), and "evolutionaries" (who, despite their respect for the constitution, criticized the government in such "irrational and unmeasured" ways that they could pass for "revolutionaries").[54]

The connection between popular sovereignty and good government remained strong, and it became a commonplace in newspapers and magazines. Citizens had the responsibility of frequently informing the government of their needs and desires; likewise, the government had to respond to their wishes and thus direct progress. Society, wrote Francisco Pi y Margall, the Spanish federalist, in *Nuevo Réjimen*, should impose its will through the state, its instrument. This concept was so ingrained in the minds of Dominican intellectuals that at least two writers argued that the government had no juridical competency to sign an agreement, further burdening the country fiscally, with the San Domingo Improvement Company. Writers called upon the ideal and the practice of democracy, narrowly defined as rule by citizens, to remind Dominicans of the value of participation and of representation. The appeal to elect candidates to the constitutional assembly, not by district but nationally, contained implicitly the bolder assertion of the implicitly modernizing president, Ramón Cáceres, upon his inauguration: the act of voting had given birth to the nation.[55]

The preponderant weight that the presidency exerted over other branches of government and over administrative units and civil society led many to conclude that a number of reforms were not only desirable but also feasible. Decentralization and the simplification of administrative services seemed like obvious measures. Likewise, the renovation of attitudes about government was in order—a newspaper column in 1892 praised the performance of the municipal government and congratulated the members of the *ayuntamiento* (town council) as *public* servants. Even earlier, the same publication had already expressed its hopes for a different balance of power at higher levels of government—discerning legislators, in touch with the people and not subservient to the executive, would heed the people's will, while the independent press kept issues alive. Upon Lilís's demise, transformations extended to ministers, who were unequivocally described as young, energetic, righteous, honest, and educated. If Heureaux had distinguished himself for governing without the consent of Dominicans, the future would be nothing but the intimate connection between society and government.

> The July revolution did not have as a goal to crush a man, but to destroy a political regime in order to institute another; to substitute the reign of force for the supremacy of law; privileges for equality before the law; arbitrariness for legality; and the misappropriation of the funds of the people for their scrupulous investment in the only legitimate objective, in the satisfaction of social needs, which behooves public administration.[56]

Various beliefs, dear to Liberals because they encapsulated the fundamental rights of every person, lined the Dominican blueprint for political change. At the strictly political level, the contract between individuals and the state was fundamental—the state gave individuals liberty, with which they obtained education and work, and citizens in turn had the responsibility of letting their preferences be known through political participation. Variety of opinion seemed as important as the multiplicity of channels through which to express them; a convention of governors and other officials (as opposed to the citizenry) did not satisfy the requirements of *El Eco de la Opinión* for total liberty of expression and participation before the presidential election. On a more practical plane, journalists and statesmen stressed the connections between the high world of politics and everyday life: work, progress, and democracy went together, not only in campaign slogans but also in the ideological map of the Liberal intelligentsia.[57] The influential Henríquez y Carvajal complained:

> And if you love liberty, [why] do you strive to not [let] it take root solidly in our country? [An] exotic plant in our land, where all the biological conditions seem to be adverse: climate, people, traditions, legends, race, confusion of ethnic elements, incipient or corrupted education, exiguous industrial development, reduced mental evolution; its cultivation demands *such* care so that it does not die in this attempt at acclimation![58]

Based on their recent experience, Dominicans of all walks of life desired, above all else, peace. Using the same line of reasoning, they also felt that a popular uprising against tyranny was a perfectly acceptable goal. In either case, citizen participation should replace authoritarian habit, and local autonomy substitute for a centralized executive. Individual rights, the hallmark of European Liberalism, were also a part of the Dominican agenda, and men of letters insisted on freedom of the press and of association as a step toward achieving the national project. More than anything, they considered "inaction the moral death of a people in this century of activity, of struggle, of work; and [Dominicans] should not any longer offer the sad spectacle of a people debilitated, indifferent, and apathetic, in the midst of the free, progressive, and republican America."[59]

ELEMENTS AT VARIANCE WITHIN THE DISCOURSE OF PROGRESS

Most historians who have written about European Liberalism in the nineteenth century have dealt with a number of generic contradictions that were inherent to the Dominican national project too. With some room to make adjustments that take into account the particularities of time and space, one could argue that all countries that pursued the Liberal formula for modernization found that freedom and equality were often at odds, and that the outcome of exercising the liberty to pursue one's desires was often unfair, if also unexpected. In the Dominican Republic, the variance between ideal and practical reality can be located in four areas of the national discourse: the apparent incongruity between the rule of the market and the government's heavy hand; the incompatibility of the goal of participatory government with contempt for the common person; the irreconcilable difference between the economic strength pursued for the country through powerful entrepreneurs at the expense of marginalized social groups, such as women and the working class; and the conflict produced by the simultaneous desire to emulate the United States and the fear it inspired.

Because Liberalism has been, as a rule, imperfectly understood, most people find that the generic Liberal state was highly interventionist, hardly ever allowing the invisible hand to work its magic and regulating the lives of people at the most intimate level. In reality, as Daniel Rodgers brilliantly lays out, Liberals treated the relationship between state and society as an organic growth and not a mechanical arrangement. Because they believed that state and citizens worked together, the intervention of the state seemed to them hardly extraneous—on the contrary, it was expected to be the result of negotiations with civil society. In the Dominican Republic, Lugo, Bonó, Hostos, Henríquez y Carvajal—most of the authors consulted for this chapter—explicitly identified as one of the obstacles to progress the difficulties that arose out of the unequal development of state and society. Safely within the

Liberal fold, these thinkers believed that the rule of law would only be achieved upon the coincidence of purpose of rulers and ruled, and toward that end they worked.[60]

The problem, of course, was that men of letters and men of state did not trust the capacity of the subalterns to make educated judgments about their own, let alone the country's, future. It is at this juncture, I think, that the contradictions between economic and political Liberalism surfaced—for Dominicans as well as for other elites who considered the prospect of general enfranchisement. Reconciling property rights under capitalism and individual rights under representative democracy was not easy, even in the abstract. Did government exist to protect the propertied or to promote the "common good"? Did propertyless men, let alone women, have anything to contribute to the decision-making process? Rodgers offers another take on this dilemma. As he explains, economic Liberalism, so-called laissez-faire, had less to do with the free economy than it did with the freely acting, moral self. Insofar as they contributed to the collective well-being, individual actions were charged with moral worth. If wise (educated) decisions were, in fact, morally superior to uninformed ones, though, the popular classes of the Dominican Republic were indeed unfit for participatory government. Lugo especially, but others as well, found that uneducated people, not surprisingly, were unable to evaluate circumstances accurately with the limited information and scant experience they had at their disposal. Because of the popular classes' disorganization and apparent lack of purpose, the intelligentsia declared them incapable of collective action. Although without a doubt enthused by the idea of government based on the cooperation of all social sectors, the intellectual class was highly suspicious of the moral worth of the uncultured, economically deprived segments of society.[61]

In the strictly economic sphere, the same dilemma repeated itself. The country's progress appeared in Liberal schemes as the sole responsibility of an entrepreneurial class with the capital and the know-how to propel the economy. But other social groups, the intelligentsia was quite aware, were busy contributing to the island's welfare through their labor: immigrants from the West Indies and Haiti, working-class men and women in the cities, and women of their own class. Economically insignificant in the formulation of the elite's ambitious plans, they could be embraced by the ideology of progress only under very rigid terms of compliance to bourgeois rules of comportment. Liberalism in the Dominican Republic, as in other Western nations, had very little room for deviance from existing hierarchies.

Finally, Dominican intellectuals straddled the abyss created by their admiration of the marks of economic progress and political evolution evident in the United States and the threat the colossal neighbor posed to Dominican sovereignty. If "the great model Republic to the North owes its greatness of being to habits of work, a never-ending peace, social order, respect for the wise economic laws that guide it, [and] the contingent of emigration that flows from all parts of Europe," then the Dominican Republic could do as well if it followed suit.[62] But the adoption of these ideals seemed to come with strings attached, and the United States had firmly set its foot on Dominican soil, first through private investments in sugar and railroads, then as a financial associate, and finally as administrator of the customshouse and fiscal agent of the government treasury. In a way, this predicament was not that thorny—once the United States infiltrated full force, the intelligentsia coalesced against it, unfortunately, in hindsight, at the expense of other political and social alternatives that may have in the long run helped form a more lasting political class. Inevitably, anti-imperialism, a rough version of nationalism, interrupted the course of economic assertion and political consolidation.

The Liberalism that Dominican intellectuals experienced fits well with Rodgers's understanding of social politics—the push for progressive legislation in a capitalist context—from 1870 to 1940. Rodgers emphasizes first of all the exchange of ideas across the Atlantic, between Europe and the United States, by flesh-and-blood individuals who were public policy experts, lobbyists, members of international think tanks, journalists, and the like. More important, he explores the reasons other historians have advanced for the existence of these movements. Given the variety of opinion expressed in Dominican sources by the very same intellectual types Rodgers studies, it is hard to categorize the efforts of the intelligentsia as responding to pressure from below; as stopgap measures to control the working classes and safeguard the regime of property; as a political reflection of the elite's class interests; as a way of not only assisting the population but also of disciplining it—the choices Rodgers offers as plausible explanations for their actions.[63] This chapter contains evidence of all these motives behind elite efforts to shape a national project and more—of a genuine commitment to lift the entire population from the torpid past and launch it toward a promising future.

The discourse of progress, regardless of how overwrought it may seem a century later, reflected accurately the hopes and anxieties of the moment. Because of their education and experience, the political commentators and social reformers who advanced their views in newspapers and other publications were aware, even if only anecdotally, of the disadvantages the country faced. Duly elected government had been a rarity, and local authorities responded more to their own interests than to those of their administrative unit. The treasury was, in fact, depleted, and no one knew for sure how much income customs brought, because Lilís, his political associates, and merchant houses disposed of approximately a third of it annually. The island appeared underpopulated—with only 435,000 inhabitants in 1888, and 638,000 in 1908—and its infrastructure nonexistent for any economic development project. Under these circumstances and given the opportunity, educated men in a position to speak and be heard would have proposals ready for consideration.[64]

The deep-seated desire for regeneration on the part of the intelligentsia could not have been more appropriate to the times. Not only was the shadow of U.S. intervention lurking in the background; the eugenics movement in the rest of Latin America had also dictated the therapeutic agenda. It made sense for the Dominican Republic to embrace the cause of progress and modernization, to gravitate toward European culture and scientific learning. To remain competitive, the island had also to adopt the accoutrements of modernization, especially evident in cities elsewhere. Men of letters and men of state, then, turned their attention to Santo Domingo and San Pedro de Macorís, two urban centers whose populations were well-positioned to join the development race.

CHAPTER TWO

The City as the Site of Citizenship

The obsession with progress resulted in particular discourses regarding the construction of a new social order out of elements and under circumstances increasingly conspicuous in growing urban areas. For those interested in these processes—turn-of-the-century intellectuals and state officials intent upon shaping modernity, and present-day scholars scrutinizing them—Santo Domingo and San Pedro de Macorís, the two cities under examination in this book, hold much promise. Both cities, according to Jaime de Jesús Domínguez, had undergone in the period between 1880 and 1899 the same processes that Santiago and Puerto Plata had evidenced between 1868 and 1874—an increase in the number of exports, growth in the value of exports followed by a rise in imports, proliferation of commercial establishments and of other businesses in the service sector, internal and external migration, emergence of light industry, establishment or increase of public services, demographic growth, and territorial expansion.[1] Because of its status as capital city, to borrow Jorge Lizardi Pollock's take on Mexico City, Santo Domingo reflected national trends and served as the gauge of the success of the state's modernizing functions. The capital was the site of power, and in the same way the Mesoamerican metropolis's architecture was "an act of representation and acquaintance with citizenship," the Dominican capital's laws and ordinances served to affirm the hegemony of the civilizing thrust and to instruct the subaltern on his or her duties.[2]

Both Santo Domingo and San Pedro de Macorís became metropolitan centers of the first order as a result of the advent of sugar in the last decades of the nineteenth century. The capital and its accessory challenged the economic primacy of Santiago, the northern seat of economic power, and by extension, threatened its monopoly as the island's political and cultural trendsetter. In their frenzied activity and diverse population, Santo Domingo and San Pedro contained, literally, the material out of which the architects of the nation-in-the-making molded their hopes and fears. For state and local officials, they represented in addition the opportunity to hold the population to the standards of modernity already witnessed in other countries. The city setting, then, further localized the national project, making it conform to its European roots, while neutralizing the African influences that obtained in Dominican soil. But if nationalism, as defined by the Dominican intelligentsia and discussed in the last chapter, was inclusive and forward-looking, citizenship, as hammered out in daily intercourse between municipal authorities and city dwellers, was exclusive and presentist.

CITIZENSHIP IN THE CITY

Two views structured Dominican intellectuals' understanding of the significance of the city to the national project. On the one hand, Santo Domingo and San Pedro de Macorís were perceived merely as commercial centers that traded in the commodities the rural areas produced, which brought the treasury much-needed revenues. From the perspective of the staunch defenders of peasant producers, such as Pedro Francisco Bonó, the cities were parasitic concentrations of people, insofar as they did not produce goods directly and so stimulate the economy, and only put pressure on the productive apparatus of the rest of the country by consuming more than they contributed. Evidence of this was the frequent alliances between rural folk and the opponents of urban-based parties, which Bonó attributed to the general aversion between city and countryside and to the injustices that were a function of proletarianization, however incomplete. In another sympathetic representation of the rural masses, Rafael J. Castillo excused the alleged depravity of peasants by accusing urban residents of having earlier set a bad example; to say that he blamed city dwellers for the ways of men and women of the countryside and for their dire situation would not be an exaggeration.[3]

Scholars have tended to agree with the assessment of the Dominican countryside as a site of production and the city as the locus of consumption. At the turn of the century, not even Santo Domingo could pass as a nucleus of industry, with the concomitant division of labor. In fact, a majority of city dwellers were still involved in agricultural and animal husbandry pursuits, and those that were not lived off the profits made through commercial transactions. This representation contrasts with that of large cities in the American continent; José Luis Romero, for example, relates how, upon the feverish and hectic explosion of productive activities in late nineteenth-century Latin American cities, the countryside turned into a place of refuge and leisure. It is safe to say, however, that in both cases the city imposed itself as the location for decisions regarding the exploitation of the rest of the country.[4]

Another view of the city held it as the depository of the elements that Liberals considered essential to modernity. Compared to the custom-bound and disperse countryside, urban centers appeared to respond to markets, to be sensitive to wage fluctuations, to alter their work rhythms according to industrial exigencies. Metropolitan concentrations may have been vulnerable to the depredations of the marketplace, but in the minds of intellectuals, they also stood for property, law, and politics. Cities were also the site of webs of interpersonal relations, and "[i]f the nation was to be reformed, it would be by first seizing the social possibilities of the cities." The values that city dwellers upheld would presumably be read in street signs, building patterns, methods of transportation, and public spaces. Order and control would eventually permeate the cityscape, and residents would truly represent themselves in their surroundings.[5]

Both visions, however, concurred in that the concentration of population and the high level of activity that marked city life held the promise of an improved political and social order. The "unitary civil model of liberal nationhood," popular all over Latin America at the turn of the century, relied on the emergence of political notions that the Dominican intelligentsia could imagine only among educated, cosmopolitan, urban populations: respect for the law, accountability of public servants, citizen participation, and civil rights. At the center of this construction was the modern concept of citizenship as a bundle of rights and obligations that bound the individual directly to the state. The adhesive agent, at the turn of the twentieth century, was not only the market of the early 1800s but also "the nation." To early nineteenth-century notions of the economic welfare of the community, then, the identification of its cultural patrimony was added as the force behind civic engagement. In terms of entitlements, it was in the city that education and public services joined, in the early twentieth century, the political rights the nineteenth century had established as markers of human progress—voting, representation, and others related to the transfer of political authority.[6]

Dominican public intellectuals could have defined membership in the polis at the turn of the century in a number of ways. According to the constitutions in effect in the period under study, Dominicans were people who had been born on Dominican soil or of Dominican parents abroad, or who had been naturalized, usually after living on the island for two years. All

Dominican males over eighteen years of age were citizens, a status that entitled them to a number of individual freedoms, including the right to vote. Modern thinkers, of course, privileged participatory citizenship over the more passive form. Those who could vote and did so were held in high esteem as a result. In between these two types were men and women who worked, owned property as a result, and were consequently upstanding members of the community.

To what extent any of these citizen-types believed they could *effectively* participate in the collective undertaking of organizing society, if they chose to, is almost impossible to determine. Most likely, the majority of the population of the Dominican Republic remained politically unimagined. The intellectual class and government authorities could hardly conceive of the general populace as a political force, believing that most Dominicans did not respect the force of law (they took up arms in the service of the first strongman who came their way) and did not consider the general welfare (meaning that of the hegemonic classes) but only their own. The masses, urban or rural, could probably not imagine themselves playing the part assigned to them either. But the point Romero makes for the larger urban centers of Latin America is pertinent here—as new social classes made their appearance in the urban milieu, they had to find political expression for their needs and aspirations outside the existing oligarchical molds, and in so doing, they became a democratic force. Political thinkers, of course, continued to believe that insofar as people lived out the rhetoric of patriotism that emanated from their pens (and that I reproduce below), they constructed the nation on a day-to-day basis. As I will argue in the rest of this book, their subalterns had other ideas.[7]

An eloquent discourse connected work, service to the country, property, self-worth, and progress to participation in the national project. Bonó, as usual, took the lead—as early as 1880, he called on the president to defend the common laborer, "who is the fatherland" (*que es la patria*), as he denounced the appropriation of peasant lands by capitalists. In 1884, he included the itinerant herding groups of the south among "the Nation" and lamented the incapacity of men to fulfill their duties as citizens and their obligations as heads of families because the sugar industry had confiscated their livelihood and dispossessed them of their "citizens' rights" (*derechos ciudadanos*). He recalled the establishment in the 1840s of training centers that would retool soldiers into craftsmen. Here the collective interest was blended with national defense as "the benefit to the individual was folded into the performance of the duty of the citizen." As the century turned, an enthusiastic columnist captured the same feeling in these words:

In what constitutes the true life of peoples and the only solid base of their progress and glory, the country offers to the gaze of the patriot who has faith and the dispassionate man who inquires and who studies under the clear and peaceful light of reason, that is "the beacon of conscience," the unequivocal testimonies of its longed-for transformation: dignifying work spreads through the entire fatherland, and the labors of the peaceful and honest citizen transform into men of duty the fanatical henchmen and the caretakers of the old tyrannies, the blind collaborators of our painful fratricidal struggles.[8]

To call themselves citizens, Dominicans had to be selfless, educated, hardworking, moral, and—one could add, to please Bonó—landholding.

As already noted, the benefits of education were almost an obsession with writers of this period, intent as they were on taking any opportunity to form the next generation of citizens. Bonó and Hostos drove this point home at every turn and linked schooling with democratic government (a function of citizenship) and individual achievement (made possible by market forces).[9] Citizenship, sometimes referred to as "civilization," required skills that were learned, not only in the course of employment but also in school halls. More important, insofar as literacy conditioned the ownership of property, a substratum of second-class citizens existed among those who could not read and write.[10] Indeed, for Francisco Henríquez y Carvajal, the ideal citizen not only worked, supported a family, and served in the armed forces because he loved his country but also was politically informed and voted. He was the man

who can talk about his individual work, about his personal labor, about his duties as a private man, about his duties as family head. He has any old job, any profession, from which he lives; he has a home and a family, of which he is the trunk, and in which prevails the moral atmosphere that gives comfort: that of domestic duties. And he is a citizen who loves his Fatherland. He laments its misfortunes and strives or longs for its welfare, because he wishes [the best] for his own children. He joins in supporting the State with a part of what his personal work produces, and he reflects on public matters with his vote. His military arm does not move except when the Fatherland is in danger or when all the rights and public liberties have been violated by an inveterate tyrant and the entire nation trembles painfully. He is delighted by that renovation of the public spirit, but he is not seduced [into] making of himself an ambitious fool who will waste his energies in ridiculous plans, of turning from a free citizen, through his own condition as a man, his personal work, and his home, into a pathetic pariah of a political situation, nor into a diminished parasite in a trunk that appears to be prospering . . . That is the worthy citizen. He reads the papers, laments the ravings of some dreamers, condemns the ill will of masked agitators and applauds the constant effort of those who really carry in their heart the true spirit of the people and who know how to adapt to current circumstances, to labor ceaselessly to procure for the country, day to day, more advantages on the road to progress. He maintains his will unscathed, and will publicly attend with it, when necessary, to deliberate with his vote on serious matters . . . That is the citizen, that is the patriot.[11]

Even at the level of ideas, the contradiction between the efforts of Liberal thinkers to institute democratic government and the state's habit of maintaining control through more autocratic, clientelistic mechanisms that undermined the foundations of citizenship revealed itself. New conceptions of the relationship between the individual and the state and between economic agents and the market required the fiction of nonhierarchical, consensual, mutually beneficial relations between producer-citizens and their governing bodies, precisely because the state was attempting to replace competing individuals (local lords) or corporate bodies (notably the church) in the management of economic life. Western states, including all of Latin America, found it easier to dismiss the incongruities caused by the interplay between authoritarianism and citizenship as if they did not exist, and the Dominican Republic followed suit.[12]

In addition, the connections between political principles imported from Europe and their applicability on American soil were tenuous. Already in the early decades of the nineteenth century, Simón Bolívar had alluded to the dangers of transplanting the precepts of the Age of Reason to the particularities of the Latin American environment. Later in the century, José Martí identified two universes in Latin America: one was carried in the head, the other moved beneath the feet; one contained ideas imported from the United States and Europe, the other was social reality. To further call attention to the even more tentative circumstances that obtained in colonial and postcolonial settings, to the perhaps insurmountable gap between the reality of would-be citizens and the values of their rulers, a scholar of Liberalism put it this way: "Misery does not produce citizens." But although the clash between high-flown notions of citizen participation and the actual monopoly of power should have invalidated the claim of elites that they operated for the benefit of the entire citizenry, "good politics," as repeated all over Latin

America, managed to articulate authority and subalternality and projected the discourse of liberation (from Spain) as the basis of the nation-state. The Dominican Republic was no exception.[13]

Santo Domingo and San Pedro de Macorís, each in its own way, possessed the full potential of citizenship, as envisioned by the Dominican intellectual class and as regulated by state officials. If anyone was positioned to take advantage of the opportunities opened up by educational institutions, by economic restructuring, and by changing political attitudes, it was the inhabitants of these urban centers, both relatively recent in terms of political weight (Santo Domingo) and of economic success (San Pedro). The two cities enjoyed an economic boom due to the growth of the sugar industry, which had spawned a number of subsidiary manufacturing operations as well as service-oriented occupations. In both, massive numbers of migrants had settled in the last decades of the century—in Santo Domingo, from other parts of the country as well as from other islands, and in San Pedro, almost exclusively from abroad. These transformations coincided with, and made urgent, the implementation of the latest ideas on human progress: universal secular education, productive employment, freedom of association, ability to vote, and so on. As did other Latin American urban concentrations at the time, both cities jumped eagerly at the chance to put into motion these processes.

SANTO DOMINGO

Santo Domingo at the close of the nineteenth century was by all accounts an ugly, insalubrious, and dangerous city. According to one 1899 visitor, all that was left of its colonial splendor were dilapidated buildings, now run-down and misused by the city's inhabitants, which "breaks the spell" the city would otherwise cast on the visitor, "because its lowliest population consists of dirty blacks and trash abounds everywhere." Another visitor, in 1908, lamented that refuse decomposed all around, utilities did not work properly, and gambling houses and taverns marred the social scene. The town council itself had targeted certain neighborhoods as eyesores and health hazards and endeavored to improve hygienic conditions there and to contribute to the material progress and aesthetic enhancement of the city. The municipal sheriff, equally concerned with safety issues, had requested the town council to clear the vegetation and debris from a number of lots "to avoid certain immoral acts that are committed in the tall grass." Residents of some of these undesirable areas lived in fear "of being hurt by the copious stones thrown around, or, what's worse, of being attacked by individuals who with their misdemeanors have duly alarmed the neighborhood."[14]

This negative vision could very well be the product of the clash between reality and expectations. Santo Domingo, at the turn of the century, was still the smallest *común* (administrative unit) on the island and had a population of, at most, twenty thousand, only 3 percent of the island's inhabitants. Local commerce on Conde Street, which continues to be the downtown commercial district, had a small-town character—buyers and sellers rode in, dropped off or picked up products, and engaged in a little conversation with the store attendant or owner, who closed shop when business was slow or he needed a break. City residents kept animals in their yards, which they milked or slaughtered for the family or for sale; hunted pigeons for food; shared water wells with their neighbors two or three streets over; disposed of their wastes in backyard latrines or in the ocean, with the help of two men designated for that purpose; and participated in public civic and religious festivities where all classes ate, drank, sang, and danced together. The pretensions of visitors and city officials may have soared almost to compensate for residents' mundane experiences and lifestyles.[15]

Santo Domingo nevertheless was showing every sign of material growth and ideological progress. Its function as the center of government since the colonial period, coupled with the establishment of several sugar mills in its vicinity, impelled business interests to concentrate there. In terms of customs revenues, the port on the Ozama River led all others in the Dominican Republic, although some large ships continued to anchor outside the bay, which was not deep enough to accommodate them. Santo Domingo was also proud to be able to educate its young people (at the Instituto Profesional, the Escuela de Bachilleres [Bachelors' School, or High School], the Escuela Normal de Maestros [Normal School for Teachers], the Instituto de Señoritas [Girls' Institute], and the Escuela Preparatoria Santo Tomás [Saint Thomas Preparatory School]); to take care of the needy (at the old-age asylum run by the Sociedad Benéfica Amiga de los Pobres [Friend of the Poor Charitable Society] and the mental asylum and orphanage established by the Junta de Caridad Padre Billini [Father Billini Board of Charity]); and to cultivate exceptional intellects at several literary clubs (Unión, Casino de la Juventud [Youth Club], Club de Damas [Ladies' Club]). The press was well established with a daily newspaper (*El Listín Diario* [The Daily Directory]), several weeklies (*El Eco de la Opinión* [The Echo of Opinion] being probably the most important), and a number of magazines with differing life spans (*Renacimiento* [Renaissance], *Blanco y Negro* [Black and White], and others). Seamstresses, caterers, machine repairmen, degreed doctors, and quacks advertised their products and services in these publications. An aqueduct had graced the old city since colonial times; a mule-drawn, one-wagon trolley transported people on steel rails beginning in 1880; electric street lighting was a reality in 1896; the telegraph, the phonograph, movies, cars, and airplanes followed in rapid succession after the turn of the century. The city, then, was a peculiar mix of carryovers from a time not yet past and portents of inescapable progress.[16]

The pace of life was confusing for business travelers who were sizing up Santo Domingo's economic potential, but it served residents well, according to historians and urban planners who have studied the city in depth. Arriving visitors at the port were usually disconcerted: they encountered narrow streets, small houses with big doors and long windows with iron bars, men with wide-brimmed hats on spirited horses, black men reclining against walls, donkeys carrying enormous haystacks, shops with extravagant merchandise. Once in the city, the disjunction between stone or masonry buildings in the urban core and wood or adobe houses with thatched roofs in the periphery provided some reassurance that class distinctions were firmly in place. Most accounts describe the city as safe, or at least apparently so—there were no street fights, robberies, or drunkenness to be seen anywhere. Tourists invariably remarked on the Spanish custom of napping at midday, the men and women retiring to hammocks in rooms that faced the courtyards, those on the street protecting themselves with parasols. Although American and some Northern European visitors found these rhythms quaint, more knowledgeable commentators recognized these routines as signaling a more sane pace in which there was room for gossip on the street, conversations with the dwellers of open-door homes, and exchanges of products with sellers or friends.[17]

The city, in fact, had a unique character that its residents liked to highlight. Certain neighborhoods were well known for the economic class, ethnic or national origin, or occupation of their inhabitants, or for some particularly memorable or regularly occurring public affair connected to the site. The center was reserved for the well-to-do families whose distinguished members had accumulated fortunes in commercial agriculture, import trade, and more recently sugar production. Navarijo, to the west, was known for its hardworking, honest population, most of whom worked in commerce. A bona fide working-class ethnic neighborhood was La Estancia, whose inhabitants hailed from Curaçao and worked as carpenters, cabinetmakers, and small-business entrepreneurs. San Lorenzo de las Minas, three miles northeast of the city, was settled in 1719 by Akan, or Mina, slaves from the Gold Coast of Africa fleeing Saint Domingue, and it reconnected with the city center yearly when its famed drummers paraded through the commercial district. Northwest of the city center, near Parque Independencia, was San

Carlos, founded by Canarians in 1684. Ponce, in the southeast corner of the colonial city and overlooking the mouth of the Ozama River, had apparently attracted women from the southern Puerto Rican city of the same name, many of whom practiced prostitution. To the west of Ponce was the "English colony," a sector of the city populated by immigrants from the British West Indies. La Fe and Galindo, on the north, were known as settlements populated by migrants from other parts of the country. Other residential quarters included, to the north, La Fajina, El Polvorín, San Lázaro, San Miguel, San Antón, and Santa Bárbara; at the center, La Catedral, Santa Clara, Las Mercedes, and El Convento; and to the south, La Misericordia and Pueblo Nuevo. Pajarito (popularly named so for a character who slipped on the wet street and whose umbrella opened wide with the wind, thus resembling a bird), now called Villa Duarte, was across the river, on the other side of Puente Mella.[18]

The reputation of alleys and streets extended to surrounding areas. La Misericordia got its name from one poet's moving description of the hangings that occurred at a spot upon which a monastery was later built. It grew to become a distinctive community, out of which spun stories and folk tales of the city's formative years. Callejón Sal-si-puedes (meaning "get out if you can") was known as "a veritable labyrinth and nocturnal passageway for suspicious and fearless people." One can safely guess that Callejón del Convento was so named for the location of the Dominican convent school at its northwestern corner. But one can only speculate on what the "m" stood for (perhaps *muerte* [death]?) in Callejón de la M, also called de las Flores, probably because cut or planted flowers adorned the spot. Callejón de la O was supposedly named after a woman who went to bathe in the river on a Good Friday and was transformed into an inlet; street boys since then have chanted "*María de la O, tu madre es puta, la mía no*" (María de la O, your mother is a whore, mine is not), and the sea would rise up.[19]

Town life developed around specific spots or happenings. The famous Parque Independencia was until 1884 only a wide, flat expanse of land with a public well in its center. Circuses and bullfights were held there—hence its old name, Placer del Conde (Leisure at Conde Street). Another memorable event was the arrival every year at Christmastime of the Minas Africans. They played the drums at Regina Church, and people would give them money, sweets, and drinks. At carnival, a local male resident would dress up as a wide-hipped woman with large buttocks and would shake his waist to mark the rhythm of a ditty children sang as he threw them candy. During those festivities, a special privilege was to summon the *diablos cajuelos* (trickster devils) to the streets to perform their pranks. The most elaborate group was the one organized by the stevedores, the Diablos de la Marina—because the occupation paid so well, they had the best costumes, with mirrors, bells, and multicolored hanging strips of cloth. In addition, *solares* (lots, housing areas) developed spontaneously as people crowded into unsafe dwellings around a single spot. The custom of erecting crosses in a public locale to mark the collective ritual space of the *solar* served to give the site a religious-civil identity. Although the archbishopric protested the demolition of these crosses at the turn of the century, the municipality saw them only as facilitating public gatherings that they could not control and quickly disposed of them or transported them to a nearby church.[20]

Two statistical renderings of the condition of the city captured the authors' measuring rods of progress (see Table 2). Construction materials, residents' occupations, and availability of urban amenities served to distinguish between the areas reserved for "decent folk" and substandard neighborhoods for the working poor. The undesirable elements of the population had been pushed to the "high" (northern) quarters, where they lived in shacks with thatched roofs. Ciudad Nueva, the new part of the city built under Lilís outside the colonial fortified wall, had houses built with foreign wood and roofed with zinc.[21]

SAN PEDRO DE MACORÍS

Sugar was the running thread in San Pedro de Macorís's short history. The settlement at the mouth of the Higuamo River grew from fishing village to bustling sugar town almost overnight in the 1880s. The first sugar mill was Angelina in 1876, followed by Porvenir, Cristóbal Colón, Puerto Rico, Santa Fe, and Consuelo. In 1882, San Pedro was made a maritime district, and in 1907, it acquired the status of province. In just twenty years, the town boasted all the amenities of a budding metropolis—large commercial houses, a good port, adequate river transport facilities, small manufacturing operations, a normal school and a girls' school, paved and lighted streets, a hospital and asylum, a theater, trolley cars, newspapers and a magazine, and several social clubs and intellectual societies. The mark of progress was such that Salvador Ross, a landowner and wealthy businessman, saw fit to donate a clock for the church tower upon his return from a business trip to the United States in 1893. By 1915, the town proudly cited among its comforts electric lighting, large concrete homes, sidewalks, a hygienic slaughterhouse and market, a fire station, a police force, and night watchmen. A mosquito eradication program and a retaining wall against the ocean were added assets.[22]

Although San Pedro had only fifteen thousand inhabitants as late as 1920,

TABLE 2
Statistical Snapshot of Santo Domingo,
1893 (and 1908)

Population

    14,702 (18,626) permanent inhabitants

    72 in transit (2,290 foreigners)

Layout

    34 (45) streets, 365 street lamps

    34 (33) public buildings

    (9 plazas or parks)

    (4 monuments)

Type of Housing

    293 (303) high (multistory?) houses

    2,361 (2,559) low houses

    2,654 (2,862) total

    1,593 with spouts to the street

Construction Material

    1,287 (1,327) masonry

    1,367 (1,535) wood

Type of Roofing

    907 thatch roofs

    868 galvanized steel roofs

    687 Roman roofs

    89 with clay tiles

    54 with slabs

    49 without a roof and in ruins

Available Services

    4 public libraries

    10 pharmacies

    11 (24) hotels, restaurants, cafés

    12 (14) newspapers

    4 (4) bookstores

    37 (43) schools

    6 (6) police stations

    15 (16) churches

    23 (90) carriages for rent

    24 (19) individually owned carriages

    135 (162) carts

TABLE 2

(continued)

Profession of Residents

  20 (44) lawyers

  5 (8) engineers

  5 (7) land surveyors

  4 (7) dentists

  5 (5) notary publics

  18 (16) physicians

  2 contractors

  (1,332 property owners)

  (23 pharmacists)

  (6 midwives)

SOURCE: Luis E. Alemar, *La ciudad de Santo Domingo (Santo Domingo, Ciudad Trujillo)* (n.d.; reprint, Santo Domingo: Editora de Santo Domingo, 1943), 274; *Censo de población y otros datos estadísticos de la ciudad de Santo Domingo*, edición oficial del ayuntamiento (Santo Domingo: Imprenta de García Hermanos, 1893), 10–19; *Censo de la ciudad de Sto. Dgo. al 20-XI-1908* [Santo Domingo?: El ayuntamiento de Santo Domingo?, 1909?].

NOTE: Available comparable information for 1908 is in parentheses.

its surrounding areas held close to forty thousand people, a situation that must have worried the town council. In an effort to manage the growth of the town, then, the occupation of city lots was a closely regulated operation. People who wanted to live in town, men and women in equal numbers, as far as I can tell from my random sample, requested permission from the town council to build a dwelling, presumably for personal use. The town council generally approved the request, requiring that construction be completed within a year, that it stay within the confines of the lot (about thirty-six feet by forty-eight feet), and that the building be at least twelve feet high. For the most part, the structures erected were *bohíos* (huts) or *puestos* (stands), generally made of wood, rarely of brick. If the person who was granted the construction permit did not fulfill the contract in the stipulated time, another person could request the same lot, which made the claim of needing a six-month extension a popular maneuver. Another common transaction was to request "possession of the *patios*" (yards) in which the houses had been built. This procedure gave the occupant title to the land for a specified amount of money (twenty-five pesos, in one instance), and at times it preceded the actual building on the property, if there ever was any. Sometimes there was disagreement between applicants, as occurred when Miguel de Soto and his neighbor claimed the same lot, although Soto had built the house that occupied it. Things could get very complicated—Margarita Chiquet requested and paid for a lot that was granted her, but she realized upon her attempt to occupy it that Nicomedes López had already built a house there. The solution the town council proposed—that she work it out with Mr. López—was doubly disconcerting. Although the procedure to occupy and then purchase a lot upon which a structure could be built, but sometimes was not, seems straightforward, it is also evident that the town council could favor one person over another in a number of ways, including drawing up the demarcation lines.[23]

The "foreign" character of San Pedro, which constantly preoccupied authorities, was evident at all levels. At the top were the owners of large sugar mills on whose success the town grew and the commercial agents that they used to market their product. They came from Puerto Rico, Spain, the United States, and Cuba after the Ten Years' War (1868–78) and had names such as Bass, Serrallés, Ross, Viccini, Bucher, Stiernstan, Fritzberg, Croisier, Phillipps, Fitzarciler, Schirmer, Locwens, Weber, Steffan, Aguayo, Fillmann, Zeloy, Balbuena, Stake, and Wiese. There were a number of other foreign family names, notable among them those of Middle Eastern or Persian origin, that circulated in the town's commercial circles or in the municipality, such as Zaglul, Kidd, Coiscou. At the bottom of the social scale were workers imported from the British West Indies and their families, who settled in sectors of the town named Jacob-Town, Sufrimiento, Villa Bergara, General Cabral, and Miramar. They are identified by name (Anita Box, Frank Salomon, Llensina Montifú, Alvina Fosie, Llimis [Jimmy?] Barcalari, Chom Lee, Lili Winquin [Wilkins?]) or appellative (Francisco el árabe [the Arab], Tomás el inglés [the Englishman, meaning an English subject, probably from the British West Indies], José el puertorriqueño [the Puerto Rican], Jamesón (chino) [Chinese]).[24]

Because of its spectacular growth, the budding metropolis was the symbol of feverish economic activity, and it cultivated this reputation. As early as 1892, El Eco de la Opinión sang its praises—in a column entitled "Correspondencia del interior" (Correspondence from the provinces), it celebrated the contract signed with the U.S. steamship company Clyde, which would provide service in San Pedro without paying dues; the rising price of land; the coming patron saint festivities; the construction of a park; and the new public clock, to be donated by Juan Serrallés (or Salvador Ross, unless the town got two new clocks from the generosity of two sugar mill owners). In a cartoon published in Renacimiento, the caption read: "In San Pedro, the drones that in other hives do well and prosper, die there because diligent life overwhelms everything and it imposes on everything a seal of activity that forces the lazy to 'ruin their shoulder.'" Joaquín Bobea, one of the founding fathers, declared with certainty that in the city's "muscular arms, the progress of the country is, one can almost say, upheld."[25]

San Pedro could brag about the modern services it offered its residents. In terms of public hygiene, officials divided their labors with precision: sweepers and weeders, garbage collectors, and yard (latrine?) inspectors. Municipal officials were also intent on recruiting the support of the well-to-do in communal improvement efforts. The report of the inspector for hygiene and sanitation noted that the administrator of the Porvenir and Santa Fe mills had been ordered to build an overpass over the drain in a town street corner. The functions of this municipal body were, in fact, wide-ranging and included overseeing the sale of prepared food and butchered meat, checking sanitary conditions in homes and backyard latrines, disinfecting sites and personal items after deaths by contagious diseases, handling sick animals, properly burying the indigent, inspecting the manufacture of medicinal compounds, managing alms begging, examining prostitutes, and vaccinating children. The members of the commission did not mince words when they filed their reports. In 1904, they found that the cemetery and slaughterhouse followed the stipulated guidelines, but the market "was a site of infection worse than the mangroves that surround the town and the latrines." The meat stands had trash and pieces of fat and meat strewn around; people slept on top of the tables; the well water was a dark green color, and a shoe sole floated in it; rumor had it that a dead animal lay in the water. The commissioners' apparent obsession with contagion was not misplaced, and city residents must have felt reassured by their exploits. The threat of a smallpox epidemic, for example, was very real in March 1904, when three cases were discovered aboard the warship Jamkee, and another ship, the Yofeka, remained under observation in Mayagüez, Puerto Rico, where another four cases had been identified.[26]

PUBLIC ORDER

Local officials, perhaps not as enthusiastic about forming citizens as men of letters, but certainly as inspired by the material indicators of progress as anyone else, were concerned with the disorder that they felt relatively new social groups in a rapidly changing economic setting would bring. As much as their counterparts in other urban centers, they were intent on showcasing in their jurisdiction the progress that would mark the country as a whole. For this reason, they set out with zeal to regulate city life and made it a point to keep abreast of similar developments in other urban centers. The Santo

Domingo town council embraced the advantages of implementing construction codes, introducing sanitary regulations, forming a constabulary, instituting street lighting, maintaining green areas, and otherwise facilitating daily life through the amenities familiar to other metropolitan centers. Smaller or more recent urban concentrations, such as San Pedro, underwent a scaled-down version of this urbanizing thrust, complete nevertheless with the enforcement of municipal ordinances, the demarcation of residential and commercial lots, and the management of public and private services.[27]

An intensified enforcement of municipal ordinances signaled the seriousness of local authorities with respect to staying competitive in the impending urban race. As always, entire *ayuntamiento* (town council) meetings in the capital and in San Pedro were filled with discussions over wandering animals, building permits, waste disposal, the quality of milk and water, butchering procedures, and disease prevention, especially cholera. A lowering of the tolerance level for infractions, however, was in order, as well as tighter control over the changes taking place all around. Using this line of reasoning, then, a member of the Santo Domingo town council demanded to know why two instances of wandering animals, whose owners should have been fined, were not duly recorded by the commissary. Likewise, another official expressed his desire to be informed of the construction of sidewalks in the city. The town council was adamant in its decision to improve sanitary conditions in the city—it denied a request to butcher animals at home from a resident whose animals were so fat he couldn't walk them to the slaughterhouse and cracked down on house animals when the threat of disease was imminent. In the neighboring *común* of San Carlos and in San Pedro, government representatives took measures to assure themselves that public dance halls paid for the required license, probably because it was a source of revenue for the municipality, perhaps as a way to get people used to the presence of government, or because they wanted to know what was going on in every corner of their jurisdiction. The minutest details of city management continued to be under the purview of town councils, and their desire to perform efficiently and effectively became ever more evident.[28]

All of the Santo Domingo town council's actions toward the administration of the markets were an exercise in the new politics of urban management. There were three markets that served the city and its suburbs: the Ozama, the 27 de febrero (February 27, the date of independence), and the Antiguo (Old). Every year, businessmen bid for the superintendence of one or more of six areas that required oversight: meat cart; ferry across the Haina River; sales tax, slaughterhouse, and weights; ferry across the Santa Cruz River; corral and pigpen; and cockpit.

TOP: The Parque Duarte in San Pedro de Macorís. (Archivo General de la Nación, Colección ADAI, album 1, photo 24.) BOTTOM: The Parque Independencia in Santo Domingo. (Archivo General de la Nación, Colección ADAI, album 5, photo 2.)

TOP: Santo Domingo slaughterhouse under construction. (Secretaría de Estado de Fomento y Obras Públicas, *Reseña de la República Dominicana* [Santo Domingo: Imp. La Cuna de América, 1906], 100.) BOTTOM: The store interior of La Industrial y Comercial (Unidentified magazine page in Archivo General de la Nación.)

TOP: The San Pedro de Macorís town council. (Unidentified magazine page in Archivo General de la Nación.) BOTTOM: The Club Unión, one of several gathering places for men of means in the capital. (Enrique Deschamps, *La República Dominicana: Directorio y guía general* [Santiago de los Caballeros: Vda. de J. Cunill, Barcelona, n.d., ca. 1906–11], 99.)

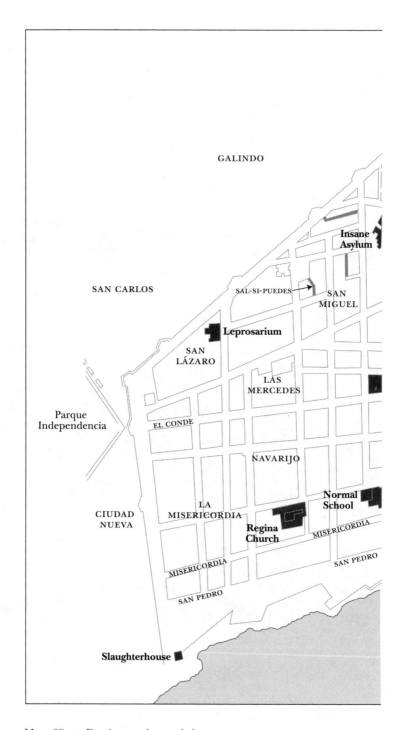

Map of Santo Domingo, early twentieth century.

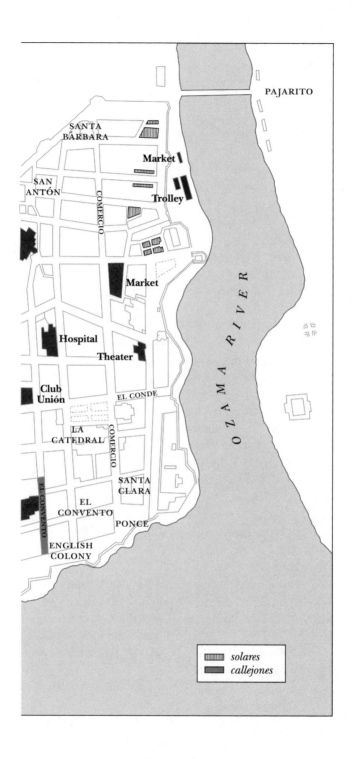

PAJARITO

SANTA
BÁRBARA

Market

SAN
ANTÓN

COMERCIO

Trolley

Market

Hospital

Theater

Club
Unión

EL CONDE

LA
CATEDRAL

COMERCIO

SANTA
CLARA

EL
CONVENTO

PONCE

EL CONVENTO

ENGLISH
COLONY

O Z A M A   R I V E R

solares
callejones

Despite this apparent transfer of authority to the private sphere, there was always some controversy that the ayuntamiento had to sort out. In 1888, administrators wanted to restrict the movement of itinerant sellers to the late morning (10:00 A.M.) because it conflicted with market sellers. In addition, and perhaps moved by the owners of market stalls, they intimated that the town council should charge street sellers a market tax, since the baskets on their heads were the equivalent of a market stand. Two years after this, a major argument ensued between sellers and management over the charge of fifty cents per week per stall. Sellers felt that they should not be charged "rent," since they had title to the booths from which they sold their products. The town council had to clarify, then, that the fifty-cent charge was not rent, but a market tax, and that the municipality could repossess the area on which the stands were located, if need be. The minister of the interior added, gratuitously, that the stalls were neither pretty nor hygienic. Yet, at the end of that year, the town council agreed to let several sellers build additional stands provided they met certain specifications—they had to be approximately two square meters and have zinc or tile roofs. It took a few more years for a commission to be formed to study the recurring safety and hygiene problems that were reported to the town council.

Disagreements with the administrators also remained a constant: in 1906, the ayuntamiento fined the person in charge of the Haina ferry, because the boat had filled with water during a storm due to his carelessness in securing it to the dock. At work in running the market, as in other aspects of city administration, were the desire for order, the self-imposed pressure to conform to modern standards of hygiene and aesthetics, the inclination to experiment with new forms of doing business, and the preservation of old patterns of fiscal prudence and personal loyalty.[29]

Conformity with the appearance of urbanity in the city core—another mark of the progress for which the city longed—was tightened up throughout the period. In Santo Domingo, thatched roofs were outlawed except in working-class neighborhoods because of the threat of uncontrolled fires, and zinc roofs were permitted in the streets surrounding the Parque Independencia, itself a very recent addition to the cityscape, only if they were hidden from view. The regulation of activities that were considered "unworthy of a cultured people," such as cockfights, bullfights, and alcohol stills were the subject of intense discussion among provincial governors, members of town councils, local mayors, and residents.

Likewise, the prohibition against animal husbandry (*crianza libre*, free-range livestock raising) was revisited over and over again. As early as 1880, a columnist advocated the reinstatement of the practice on the part of public officials of capturing animals that were roaming about, as an incentive to the owners of such animals to keep them fenced in. Not only were animals, especially pigs, that were kept in backyards (let alone those roaming around in front of a house or in public areas) an unseemly sight; they also promoted uncleanliness within the city boundaries because of what they ate and the wastes they produced. In San Pedro, the police superintendent found it hard to convince a town dweller that his cow and newborn calves were disturbing the peace when they bellowed to find each other during the night. Along with the testimony of twenty-one neighbors, he sent a moving note to the town council, explaining that he needed to have fresh milk for health reasons and defending the cow: "Being it public and notorious that this is, without peer, the most docile and friendly [cow]; so that from its pastures it comes to my house and from here to the pastures without harming anybody; what's more, so domestic that it crosses through the center of the house and in the midst of my family as if it were an animal raised by hand." Eventually, the ayuntamiento ruled that owners of cows that had just given birth would be fined five pesos each time the animal made too much noise and double that for subsequent transgressions. In 1893, stray dogs were exterminated in San Pedro, and in 1908, roaming pigs were caught and their owners fined in Santo Domingo. A cleanup campaign focusing on yards and latrines ensued. Three years later, more legislation reinforced the same principles: animals had to be fenced in if their owners lived within a radius of four kilometers of provincial capitals or in population centers that were the seats of town councils; in agricultural areas; or in places where crops for export or for internal consumption were planted in more than two *caballerías* (about sixty-six acres).[30]

Another noticeable change in this period was the promotion of standards of living (and their material accoutrements) that were believed to be a commonplace elsewhere. Although the ayuntamiento had always eagerly taken up the causes of public hygiene, safety, services, entertainment, and order, new operations began to fall under its purview toward the end of the nineteenth century. In mid-1892, for example, the weekly *El Eco de la Opinión* floated the idea of vaccinating the entire population against smallpox by having a doctor traverse the country accompanied by a cow with live pustules and following up by not accepting children in school who had not been inoculated. It later published a list of measures to avoid the croup, considered the most contagious of diseases; and congratulated the town council for a number of successes, among which were the purchase of street-cleaning equipment and a fire engine. A code that regulated the sale of prepared foods on the street was published in 1906—it stipulated the suitable means of carrying the products, the conditions in which the food should be kept, and the proper attire for the sellers. In 1909, the new position of municipal doctor was created, and in 1915, a leprosarium and a crematory for animals were founded.

Throughout the period, roads were furiously repaired, not only to make them more passable for residents but also to open them up for the first time to the passage of carriages and carts. This process was especially important, and particularly significant, in those instances where the road in question was on a hill with houses on either side, an accomplishment for engineers at the time and a challenge for urban planners up until the 1930s. A resolution that was undoubtedly ahead of its time required the movie theater to increase the number of exits for safety reasons in case of fire, to widen the aisles for the comfort of the public, and to place a zinc division instead of a curtain to separate the projection booth from the audience. Another new project, at least in conceptualization, was the deliberate construction of green areas, usually in existing *plazas*, complete with benches to sit on, electric lighting, trees for shade, and tiled paths. The crowning achievement, a sewer system, was in the works in 1906. The objectives were not new, but the level of execution was certainly unparalleled compared to previous years.[31]

Officials were also observing behavior to measure the extent of progress in the Dominican Republic, especially in urban areas. One early basis of concern was the marked presence of children on the street (as opposed to in school). There was certainly a public-order motivation behind this preoccupation, but the appeal was to those who believed that the mark of a progressive nation was universal school attendance. Similarly, popular wisdom urged that civilized people should treat animals, including beasts of burden, with care and a degree of respect. The same columnist lamented that cart operators and itinerant sellers of goods placed excessive burdens on their animals and beat them to make them move faster. A lively discussion ensued in the town councils of both Santo Domingo and San Pedro over the habit of cart drivers of riding on the vehicle rather than walking beside the animal. Seemingly a safety precaution, it also suggests that only "decent" people should ride, as was the custom in colonial Spanish America, and that their appearance should be pleasing to the eye. In the same vein, the rehabilitation of Santo Domingo's central plaza, located in front of the cathedral, was hailed as a necessary measure "demanded in unison by the advances of the century, [and] taking into account the degree of civilization that societies have achieved in sociability."[32]

Municipal codes were frankly understood as guidelines for a civilized urban existence, and an ordinance prohibiting dances when there were sick people in the neighborhood or that required the use of bathing suits in the ocean and rivers was not too small a matter for the attention of the town council. The president of the Santo Domingo town council moved in 1884 that the governor of the province prohibit *bailes de cueros* (drumming dances, although the word *cuero* can refer both to the skin of the drum and to nudity), apparently a diversion licensed by the municipal council prior to that time, "as these end up being an opportunity for very lamentable disorders that tend to lead to the relaxation of good customs that have up to now distinguished us." The municipal prefect of San Pedro did not mince words when he tried to suppress the dances in which drums were played. He was moved by "the many complaints that I have received daily due to the scandal caused by the *plenas* [a type of African-derived dance] and amusements in which the drum is played, reminding [one] of the times of the *congos*, and tormenting hundreds of families . . . I have wanted to carry out what the other town council proposed, which was to permit them their amusements, but not with the inappropriate drum, because neither morals nor the times embrace [this measure]."[33]

It should have been no surprise for city residents, then, that civil authorities were changing their attitudes with respect to the degree of control they wanted to exert over the city's diverse populations. Progress necessitated a change in the definition of problematic matters and in the procedures used to deal with them, so that tolerance gave way to the desire to manage and, in some instances, to prevent situations. A growing sense that an agreed-upon moral economy and social pressure were not enough to maintain the desired public order pervaded the conversations of town councillors. A few examples follow.

Whereas some felt that disturbances to the peace in working-class neighborhoods could be contained, in one instance, by the simple construction of stocks to be administered by residents who took on the attributes of a municipal guard, others demanded increases in the number of rural and urban police to control the growing population and the social problems it caused. The governor of Santo Domingo province asked the central government to recognize that a city of sixteen thousand was bound to attract much crime if vigilance was lax; to appoint more night watchmen; and to increase the number of police officers in the inner city, where robberies and fires had become more frequent. The prefect of San Pedro requested the purchase of five revolvers so that all twenty agents would be armed. A new city official, the municipal doctor, did not see patients, at least not as part of his public functions, but rather inspected foods, oversaw vaccinations, recorded deaths, visited asylums, checked prostitutes, and "cooperate[d] with the police."

Acting on the concern of local mothers, who felt that the police presence in the Santo Domingo slaughterhouse was insufficient to prevent the street children and young people who gathered there from horsing around and picking fights that sometimes moved dangerously close to the bluff, the town council decided that troublemakers would be summarily picked up if they had no occupation. Years later, officials in nearby San Carlos considered detention facilities so inadequate that a dungeon in the military headquarters was rehabilitated. Perceived increases in disorderliness led to increased state control.[34]

A parallel development was the understanding that the functions of the police extended further than merely ensuring compliance with the letter of the law and that they required a degree of discernment that would permit officers to stand above the general populace. In bills redefining the attributions of the rural and urban police, which early in this period shared jurisdictions by virtue of the types of situations with which they dealt, legislators cast law enforcement officers as models of the highest virtues of citizenship. Rural police deputies, for example, had to be Dominican, older than twenty-five years of age, familiar with agricultural practices, moral, and have good habits. They should visit the area's denizens, proffer advice regarding crops, prevent gambling, mediate conflicts, and ensure that roads were free of debris. Urban police should not only ensure that the law itself was being followed but also watch that residents behave with moderation during public festivities. The law contained stipulations regarding the appearance of building fronts, waste disposal, transit of animals in the urban core, proper language and comportment, acceptable activities for children (school or a trade), public entertainment (namely, cockfights, which could take place only on Sundays or holidays, and games of chance, which were prohibited), and more.

The creation in 1908 of the Guardia Republicana (Republican Guard), a corps of volunteers that would guarantee the social order and impose work discipline in urban and rural areas alike, reiterated the moral and physical superiority of police deputies—they were required to be Dominican, between the ages of eighteen and fifty, of a certain height and weight, have good habits, and be healthy. The reasoning behind this selectivity, a writer suggests, was the desire to increase the number of agents that could be trained "to respond thoroughly to the obligations they were entrusted to carry out. When this occurs, the police service . . . will satisfy the demands [imposed by] circumstances, and [the objectives of] communal hygiene and safety will reach even greater heights in the scale of culture that civilization demands." A list of their functions confirms their role as enforcers of appropriate behavior: regulation of cockfights, prosecution of games of chance, imposition of monetary or work levies for the construction of roads, eradication of the insurrectionary tendencies of the population, prohibition of religious acts such as wakes, prayer meetings, or all-night affairs where alcohol was consumed in excess, among others.[35]

Similarly, the ayuntamiento expanded its jurisdiction to include previously unimaginable functions. Education and hygiene, of course, had been under the purview of municipal authorities since colonial times. But whereas those categories had originally referred to not much more than building schools and keeping the market clean, by the early twentieth-century, education included instilling in the citizenry the basic rules of urbanity and providing them with the spaces in which to exercise them, such as sidewalks, gardens, and public parks. Similarly, hygiene extended to health, and the town council took charge of hospitals, cemeteries, and asylums previously run by the church and distributed vaccine fluid to control disease. Stretching even further definitions of the public welfare, in 1912 Santo Domingo's municipal council listed among its functions promoting immigration and drawing up a registry of city residents.[36] Convinced that the times demanded inspired leadership, public officials cast themselves in the role of guides of the population at large.

Well into the second decade of the twentieth century, Santo Domingo and San Pedro de Macorís boasted the entire panoply of indicators of material growth and well-being—electricity, port facilities, educational institutions, newspapers, paved roads, and parks. Both cities, moreover, strictly regulated economic and social activity through the enforcement of standards for building, for selling in the market, even for public conduct. In their eagerness to control the quality and the pace of urban life, public authorities engaged as well in molding the behavior of city residents. As they endeavored to make it possible for everyone to belong to the community, as they defined it, they insisted on conformity with standards of living that may not have appealed or been accessible to the population at large. As one can tell from their continued campaigns to clean up the market, to capture stray animals, to control traffic, and to enforce dress codes, their will remained unbent.

THE CITY'S CITIZENS

As it is all too easy to predict with hindsight, the high dreams of the intellectual class and the focused efforts of local authorities to make urban residents into modern citizens did not proceed as smoothly as the first two would have wanted. For their part, the subalterns were going to reject the official perception of their persons and their situation as problematic, based as it was on the authorities' mental association between environment and people. As explained earlier, the division of Santo Domingo (and of San Pedro de Macorís, for that matter) into a cultured and well-off center and a working-class, if not poor, periphery reinforced social boundaries. "Geographies of exclusion" were at work in the Dominican Republic, as in much of Latin America, and cities became "the historical layout of the lines of the urban social classes and the spatial drawing of the moral precepts of the dominant classes." Disorderly and dirty people lived in untidy and unsanitary spaces. Although the Latin American eugenics movement did not suggest that these undesirable characteristics were being passed on biologically, another equally dangerous leap in logic was made. The physical disarray and confusion that was the norm in working-class neighborhoods pointed to a lack of morals and disrespect for the law.[37]

The other representation working-class city dwellers would refute was that their standing was inferior because the space they occupied belonged to the state. From the perspective of the government, scholars have pointed out, people who lived in poor sectors were less than respectable, not only because their limited choice of residence showed they had few resources but also because, by virtue of occupying land without holding legal title, they were open to intervention at any time. Government officials, as already noted, were fond of reminding the working poor that, unless they held legal title to the plot in which they had built a house or a business, the land belonged to the state. For the government, public (in the sense of not private) space signaled permission to interfere. Poor people, whose living space was constantly violated, created another kind of public space, one that they could control. This was everybody's space, the zone of sociability, composed of stores, cafés, pubs, market stands, plazas, and street corners, where people conversed, exchanged money or goods, kissed, argued, played, or worked. In it, personal dignity remained intact, as municipal officials could hardly invade such public activity.[38]

Despite subaltern resistance to control from above, government forces had a stronger hand. For one thing, the city was easy to police. Compared to the countryside, it was a compact area, with a diverse and disorganized population, that functioned comparatively well through patron-client relations and whose access to social services was, after all, more tangible than it was for rural dwellers. Secondly, and this was especially true in Santo Domingo, the stakes were high—the civility index to which the state aspired was intimately linked to the disciplining of urban space. As mentioned earlier, it was in the city where statesmen had placed the gauge of material progress and where they expected to see results incarnated. To the extent that city dwellers did not conform to the exigencies of the moment, the success of the ideology of progress was at risk. It is not surprising, then, that force, the third motor behind state action, was used more liberally with migrants and itinerants—from the perspective of the authorities, these shifting populations were the true masters of space and as such required discipline.[39]

In reality, both high and low, powerful and powerless, and everyone in between were making sense of their surroundings, which brought about, at one and the same time, modernization and the distancing of most of the population from that process. Despite the seemingly endless offer of opportunities and services that could be obtained in the city, the urban core remained for the marginal classes a small, limiting place, where their mobility was constrained by the resources accessible to them, by their insufficient knowledge of how to tap available benefits, and by the very real physical restrictions, almost persecution, imposed on them by police officers. The city, then, was not only the site of modernity, and as such, the not-countryside. Contrary to the assertions of historians who discern a deep divide between rural and urban settings, I maintain that the city, like its rural counterpart, was a place for the expression of conflicts, a space where "expressive phenomena . . . come into tension with the rationalization of social life." In both settings, marginality was becoming universal, or one could say more positively, diversity was more widespread.[40]

Ultimately, it was the complicated web of relationships that city dwellers engaged in—with peers, municipal authorities, social superiors, the state, economic associates, and so on—that formed the basis of citizenship. The city had to "work" because its inhabitants had to obtain services, solve conflicts, make a living, amuse themselves, and connect with each other. More than town council meetings or municipal codes or prosecution of inappropriate behavior, the everyday interactions of urban residents molded notions of citizenship.[41] The following chapters explore the forces from above and below, internal and external, that defined this process for three subaltern groups: immigrants, bourgeois women, and working-class men and women.

CHAPTER THREE

Race in the Formation of Nationality

Indispensable to the blueprint for progress, as one would expect, given its proponents' preoccupations, was the regeneration not only of the country's economic base but of the population as well. Immigration was one of the proposed solutions to economic and social ills, and the Argentine dictum "*poblar es gobernar*" (to populate is to govern) became a commonplace among Dominican policy setters. Reality set in, however, and faced with thousands of black workers from the West Indies and Haiti in the first decade of the twentieth century, both men of letters and men of state had to reconcile their presence with the stipulations of the national project. In sorting out the place of immigrants in the social, economic, and racial hierarchy, the intelligentsia forged political categories that would be used and abused, with some variations, for years to come. The nature of "the national character" as a work in progress, constantly under revision to fit the circumstances its shapers confronted both in the abstract and in the day-to-day, was set, I would argue, in this period.

THE THRUST FOR IMMIGRATION

Immigration was imperative, in the first place, to make the island produce more and accumulate riches. With that in mind, social reformers and state officials envisioned modern agricultural projects on previously uncultivated land, farms whose technology and methods would be the most advanced. Hostos appealed to strictly material interests when he advocated the creation of an immigration society formed by creditors of the state and linked immigration to the reduction of domestic debt. The hardworking, honest, skilled, and economically stable colonists that the Dominican Republic expected to attract would compensate for the unwillingness of Dominicans to work. As explained by a journalist, the heat prompted people to go lie down after 11:00 A.M.; rural folk had enough to eat for a year by working the fields for a month; and they had few needs that they had to meet with money, so they refused to work. This analysis failed to mention, of course, that Dominican peasants saw no reason to work the property of others when they had their own fields to cultivate.[1]

The second goal of immigration, to "populate the island," was perhaps even more urgent, if we follow the logic of the moment. According to Hostos, without a critical mass, that group of men whose destiny it would be to lead the country by transcending their individual interests and imagining the common good, would never be a reality. The supporters of immigration schemes, moreover, expected white European settlers to bring to the Dominican Republic their own notions of "organization," a term that suggested not only that local production methods were careless and deficient but also that social relations could be strengthened through active community building. Hostos went so far as to assert that these "organized families" would serve as an "economic, domestic, and civic model" for their neighbors. "That industrious, intelligent, and honest immigrant [population] that might come to populate our fields, to figure out the future of our fecund soil, to give practical lessons to our farmers, [who are] settled in the fatal and dreadful routine in which they live, consigned [to it], without hope," was the key to the improvement of the country. In addition, immigration would serve as a "biological element [to] increase the vitality of [the Dominican] race with a contingent of new blood that [will] activate and strengthen that which circulated in [its] veins." As late as 1916, the president of the republic wanted to solve "the vital problem of repopulating—with healthy and vigorous people—the loneliness of our countryside."[2]

The debate over how to attract immigrants reinforced these two thrusts, which dominated the discourse from the late nineteenth to the early twentieth centuries. If the Dominican Republic was going to successfully target "the white, healthy and hardworking people [it] want[ed] to attract," some major social and economic reforms were in order. The Dominican population, for one thing, must cleanse itself "in body and soul," according to Francisco Peynado, the future secretary of state. Cleanliness of body had to be total. It was not enough to prepare the areas where the immigrants would settle—"the entire country [had] to be sanitized [*higienizarse*]." Cleanliness of soul referred to the political apparatus that ensured equal treatment for all citizens—the laws and institutions that promoted social justice, such as schools, jails, and charitable organizations, which, according to the author, were not securely in place.[3]

Economically, the Dominican Republic had to undergo certain transformations before it could convince any future residents that there were profits to be gained by settling there. Writers recited the same litany in their pleas for action: roads, transportation, property ownership, disease control, taxation, tariffs, salaries, cultivation methods, capital investment—all had to improve in order to function properly and to result in economic growth. It did not allay the concerns of the advocates of immigration at all that a Haitian newspaper considered the Dominican Republic "worthy" of immigrants because of its natural resources, internal peace, increased commerce, rise in property values, concessions to enterprises, and equal civil rights for citizens and foreigners—they considered this inventory their wish list. Echoing their own formulas for progress, Dominican intellectuals placed their hopes on the human and economic impetus they would gain with immigration.[4]

A number of immigration laws or decrees were approved in this period that responded primarily to changing circumstances in the sugar industry and to the shifting demographics of the Dominican population. In 1879, an executive decree allowed planters to directly contract with laborers from other countries. The minister of development worked out one such agreement in 1884, when families from the Canary Islands were imported to work in the sugar industry, at a time when prices had dropped and wages followed suit. The planter would provide rooms or materials to build a dwelling, oxen and farming equipment, crops and land for subsistence purposes, and $2.50 to $3.00 per one hundred *arrobas* (between 2,400 and 3,600 pounds) of cane. The wage workers were bound to work only for the planter with whom they had contracted. Agricultural settlers had more flexibility, as the government gave 50 *tareas* (about 8 acres) to every adult male who wanted to settle independently, 100 to childless couples, and 125 to couples with children.

The stipulations became a bit stricter in 1905 because up until then there was no law against "criminals, invalids, lepers, prostitutes, and all kinds of people with bad past histories or suffering from contagious diseases" coming to the island. The 1905 law, then, required a certificate of good conduct, thirty pesos in gold or a contract with an agricultural enterprise or with the government, and no evidence of contagious diseases. Foreigners from Europe and the United States had sixty days to comply with these requirements, whereas West Indians had thirty days. By 1909, interested parties were advocating openly for European colonists, who they felt should be provided with transportation to the Dominican Republic, land, seeds, animals, and agricultural equipment. Preference should be given to

> families with experience in the great crops over those with pastoral backgrounds, in which still prevail communist traditions, seldom appropriate to the development of strong individual [efforts], and over those who live in fruit [producing] zones, whose labor is reduced to gather the fruit, [therefore] being little apt for large-scale commerce and for the transformation of those products in industrial [settings].

In 1912, the island opened its door to "all civilized people in good health," although non-Caucasians needed a permit prior to entry. Recruiting offices were to be established in Europe, the United States, and the former Spanish islands, which would negotiate contracts with farmers, who had to be stable, educated, in good health, and in possession of five hundred pesos.[5]

The newspaper record gives the impression that none of these schemes was entirely successful. The German consul to the Dominican Republic inquired in 1880 about the best lands, the fertility of the soil, the climate, and the cultivation of certain crops; *El Eco de la Opinión* wistfully hoped the matter would be resolved in a way that was beneficial to both parties. In 1884, as the enthusiastic supporter of immigration that it was, it boldly opined about the national origins of possible immigrants. The Spanish were desired because of historic ties; people from the Canary Islands and Navarra, because they were industrious, healthy in body, and strong of spirit; Belgians, because they were good workers and had good judgment; and there was no justification given, perhaps because none was needed, for the preference for immigrants from Alsace-Lorraine, Austria, Germany, or Hungary. At that time, the government approved, as *El Eco* had advocated, the allocation of 30 percent of export duties to immigration efforts. But that money, like much of Heureaux's most promising projects, never materialized. In the 1890s, there was talk and some movement to tap into Puerto Rico. But by 1893, the ayuntamientos were released from the requirement of setting aside 5 percent of their income for immigration and agricultural purposes; much to their relief, they could now use this money to meet other obligations, especially as concerned education. In 1908, the minister of agriculture, responding to the president's call, asked the ayuntamientos to report on vacant lands: Which could be available for immigrants? What crops could be planted in them? What river or transportation systems were at hand? What was the distance from other settlements? Evidently, the work of immigration was yet to be done.[6]

What the Dominican Republic sought and what it got were two very different things, although, as noted above, proponents of European immigration continued to seek *dei ex machina*. Sources do not always provide consistent information, but it is easy to conclude that the island as a whole, and especially Santo Domingo and San Pedro de Macorís, became the preferred destination of men and women from the British West Indies and from Puerto Rico prior to the turn of the century, and after 1910, of Haitians and less so of residents of the former English colonies (see Table 3). Migrants from the Lesser Antilles arrived in large numbers earlier than any, because of the land and employment crisis in their own home islands. They worked as stevedores in Puerto Plata, and the women in their group functioned as laundresses. British West Indians were disparagingly called "*cocolos,*" conceivably a corruption of the name of one of their islands of origin, Tortola. (The name has stuck, and it no longer carries negative connotations in the Dominican Republic.) Cubans and Puerto Ricans were both manual laborers and middle-class "professionals" (teachers, skilled artisans, and the like), also escaping a contracting economy and political turmoil at home. "Turks" or "Arabs," who do not appear in significant numbers in statistical data, dominated the itinerant vendor market, some owning prosperous businesses in Conde Street and Mella Avenue in the capital. Only a small contingent of Swiss immigrants grew cocoa in Samaná, and Germans cultivated rice in Sabana de la Mar, true to the dreams of immigration proponents.[7]

Needless to say, immigration proponents were very disappointed. Almost in defiance of the orderly schemes that floated around at the time, men from Tortola, St. Kitts, Grenada, St. Vincent, St. Martin, Aruba, St. Thomas, and Curaçao arrived by the thousands on the island, in sailboats run by pilot-entrepreneurs who charged the one hundred or so workers they packed into the boat ten pesos each for the trip alone. Travel lasted seven to eight days if the weather was good, twice as long if the winds were contrary. Cocolos replaced Puerto Rican laborers in the early days of the sugar crisis of the 1880s, when neither the latter nor Dominican peasants would work for the wages offered. They came alone and, after a few years, brought their families or married into the Dominican peasant class. Those early arrivals, some of whom stayed in the Dominican Republic year-round, not only cut cane but also worked as carpenters, masons, mechanics, petty traders, and the like. They settled in particular neighborhoods of San Pedro—on the southern edge of town by the sea, in Miramar and Yokoton (Jacob-Town). In Santo Domingo, the "English colony" was undoubtedly space claimed by immigrants from the British islands. By the 1890s, a steady influx of cocolos arrived each year for the harvest and left soon afterwards, a flow that raised suspicions among some sectors of Dominican society.[8]

ANTI-IMMIGRANT SENTIMENT

A vigorous anti-immigration campaign filled the pages of *El Listín Diario*, which appeared to be speaking for the working class and for the country as a whole. Cocolos were accused of not spending money in the Dominican economy, sending their savings abroad, begging, being dirty, spreading disease, monopolizing the industry, and depressing salaries. Puerto Ricans too were "a phalanx of unemployed and vicious [men], who swarm in the streets of [San Pedro de] Macorís or who live holed up in a hellish gambling den." In a rare anti-immigration statement, *El Eco de la Opinión* also called immigrants "bad elements, perturbers of the economic order, vicious in the social order." Merchants did not like immigrants, because they did not buy much—they saved all their money to take home. Dominican workers presumably were well aware that the immigrants' presence reduced wages and restricted their own bargaining power vis-à-vis their employers, so much so that cocolo demands for better pay in 1911 went unendorsed. The Sociedad de Propaganda en Favor del Bracero Dominicano (Society for Propaganda in Favor of Dominican Workers) tried to "intimidate" laborers who wanted better working conditions during the strike at the Angelina mill. For his part, the governor of San Pedro asked the minister of the interior and police to put a stop to cocolo immigration to avoid further divisions. Cocolos especially were marginalized because of their "strange" practices. The head of the Republican Guard issued a prohibition against religious practices outside of Catholic or Protestant church buildings, claiming that they led to vagrancy and corruption. Wakes, puberty ceremonies, and other acts "of savagery that provide the opportunity for drunkenness and entertainment that undermine good habits"—clearly a reference to African religious traditions—were proscribed.[9]

Landowners defended the importation of foreign workers, and historians have registered its positive effects. William Bass, who in 1893 placed an ad in *El Eco de la Opinión* for one thousand men—specifying "no slackers"—justified his hiring of "Englishmen" by arguing, in his characteristic broken Spanish, that worker competence was in everyone's interest and that his top posts were filled by Dominicans. In his appeal for support to the Dominican government, he addressed a number of popular concerns. Immigrants were not competing with Dominicans for jobs, since the latter were only interested in working in their *conucos*. He also expected migrants from the French,

TABLE 3

Immigrants and Foreign Residents in Santo Domingo
and San Pedro de Macorís, 1882–1916

1882	1,953 immigrants, among them:
	– 847 "Spaniards" (probably from Puerto Rico and Cuba)
	– 379 "English" (from the islands)
	– 215 "Dutch" (from the islands)
	– 117 "Danish" (from the islands)
1884	500 foreigners, mostly cocolos, in sugar mills
1893	3,111 cocolos in San Pedro de Macorís
	William Bass imports 100 cocolos for Consuelo sugar mill
	Immigration Society of San Pedro de Macorís brings 250 Puerto Ricans
1900	1,500 cocolos in San Pedro de Macorís
1902–3	2,967 cocolos in San Pedro de Macorís, 1,500 cocolos in Santo Domingo
	4,500 cocolos imported for harvest
1910	3,000–4,000 foreigners in sugar mills
1912	5,000 cocolos in sugar mills
	4,885 wage workers in sugar mills
	4,000 British workers in San Pedro de Macorís
1913	5,000 cocolos in sugar mills
	4,885 wage workers in sugar mills
	750 wage workers from the islands for Angelina sugar mill, 300 wage workers for Cristóbal Colón sugar mill
1914	5,000 cocolos in sugar mills
	4,885 wage workers in sugar mills
	3,980 immigrants
	11,800 cocolos in Santo Domingo and San Pedro de Macorís
	2,000 cocolos and families arrive in the Dominican Republic
1915	5,000 cocolos in sugar mills
	4,885 wage workers in sugar mills
	6,448 immigrants, among them:
	– 1,315 from the British, Dutch, Danish, and French islands (but more probably 2,315, due to an arithmetical error in the source)
	– 2,020 Puerto Ricans
1916	5,000 cocolos in sugar mills
	4,885 wage workers in sugar mills

SOURCES: *Revista de Agricultura* (1913): 519–20, 522; José del Castillo, "Las inmigraciones y su aporte a la cultura dominicana (finales del siglo XIX y principios del XX)," in *Ensayos sobre cultura dominicana*, ed. Bernardo Vega et al., 4th ed. (Santo Domingo: Fundación Cultural Dominicana, Museo del Hombre Dominicano, 1996), 185; José del Castillo, *La inmigración de braceros azucareros en la República dominicana, 1900–1930* (Santo Domingo: Cuadernos del Centro

Danish, and English islands to be accustomed to respecting authority, to want to settle permanently in the Dominican Republic, and to not get involved in the occupations or aspirations of Dominicans. José Ramón López, director of statistics and respected commentator of the agricultural scene, considered foreign laborers "docile and hardworking," well-educated, disciplined, and possessing good hygiene. The British consul also acted as a buffer to verbal and physical attack on the cocolos—in 1895, 356 of them wrote to the queen to ask the protection of the consul because they were afraid their employers would imprison them arbitrarily.[10]

Most historians will agree that the negative labels foreign workers suffered reflected internal conflicts within Dominican society, and not the immigrants' particular history. Patrick Bryan, for example, suggests that the mixed-race Dominican elite felt a degree of discomfort in allowing entry to thousands of black workers from "Africanized" areas of the Caribbean—therefore opposing what was, from an economic standpoint, a perfectly tenable state of affairs. Harry Hoetink goes further, intimating that the reason the elite resented certain groups of immigrants was that the newcomers rivaled their control over their own Dominican "clients." The case of Costa Rica is illustrative of yet another alternative explanation for anti-immigrant sentiment in the Dominican Republic. As a device to divert the animosity of local workers toward the firm, the U.S. Mining Company imported West Indian laborers and gave them preferred status. Costa Rican workers, then, coalesced against their immediate oppressors, the West Indian guards used to control unrest. Hostility toward immigrants, then, had little to do with the immigrants themselves, but rather with elite dissatisfaction over their own position in the economic game. Cocolos, moreover, have left a very positive legacy in island culture, insofar as they established strong family networks, formed mutual-aid societies (notably, the Odd Fellows' lodges), founded Protestant churches (the famous "*chorchas*"), projected austere discipline in money matters, and deployed a strong sense of political activism. Despite the

Dominicano de Investigaciones Antropológicas, UASD, no. 7, 1978), 15, 38, 39, 50–51, 52–53, 56–57; Orlando Inoa, *Azúcar: Arabes, cocolos y haitianos* (Santo Domingo: Editora Cole y FLACSO, 1999), 122–23; Julio César Mota Acosta, *Los cocolos en Santo Domingo: Carta anti-prólogo de Pedro Mir* (Santo Domingo: Editorial La Gaviota, 1977), 12; María Elena Muñoz, *Las relaciones domínico-haitianas: Geopolítica y migración* (Santo Domingo: Editora Alfa y Omega, 1995), 76; Patrick Bryan, "La cuestión obrera en la industria azucarera de la República Dominicana," *Eme Eme* 7.41 (1979): 62, 64; José del Castillo, "Azúcar y braceros: Historia de un problema," *Eme Eme* 10.58 (1982): 15.
NOTE: I have remained faithful to the wording used by the authors.

isolation visited upon West Indians because of their language, religion, and other cultural practices, the very image of a closed community, diligent and self-sufficient, gained them the respect of Dominicans.[11]

Other immigrant groups, equally maligned at the time, also appear to have integrated into the Dominican context in a healthy way. In the case of "Turks" or "Arabs," classifications that included people from a number of African and Middle Eastern countries and probably Jews as well, it was not their numbers that made their presence noticeable, but their activities. As small-time traders, they were probably very aggressive and were considered boorish, unrefined, dirty, and afflicted with bad habits. Because the San Pedro contingent sold their products at a lower price than other merchants, *Nuevo Réjimen* suspected they were cheating the treasury—not paying duties on merchandise imported from wholesalers in the United States. The market merchants in Santo Domingo also felt Middle Eastern immigrants were taking advantage of the government; in 1905, they asked the ayuntamiento to have those sellers located on the beach of the Ozama River pay the same amount market vendors paid for their stalls in the market. "Turks," neverthe-less, became indispensable to the poor residents of Santo Domingo, whom they visited in their homes and sold merchandise to on credit. And as did Dominican citizens, "*árabes*" complained because they felt they were being charged too much for their business licenses; asked the president to exempt them from prohibitions against marrying close relatives; requested building materials from the ayuntamiento; obtained permission to settle permanently in the Dominican Republic; and were summoned to court as witnesses or for selling foods in unsanitary conditions. Their profile, indeed, is no different from that of other city residents, including Dominicans.[12]

This uneven but steady blending of newcomers into a larger immigrant milieu was the rule during the last decades of the nineteenth century and the first years of the twentieth. Puerto Ricans, Cubans, and Spaniards emerge in the documentary record as especially active in soliciting residency status, applying for public service jobs (e.g., chief of police, municipal guard), and initiating citizenship procedures—not surprising, given the language and cultural parity they shared with Dominicans. The Puerto Rican community especially had an enduring relationship with the Dominican Republic, as the first efforts to recruit cane workers were directed at the smaller island. By the early twentieth century, Santo Domingo had a "Puerto Rican Colony," an organization that oversaw activities that addressed Puerto Rican concerns.

Although less frequently, members of other immigrant groups requested citizenship status and applied for permanent municipal posts. All immigrant groups appear prominently in citations for minor civic-order offenses or public-health notations, where their ethnic identity serves as an identifying characteristic. Because "*el curazoleño*" (from Curaçao) Isidoro Mambre died with no money or relatives to cover his burial, a municipal official collected $3.75 among "*sirios*" (Syrians) and "*curazoleños*." "José *el inglés*," "Jamesón (*chino*)," "Nicola *el italiano*," "*el turco* Antonio Abdala," and "Eugenia Bieni, Leonie Didass, and Lrien [*sic*] Pedro, *martiniquesas*" were among the hundreds of people detained every year for selling adulterated milk, or yelling at each other, or letting animals roam unattended. Although it is telling that their nationality serves as a signifier for public-order purposes, their activities and the treatment they received are no different from those of other city residents.[13]

Despite the apparent integration of immigrant groups, so that they are virtually indistinguishable in the historical record from Dominicans themselves, there are many indications that the presence of foreigners on Dominican soil was indeed suspect. Not only were immigrants of the popular classes identified by nationality or ethnic origin in police records, as shown above, but there was also anti-immigrant rhetoric that emphasized the privileges they and well-to-do foreigners enjoyed vis-à-vis Dominicans. They did not, for example, have to serve in the army—although belonging to the National Guard would be a good way for them to earn a living, the author of a piece opposing universal conscription offered. Noticeably so during Cáceres's presidency (1905–11), foreign sugar planters were exempted from production and export taxes, while Dominican entrepreneurs and merchants felt burdened by new levies created to provide larger revenues for the state. A *Nuevo Réjimen* writer acknowledged that immigrants contributed to the "culture and progress of the country," but he was wary of their involvement in politics—under Lilís's regime, their influence was "great and corrupt." The impression that immigrants enjoyed a privileged existence continued until the end of this period—in 1915, the author of a piece on the price of land noted that civil strife did not affect foreigners (one assumes because they took no side), and as Dominicans respected private property, foreign investments were always safe.[14]

A public dispute between an *El Eco de la Opinión* columnist, his readers, and the newspaper's management allows a quick glimpse at how sensitive an issue the presence and actions of foreigners could be, at least in the early period. C. T. Wayo's gossip-type column, "Cosas," criticized the lack of attendance, especially by foreigners, at a circus function whose proceeds would be used to rebuild the avenue that led to the cathedral square. A reader riposted that many foreigners contributed to public works projects; that contributions were strictly voluntary; and that many Dominicans failed to show up at the benefit function, although they did go to the circus another day. Wayo countered by extending his condemnation of foreigners to "false foreigners"—those who declared themselves Dominican when there was something to be gained, but who claimed the citizenship of one of their parents when it was more convenient—and invited those who had opinions contrary to his to write in. The argument was put to rest by the intervention of the editor, who stated unequivocally that the newspaper disagreed totally with the columnist's view and "[would not] permit any more talk against foreigners."[15]

Even Eugenio María de Hostos, the Puerto Rican thinker whose commitment to the Dominican Republic was a given in certain circles, was attacked as an outsider. F. X. Amiama lamented that the education bill submitted to the legislature was written by a foreigner (Hostos had been appointed superintendent of public education). In Hostos's defense, an anonymous writer emphasized Hostos's dedication to the fatherland and pointed to the universal nature of his knowledge. In another writing, Rafael J. Castillo, editor of *Nuevo Réjimen*, challenged the use of the word "dominicanize" on the part of Hostos's opponents to suggest that his plans still had to conform to the needs of the Dominican population. Castillo declared himself against the "Dominican" system of learning, where children sat motionless and memorized, shaking in fear. Amiama continued his attack, calling Hostos an "American citizen" and his appointment a violation of the law. A *Nuevo Réjimen* writer reminded him that "America" referred to the entire continent and that Hostos had long advocated for the independence of all the islands—he was not a "Yankee." He was, in fact, ideal for the position, and even though there were some administrative posts that should have been filled by Dominicans, the superintendency of education was not one of them. It is telling that, although the root of the opposition to Hostos's ideas was that they were secular and undermined traditional values, they were attacked as alien to the Dominican spirit. Likewise, character assassination took the form of outsider status.[16]

One group of immigrants whose presence raised the highest expectations was planters. Only once, when William Bass went directly to the minister of the interior to complain about an incident at his mill, did *El Eco de la Opinión* criticize his actions: it denounced his behavior as alarmist and out of proportion because he had not first informed the provincial governor of the matter. The newspaper's opinion the rest of the time was, as expected, quite positive. Bass himself was admired for his dedication to work and the force of his capital investment, precisely "what the Dominican people needed to make it to the top." He was not above calling attention to himself, and he gave opinions and commanded notice, claiming that "all foreigners who have entrenched interests in the country are Dominican" and appealing to the universal character of business (in his words, "industry knows no nationality"). Salvador Ross, owner of Santa Fe, despite being a foreigner, collaborated in municipal public works efforts and toward the progress of the country. This behavior gained him a place as a "favored offspring" of the Dominican Republic.[17]

ANTI-HAITIANISM

Despite the conflicts that emerged, at both the abstract and the practical level, around the issue of immigration, only one group was truly vilified in this period, and that was Haitians. This is almost inexplicable, because their numbers were so small that the impact they could have had on the social order, or the influence they could have exercised on culture, were insignificant. But as the following paragraphs show, anti-Haitianism was a complicated sentiment that served well to accommodate worries about national security, disdain for Haiti's historical and economic development, and condescension for their cultural expressions.

Every expert on immigration in this period is agreed on the fact that Haitians began to arrive in Dominican cane fields late in the first decade of the twentieth century and were actively recruited as workers only after the U.S. occupation of the island. By 1919, ten thousand of the fourteen thousand wage workers in the sugar industry were Haitian, but there are no comparable figures before that year. Prior to 1916, however, a few traces of efforts to import Haitians as workers exist. María Elena Muñoz asserts, for example, that the 1912 law that allowed immigrants who were civilized and in good health but required permission for nonwhites was supplemented by a number of executive decrees, which insinuated that official recruitment efforts through agents should stop, but individual attempts to simply cross the border were welcome. Orlando Inoa also offers fragmentary evidence to confirm the increasing Haitian input into the operation of cane mills. In 1910, the *Gaceta Oficial* mentions not only cocolos but also Haitians among the "inferior" laborers whose presence discouraged Dominicans from working in the fields. The founding of *centrales* (modern industrialized sugar mills) on the island beginning in 1911 and the concomitant migration of workers to Cuba after 1912 encouraged Haitians to cross over to Dominican cane fields. In 1913, *El Listín Diario*, ever the enemy of migrant laborers, noted how the Dominican Republic served as the place "where the Haitian working masses flowed." In 1914, Inoa states, immigration from Haiti picked up rapidly, and by 1917, companies were sending agents to the western part of the island.

Although Haitian immigration to the Dominican Republic has always been seen as a function of U.S. capitalist penetration on the island, and it is clear that the numbers shot up during the American military intervention, the discreet presence of Haitians prior to 1916 is very much a part of the history of the Dominican Republic in this period.[18]

Haitians were treated to all kinds of insults in the Dominican press. In one single article in *El Eco de la Opinión*, the length of the list is only matched by the intensity of the language.

– "a people grotesquely carnivalesque in its way of being, and in its clumsy aspirations to potential singular grandeur"
– "Haitians are pretentious, arrogant, and contrary to the simplicity and morality of [Dominican] habits [and do] not want to submit nor to adjust to them; and as a consequence, only think of the absorbing [desire for] domination of the conquerors"
– "greedy neighbors"
– "neither their political education, nor their social customs, nor their pretentious arrogance, nor their crazy extravagances, nor their paltry and unusual objective of political-social isolation will be accepted"
– "eager to possess a more spacious field, in which to spill the exodus of its numerous population and the plethora of its ridiculous arrogance."

In that same year, another journalist added to the inventory: "aggressors, infractors, and violators of . . . rights and international conventions."[19] As a catalogue of Dominican fears of their neighbors, these insults correctly identified the resentment over Haitian rule from 1822 to 1844; the rejection of Haitian racial politics; the contempt for Haiti's economic situation; and the sense of Dominican superiority due to a perceived proximity to modern European political, social, economic, legal, and cultural practices, to which I now turn.

The simplest manifestation of anti-Haitianism came in the form of detestation of Haiti's political rule over the Dominican people in the early nineteenth century. The period from 1822 to 1844 is remembered in Dominican history, to this day, as "the Haitian Domination" (*la dominación haitiana*), a parenthesis in the development of native institutions during which alien laws based on unfamiliar principles turned social and political life upside down. At this time, in the words of an admirer of Juan Pablo Duarte, one of the men who led the movement to oust the Haitians,

the principal elements of society, the rich, the wise, the conspicuous, the well-to-do, fled abroad in search of guarantees for their interests, of respite for their lives, of respect for their homes. White peoples, manly peoples, made way for lucrative jobs for the Haitian. What desolation for patriotism! What a long and ignominious night! What a deep descent! What a great ruin filled the fatherland made a slave!

Hostos was alone in promoting the idea that Haitian rule, despite the damage it caused to family, property, and progress, performed on political society "the inestimable benefit of democratizing and equalizing to the point of erasing [at the level of] ideas and customs the notion of privileged authority and caste difference." The fear that history would repeat itself lurked in the background: "All the elements of Haitian society nurture the greedy thought of subjugating the Dominican people, turning it into a vile slave and a passive instrument of its retrograde intentions and of its exceptionally anti-cosmopolitan ends, at [a] time of universal expansion and fraternal ties of international friendship." Past experience had shown Dominicans that not only did they not want to be ruled by an outside power but also that their political trajectory was incompatible with Haiti's. "If the confusion [of others regarding the Dominican Republic and Haiti], (as different as they are in language, history, and republican ways), hurt the Dominican Republic, imagine what political union would [do]." The political opposition to Haiti had many levels indeed.[20]

Another key element of anti-Haitianism was the accusation of racial exclusivism, of isolationism, of anti-Europeanism. In this respect, Dominicans would always point to Haiti's birth as the result of a race war in which, according to the common wisdom, the savage destroyed the civilized. In the Dominican Republic, on the other hand, "the incendiary torch did not drag through villages, hamlets, or cities; nor —— [illegible] its fields with torrents of human blood, nor did it eradicate, so to speak, the vigorous vitality of the European race: colonizing, progressive, creative, and civilizing." For this reason, blacks and mulattoes in Haiti hated each other and continued to fight, condemning the country to material poverty. Dominicans, according to their own account, welcomed racial mixture and did not obsess about it, while Haitians prohibited confraternization, the mark of advanced societies. Because of the Dominican Republic's "cosmopolitanism" (read "European ideological influence"), Haiti would always resent its eastern neighbor and try to neutralize it.[21]

Haitians were despised for economic reasons as well. While most Dominicans were in awe of the rebellious slaves at the turn of the nineteenth century and feared the invading armies at midcentury, they looked at the working masses of the early twentieth century with nothing but contempt. Haitians who crossed the border to work in public projects or in the sugar industry were poor, illiterate, and performed slavelike labor. Dominicans who rejected the "peaceful invasion," as it was called, talked about this migration in bellicose terms—a proposed railroad from Enriquillo to Barahona was considered a potential weapon of war, which could fall into enemy hands, an outcome that was inevitable, given its location. Américo Lugo reiterated the idea of a Haitian takeover but used the opportunity to revisit the situation of the Dominican Republic itself. He denied that the Haitian government might be plotting to colonize the eastern half of the island. What was happening instead, he explained, was that Haitians valued land more than Dominicans, who persisted in owning land collectively—the ill-famed *terrenos comuneros*. For that reason, Haitians were settling in large numbers on unclaimed land and becoming a majority of the population in those areas.[22]

Probably the most eloquent expression of the condescension with which Dominicans approached their neighbors was the bundle of characteristics gathered under the label "culture." As always, Dominicans at the turn of the century were careful to deny that they disdained Haitians because they were black. Rather, they insisted, the differences that made the two peoples incompatible resided in "culture"—language, religion, body of laws, social practices. Vodou and cannibalism, two "germs even more barbarian and solvent [of culture than race is] . . . placed [Haiti] at the very bottom of civilized nations." Most writers were convinced that Haiti was, and was destined to be, "a land of cannibals," an anomaly in "the hospitable and republican [terrain of] America."[23]

What Dominicans were describing inadvertently, however, was their vision of modernity. In a fiery debate conducted between *El Eco de la Opinión* and *L'Opinion Nationale*, the Dominican newspaper spelled out what made Dominicans superior to Haitians. One insistent theme was in the area of individual liberties: the existence of an ethical component to a free press. *El Eco* patronized its counterpart by suggesting that the Haitian newspaper might not understand that an independent journal, unlike an official publication, reflected and responded to the opinions of its readers. It criticized *L'Opinion* for its lack of "collegiality" when it attacked *El Eco*, apparently insulting particular columnists. The culmination of this unprincipled behavior, *El Eco* complained, was when the Haitian journalist did not sign his article. For *El Eco*'s editor to obtain satisfaction,

> it was enough to know what the distance was that had perforce to exist between him, who had always maintained himself in the limits of decency by signing his writings, and the other [journalist] who, hiding in the black shadow of anonymity, had barked from there as a dog with

rabies, taking refuge under the protective shield of Mr. Lafleur, director editor of "*L'Opinion Nationale*" of Port-au-Prince, a city in which they would *eat* our friend.[24]

Another area in which Dominicans had the upper hand, at least in the opinion of *El Eco*, was material well-being. In matters of "social order, . . . public administration, . . . agriculture, commerce and industry, and . . . public schooling," Dominicans were superior to Haitians, who with "excessive conceit" had claimed otherwise. "The antagonism of laws, morals, customs, social spirit, and all that constitutes or gives the right to a people to call itself a civilized nation, is as evident as the instinctive repugnance that both peoples feel reciprocally." It was enough to compare the foundations of independence for both countries, and the "spirit that supposedly drives each nation . . . in [matters] concerning progress and humanitarian tendencies of the age."

Finally, there was patriotic sentiment. *El Eco* acknowledged its "exaggerated patriotism" but distinguished it from "the shortcut of passion," which presumably was the mark of Haitians. It prided itself, in fact, "in having expressed the beautiful, noble, praiseworthy, patriotic passion that raises the level of nations, making them great and respectable, and whose exaggerations are admissible in view of the sacred and powerful motive that inspires them." *El Eco* considered preferable "the burst of thunder and the martial roar of a people mindful of its independence, to the mortal silence of debilitated and indifferent societies and to the cold ramblings of an outdated and lightweight diplomacy." This ardent rhetoric served not so much to pile praise on the Dominican Republic as to put down Haiti, not quite to describe how far Dominicans had traveled on the path to civilization, but rather to point out that Haitians were outside that road map.

Expressions of anti-Haitianism contained a good dosage of nationalism— such as it existed, was understood, and was being shaped at the time. Dominican independence, the reputed birth of the nation, occurred the moment the Haitian occupying forces were permanently repelled, on 27 February 1844—the culmination of "the epic journey that gave [Dominicans] a free and independent fatherland." The Haitian army served as the enemy that facilitated an organized opposition, and Haitians generally became "the other" against which to form a sense of community. The image of "[Haitian president Charles] Hérard cross[ing] the northern frontier at the head of a numerous troop with the intention of drowning in the foul-smelling breath of his lineage the delicate fetus of nationhood that already palpitated in the heart of [the Dominican Republic's] illustrious champions" was likely to inflame strong nationalist sentiments. In a more immediately current account of Haiti as a foreign threat, Bonó suggested that the "war machine" on the Dominican Republic's west side was collaborating with the United States in its attempt to control access to the region and to the future canal zone. Because the "African race that does not want to blend with other races nor to fully enter [the path of] civilization" dominated Haiti, Haitians were "the most suitable group to frighten [Dominicans], to startle [them], and to serve as instrument [of American foreign policy]."[25]

The paragraphs above have laid out the broad outlines of what experts on the formation of national identity will readily recognize as the Trujillista anti-Haitian nationalist discourse. As related in the introduction, Trujillo and his ideologues, notably Manuel Arturo Peña Batlle and Joaquín Balaguer, constructed a unique brand of nationalism in the 1930s, based on Hispanophilia and anti-Haitianism. The same litany recorded above—the threat of alien domination, backward cultural practices, material poverty, antimodern values—became useful to the later version of self-proclaimed builders of the country's future. Identical words filled the writings of essayists of the early twentieth century and of those three decades later—exclusivism, cosmopolitanism, peaceful invasion. Anti-Haitianism was "the nectar that nourished—and continues to nourish—'nationalism' [in the Dominican Republic]."[26]

Historians have examined these outbursts of "nationalist" sentiment in an attempt to grasp its roots. One sizable group of authors explains anti-Haitianism as a function of the efforts of the dominant classes to remain firmly at the top of the hierarchy. In the phrase "*pensamiento colonialista de la oligarquía gobernante*" (colonialist thought of the ruling oligarchy), Franklin J. Franco Pichardo alludes to both the racist, classist, statist colonial legacy and the refashioned republican ruling-class interests present in anti-Haitianism. Ernesto Sagás goes further to say that the annexationist schemes of midcentury, which used the Haitian "menace" as a scare tactic, were nothing more than an attempt to preserve power as defined by traditional colonialist frameworks, in the interest of old or new imperial masters. The "tendentious and antinational manipulations of pro-Hispanic oligarchic thought" (*manipulación tendenciosa antinacional del pensamiento oligárquico prohispano*), to quote Franco Pichardo again, also made it possible to deflect class conflict, as darker Dominicans from the popular classes could always find in Haitians people who were even lower than they were.[27]

Another very convincing position, not necessarily exclusive of others, is that negative identification was a logical step when a more positive one was impossible. "We prefer anything to being Haitian," one of the advocates of

Dominican sovereignty allegedly said. Faced with the foreign occupation and its attendant institutions, the leaders of Dominican independence expressed their desire to revert to the familiar—Spanish traditions and colonial structures of domination—not necessarily by choice, but by default. The Trinitarian manifesto of January 1844, then, ended up as a primarily anti-Haitian document. Other patriotic decrees emphasized the cultural differences between the two countries and the aggression of Haiti toward the Dominican Republic. The advantages of this alignment became clear later in the century, when the United States might have treated Haitians and Dominicans in the same way, had it not been for the vehement protests of Dominicans. Just about every visitor to both sides of the island commented on the differences between the two societies and was usually more generous, although not by much, in his or her evaluation of Dominicans. Many circumstances reinforced the Dominican hostility toward Haitians.[28]

A third explanation for anti-Haitianism, less directly pertinent to my study, is the development of world capitalism. The unequal development of both parts of the island, that is, the growth of Saint Domingue into a plantation economy as Santo Domingo reverted, so to speak, to subsistence farming and cattle raising, allowed for a more conflictive and eventually destructive relationship between African slaves and masters. The Dominican Republic, in turn, developed more harmonious race relations and, conceivably, a more egalitarian society and form of government.[29]

Despite the deliberateness with which historians have tried to dissect the problem, there is still an enormous contempt for Haitians in the Dominican Republic, even in academic writing. Little explanation is offered in Dominican texts regarding the historical choices the Haitian people or its leaders made. Invariably, race or color infiltrates the narration, presumably as a minor point to be qualified but never challenged. A few examples, selected for their choice of words, will suffice: "The Dominican army that repelled the constant invasions of the army of Haiti during the independence war, triumphed because its cause was that of the entire Dominican people, while the army of Haiti, at that time, defended a lost cause: the cause that attempted to restore the interests of the militarist oligarchy of that country in our territory."[30] "It is true, Haitians are really black, with a very consistent epidermis that covers an equally solid and defined identity. There is no doubt about it: they are black indeed."[31] "Contrary to what is commonly thought, Dominicans started feeling disdain toward Haitians not because of matters of color, but because of their despotic administration of Santo Domingo."[32] A few historians have written about alliances or commonalities of interest that occurred between Haitians and Dominicans during the Haitian occupation and beyond, but these instances fill less than a page in any one of their books.[33]

Several writers have cleverly turned the issue on its head, and rather than trying to explain why anti-Haitianism is or is not a racist ideology, they have simply examined anti-Haitianism as one more element in the panoply of racist expression current at the time and to this day. For many decades, the efforts of scholars of the independence period and beyond targeted the coincidence of hated-enemy status and black color as the key element in understanding why Dominicans, who themselves are descendants of African slaves, despised Haitians and considered them, and not themselves, black.[34] It has only been in the last ten years that historians have examined racial prejudice in the Spanish Caribbean at the turn of the twentieth century and valiantly confronted the conundrum that bedeviled every island and still continues to haunt them: how to incorporate the large colored population into the elite vision of the national project. The centrality of race in the praxis of rule by the Spanish came to the foreground. In Cuba, independence leaders had to figure out how to overcome the racial divisions that the Spanish had imposed on them without allowing colored peoples an equal footing in the political arena—hence, the erasure of race in notions of Cuban citizenship.[35] In the Dominican Republic, the Creole elites, operating on the (Spanish) white somatic norm, were tolerant of people with darker hues, especially if they remained at the bottom, and privileged whiteness much as other European-descent populations did at the time. Based on this logic of hierarchy, anti-Haitianism can easily be understood as a "manifestation of the long-term evolution of racial prejudices, . . . and [the] creation of a nationalist Dominican 'false consciousness.' "[36]

The racism that some scholars have come to accept as a component of the national consciousness had particularly damaging consequences for the national project in the early twentieth century. The pessimistic forecast for the future that some of the ideologues of progress put out was based on racial mixture. Francisco Henríquez y Carvajal, Américo Lugo, Francisco Moscoso Puello, Eugenio María de Hostos, and Federico García Godoy worried about the incapacity for civilization of the popular classes. Dominicans were weak and easily manipulated; the physical and mental degeneration that was a function of miscegenation translated into "social anemia." What was worse, the Spanish element in the mix was more Semitic than Aryan—an additional negative characteristic.[37]

The discomfort with hybridity that Dominicans exhibited was not at all exceptional in this period. As Nancy Leys Stepan affirms for the region as a whole, the European stereotypes of Latin American societies as not yet fixed and therefore not biologically stable were absorbed by Latin American elites, who blamed their subordinates for the negative traits that racial impurity carried with it. In Ann Stoler's precise words, "[racial] mixing called into question the very criteria by which Europeanness could be identified, citizenship should be accorded, and nationality assigned." The mere insinuation of extraneous elements into the genetic pool of the powerful challenged the monopoly of European domination. At the same time, capitalism allowed status to be determined by acquired characteristics, and purity of blood and birthright could no longer justify the domination of people of color by Europeans. The privileges of whiteness had to be reallocated, and another way to explain inequalities had to be put into effect. Scientific racism met this need, in the Dominican Republic as well as in the rest of Latin America, by recasting hierarchy as a function of biological (and not material) inheritance. It legitimized the rule of the powerful over their subordinates, country over country through the auspices of colonialism, one social group over another as a function of economic and political supremacy. In a perverse twist, "the idea of race" filtered down to the popular classes, who, aware of the value of whiteness, aspired to climb to the top by deriding their inferiors and taking on the attributes of their superiors. The Liberal emphasis on the capacity of the individual to improve only confirmed that those at the bottom were morally deficient—no surprise, since they were also not white.[38]

The Dominican eugenics movement, although the ideologues of progress would never have referred to their efforts in that way, lamented that racial mixing had had such dire consequences and submitted that European immigrants would provide the new blood necessary to rectify the situation. While the process of racial definition was put into motion, however, Dominicans worked on both celebrating their mixed heritage and minimizing their African origins. Haitians came in handy to accomplish this sleight of hand. If Dominicans could embrace their *mulatez* ("brownness," black-and-white mix), it was only because they could look down on "truly black" Haitians. True, there were plenty of very dark Dominicans, as dark as some Haitians were—if we buy the notion that color is an objective category of analysis. But if Dominicans were dark, they could claim it was because of their Indian, not African, ancestors. There was precedent for this adroit manipulation of reality. As Meindert Fennema and Troetje Loewenthal reconstruct the historical record, runaway slaves from Haiti, who wanted to disassociate from their slave past, called themselves "Indians." Closer to the turn of the century, the novel *Enriquillo* lauded the archetypical person of color, in this case an Arawak chief, who recognized the superior European culture and aspired to become "civilized." In labeling themselves "*indios*," Dominicans of color both rejected the very negative characteristics associated with Africanness and approached, even if figuratively, the European cultural ideal. After all, as was the case for Cuba, Spain might have been backward, but Africa was primitive; Spain could be holding the island back, but Africa could drag it down; Spain was an obstacle to nationalist dreams, but Africa was a real threat to the persistence of national unity. The collapse of the categories of race, culture, and nation held promise not only for people of color, who protected themselves from the overt exercise of racism by practicing their own, milder version of it, but also for the elite, who used this identification with European ideals to prevent political alliances based on color, and consequently and perhaps more important, class. Anti-Haitianism made racism safe—since Dominicans were descended from the Spanish, they could discriminate against black people without having to look at themselves.[39]

Dominican scientific racism worked deftly through another apparent contradiction. Just like Brazil's myth of racial democracy, the flexibility of racial categories in the Dominican Republic both ensured tolerance and reinforced the value of whiteness. Joaquín María Bobea, after establishing that all people were part of the human race, justified the universal practice of gravitating toward one's peers. "Nobility, bourgeoisie, and [common] people, [all] have their blood ties and affinity intermingled in such a way that ultimately we are one human family, but in the face of the conventions that money, aristocracy, pride, and the vanity of men institute, each sheep must walk with its partner [*cada oveja con su pareja*]." Bonó was more subtle—recognizing social inequalities without identifying them as ascribed or acquired, he believed they were softened by the tolerance that was the product of Creole indolence and Spanish compassion. Lugo declared unequivocally that white people were superior, a logic that allowed that lighter people could achieve some worth. Hostos envisioned a glorious future for the Dominican Republic with the importation of white immigrants, but he also built his entire political legacy around the notion of advancement through education. Because the racial construction of any one person depended, and still does, on their phenotypical approximation to a white somatic ideal, there was no either-or quality to the process. Rather, one could be more or less white or black, depending on social skills, such as education or comportment. Everyone, of course, aspired to move toward, and perhaps even to enter, the white category, as it guaranteed access to privilege. The fluidity of the process both prevented a harsh racism and paved the way for a practice of racism. And so Negrophobia existed without racial oppression.[40]

The legerdemain required to perform such feats of logic resides in notions of culture as consisting of traits passed on from one generation to another, almost as if genetically. Scholars of culture have devoted numerous pages to the differences between its high and low iterations and to the range of human activity that one can place (or should examine) under the label. These notions of what constitutes culture have tended to be static and, more pertinent to my argument, passive. Recently, Latin American historians have uncovered a very active formulation of national culture, not just on the part of the intellectual class in the service of the state but among the popular classes in their attempts to position themselves advantageously vis-à-vis their "inferiors." Mexico would not have been able to claim its indigenous population under the mantle of *mestizaje* (race mixture) had it not been for the shift in emphasis from race in the nineteenth century to ethnicity in the twentieth. In Peru, *mestizos*, who were by definition racially mixed, acquired status by virtue of a high-school education and birth into a new "racial" category, "*mestizos, pero no cholos*." They were superior to *cholos*, urban market sellers, who could also be mixed, but who were considered indigenous because of their unrefined ways. Eventually, as Marisol de la Cadena argues in an interesting twist, racial mixture in Peru acquired a spiritual component that was inseparable from notions of virility, national culture, personal pride, and respect for the community and that ignored purity of blood.[41]

Mexicans and Peruvians were not alone in taking these leaps of faith. If we understand the study of race to be the study of "European thinking about difference," the successful disassociation of mulattoes from African ancestry and the peaceful coexistence of racism and racial tolerance in the Dominican Republic appear reasonable, even inevitable, given the demographics of the island at independence and the Spanish colonial legacy. "Impurities of blood" could be easily forgiven, becoming irrelevant, if the cultural patrimony was certifiably European—in the Dominican case, Hispanic. It was not until 1930 that Trujillo crystallized this line of reasoning to the level of state ideology, but its roots were carefully secured by the proponents of progress, first as anti-Haitianism and then as a nascent nationalism, complete with strength of character, capacity for work, and willingness to advance.[42]

The emphasis on Hispanic culture served Dominicans well in their efforts to move forward in the early twentieth century as well as in the 1930s. They had not only avoided the pitfalls of hybridity by denying their African ancestry and substituting it with a heavily Europeanized, "civilized" indigenous element; they had also been able to eradicate the troublesome racial questions from the discourse of national unity, subsumed as they were by culture. But the more positive spin on miscegenation did not erase race, as *mulatez* remained ultimately racially deterministic, albeit not purist. And the emphasis on culture only shifted the locus of essentialist notions. In the end, the image of national unity, the celebration of cultural sameness, and the projection of an identity of interests were achieved by articulating racialized notions of culture. This is the Dominican version of Paul Gilroy's "racism without race" or Verena Stolcke's "cultural fundamentalism." In that these notions of cultural difference were accorded moral weight and became transferable by blood, the national project remained one of forced conformity or exclusion.[43]

For the elite, among which one must include the intellectual class, the shift to culture as the site of difference was expedient indeed. As was the case with anti-Haitianism, focusing on culture displaced attention to a more manageable arena of internal politics. Collecting all Dominicans under the cover of Hispanic culture both facilitated denying access to privilege to those who did not conform to Europeanized practices and conceivably allowed full participation in the life of the country to those who complied. The mantra of culture, moreover, reinforced the possibility that Dominicans could form a nation, with distinctive characteristics, shared by all, something a strictly racial definition of Dominicanness could not do. Culture, one into which Dominicans were born and that could pass from generation to generation, placed Dominicans just a notch away from "biopolitical homogeneity," from becoming a cosmic racelike people destined for a bright future.[44]

Conscious of it or not, Dominican intellectuals were forging political categories as they chiseled out the racial-cultural characteristics that defined the nation and that distinguished Dominicans from Haitians. Although they may have intended to come up once and for all with the formula for progress that would see the country into the future, the process they were engaged in was not finite. The very people they found so difficult to integrate, albeit figuratively, into the discourse of progress would themselves have their say regarding their participation in the nation. The following chapters interlace elite and popular efforts to inject gender and class into the national project.

CHAPTER FOUR

Representing Bourgeois

Womanhood

B ourgeois women, because of their "culture" and by association with
the very masterminds of the ideology of progress, were predictably
part of the Dominican national project. But the roles they were assigned, principally as wives and mothers of the country's patriarchs, ultimately served men's political objectives and denied women autonomous
participation in the nation to be. "Ladies" of the upper and middle classes
throughout this period showed themselves to be forthright collaborators of
men and to subscribe to their expectations. Their increased presence in the
public sphere, however, must have alarmed their male peers, who proceeded
to restrict their activities, not physically, but discursively. The depiction of
women in occasional literary pieces and regular daily columns fixed them
unequivocally within the home, under the patriarch's vigilant gaze.

Newspaper and magazine representations of bourgeois women located
citizenship beyond their reach, figuratively and literally. Upper- and middle-
class women invariably appeared in short stories, advertisements, or anec-
dotal columns as objects of men's political schemes or as obstacles to the
formation of the nation. The elite men who put out these publications projected onto bourgeois women formulaic roles in the preconceived social
order they controlled. As the intelligentsia took it upon themselves to fix the
limits of national difference, so as to control for certain traits that subaltern groups might exhibit, they pronounced educated "white" women the
beneficiaries of their guidance and working-class women marginal to the
polity.

THE ROLE OF BOURGEOIS WOMEN IN
THE FORGING OF THE NEW NATION

Nobody doubted that the process of civic regeneration required the insertion of women into reformulations of the nation-in-the-making. As everywhere else, women were recognized first and foremost for their biological and social reproductive functions. As mothers, they were directly responsible for nation-building: they literally brought into the world the next generation of (male) citizens. As the companions of men (their husbands, brothers, uncles, cousins, male family friends), they offered the material and emotional support that allowed men to engage in the more public functions of state-building.

Several Dominican women had obtained national standing by extending these household roles to the public sphere, beginning with the school system and eventually penetrating the arena of politics. Salomé Ureña de Henríquez (1850–97), founder in 1881 of the Instituto de Señoritas (Girls' Institute) under the auspices of Eugenio María de Hostos and wife of political figure Francisco Henríquez y Carvajal, was dubbed in her own time "national poet," having distinguished herself by her inspiring patriotic verses. At the institute, she trained six teachers who, in turn, educated a number of young women who opened schools for girls in the early twentieth century. Among them was Mercedes Moscoso, who along with her sister founded a girls' institute in San Pedro de Macorís. Another well-known name was Luisa Ozema Pellerano, who protested Lilís's continuous concessions to foreign interests and became an outspoken critic of the U.S. intervention in 1916. Others had less of an impact, founding elementary schools or libraries for girls and women and so advocating equality in more limited settings.

The majority of women, however, regardless of their class and education, restricted their activities to managing households, raising children, cultivating the family's ties to the larger community, and comforting the men in their lives. Not expected to contribute much by way of the originality of their intellect, the female associates of upper- and middle-class men were particularly instrumental insofar as they reproduced the genetic pool and the social values necessary for the country's development. Dominican working-class women, with fewer resources available for these tasks, served to demarcate class and race lines for their bourgeois sisters and their husbands, as detailed in chapter 5. In a way not very different from what Partha Chatterjee describes for Indian women in Bengal, the nationalist discourse prescribed the role of women, that is, of a particular kind of woman (educated, connected to the home, spiritually strong, different from both "the vulgar western woman" and the common Indian woman), with very little input from the women it was meant to affect.[1]

Given that most women, even if upper class, were not considered suited to carry out any duties of consequence, Dominican literati aimed to cover a broad band of the elements necessary for the attainment of the correct social order. Local magazines and newspapers dedicated sections to the "fairer sex" and published pieces that presumably depicted universal human conditions and thus reinforced expected gender roles and denounced aberrant behavior. Some of the authors of essays and short stories were foreigners— most notably, Emilia Pardo Bazán and Jacinto Benavente (Spanish), Froilán Turcios (Ecuadorian), Manuel Díaz Rodríguez (Venezuelan), and Catulle Mendes (French). But many of the plethora of short stories on the virtues and vices of women were written by Dominicans—writers who will never be remembered for their literary endeavors, but who were at the time certainly well-connected socially and, significantly, advocated Dominican autonomy from the United States. In many cases, the same men who wrote about politics also published gushing fiction and poetry meant to establish for the new nation a safe and moral social order.[2]

The stories and periodic columns these men wrote appeared regularly both in magazines directed at a general readership and in more politically minded publications. Most of the fictional pieces were set in faraway lands or times, although the men, women, and children in them were intended to be universally familiar. With only a few exceptions, good women inspired their mates with their obedience, persistence, understanding, honesty, and impeccable homemaking, *or* beautiful women ruined men because of their greed, vanity, ignorance, frivolity, and inconstancy. Men, in all cases noble beings whose sense of duty was their most transparent quality, either found solace in faithful female companions *or* were victimized by treacherous women.

The sole story line that illustrated a nonconflictive relationship between the sexes emphasized a woman's nurturing role, her limited but personally satisfying domain, and men's responsibility (and assumed capacity) to make women happy. Francisco and Josefa were scheduled to marry when Francisco disappeared. Ten years later, the author finds him in Barcelona, where Francisco reveals the reason for eluding his commitment: he had fallen in love with his fiancée's sister, who was dying of tuberculosis. The honorable thing to do, he reasoned at the time, was to flee the situation. He feels certain that he made the right decision, having learned that Josefa, who had worried about his change in temperament, continued to care for her sister until she died and later married a man who made her happy. In another of these accounts of harmonious family and love relationships, a young couple kisses passionately on an outing in the evening; at 9:00 P.M., the woman goes home, kisses her sleeping grandmother warmly on the cheek, and goes to bed to dream of her loved one. Domesticity, duty, innocence, loyalty—these were the forces that made women good.[3]

Women also served as nothing more than love objects for men in these literary pieces, although disappointment or hardship formed a part of the drama. Conventional wisdom averred that women "walk on this earth stealing the wills [of men] with the [red] carnation of the[ir] cheeks and the light of the[ir] eyes." Addressing a fictional woman, another romantic commented: "It's just that your eyes are a duplicate image of your soul, and the soul is that fanciful flare-up that burns in your body as does a lamp in a temple consecrated to the cult of Aphrodite in the inviolate secret of discreet offerings." Not all women provided unequivocal desire, another author cautioned: "A woman is like a verse. A sonorous hexameter, a brilliant hendecasyllable. A dull line, composed by a poor lyricist. One can find anything." But, another counseled, "To try to extinguish the passion for a woman one adores by leaving her is to want to quench your thirst without drinking." The effect of failed relationships was such on men that they "avenge on tender women their not having been loved by the tramps. This," the author lamented, "is what we [men] call being very strong." Relationships between men and women were undoubtedly problematic: one writer bemoaned having passed up the opportunity to share life with a gypsy who silently observed his flirtations with other women. The only safe place for men, it appeared, was the male imagination: one poet shared with readers "brides of all colors who give him hopes in a life of misfortune, give him strength, warmth, [and] inspire him with their caresses and kisses." Real or not, the leads in these tales were men whose intentions were honorable and their longing for companionship honest. The women characters who incited their introspection were, remarkably, exemplary of their gender: warm, pleasurable, modest, vigilant of their reputation.[4]

It seemed a more pressing matter, however, to portray the uglier aspects of the female psyche. The stories of scheming and alluring women not only outnumbered the ones referred to above; they were also more elaborate in plot, more selective in the use of language, richer in detail, more precise in structure, and transparently didactic—none of which should suggest that they were "better" literature. An extreme example of this other depiction of women focuses on female lasciviousness and capriciousness. A man contemplates suicide because his wife, who is a prostitute, will not spend time with him unless he pays her. Eighteen and a virgin when they married, the reader learns, she was already well versed in carnal matters. The couple now have two children, and he has spent his entire fortune on her whims; but she continues to live a decadent life.[5]

Oversexed females were a commonplace in these tales. In one of the few stories with a local setting, the young and eager wife of a seaman who is tired from traveling constantly from Santo Domingo to San Pedro de Macorís takes out her frustration by throwing a stick at a rooster that was not responding to the sexual advances of a hen in the yard—conceivably a duplication of the wife's own situation. In more cosmopolitan surroundings, an equally sex-driven "little baroness" rushes to confess the previous night's excesses to a priest and apparently delights so much in revisiting the experience that she forgets the corset she has been holding in her hand inside the confessional. As she leaves the church, a statue of Satan appears to smirk at her predicament. In a not entirely tasteless and very pointedly political humorous aside, allegedly found scribbled on a statue in Rome, a farmer claims he supports the pope and the emperor; a merchant confesses he steals from the previous three; a lawyer deceives all four; a physician can drive the foregoing five to their deaths; a woman serves as temptation for the previous six; a priest absolves all seven; and the devil takes the full eight to hell with him. Although men have no actual interaction with the female characters in the course of these stories, the reader has enough circumstantial evidence to condemn women's behavior and speculate on its consequences.[6]

Magnifying the danger of women's uncontrollable sex drive were their coquettish manner, fickleness, and capacity for deceit. Flor de Oro (Golden Flower), apparently so named for her blond tresses, sets her sights on a New York millionaire (Mr. Love), to whom her uncle hopes to marry her sister off. Defying the contradiction between her objective and his name, she schemes to have the house cat attack her sister, who becomes blind and then insane. Flor de Oro confesses her crime only when Mr. Love sends her uncle a telegram inviting him to his wedding. In another tale of disingenuousness, a thirty-year-old "Yankee" woman, married and with two daughters, proposes to her Dominican tenant, the presumed author, that they have an affair. Although he initially embarks on this forbidden jaunt without any vacillation, he begins to get jealous of her husband and suggests that they elope. The woman "fixed on [him] her deep and serene ocean-blue eyes, laden with satisfied desire" and explained that their romance has only been a whim, and that she loves her husband and adores her daughters. Although it is significant that the woman in the last story is American, the moral of both literary pieces appears to be that the female sex is untrustworthy and capable of the most inexplicable actions. Another not-so-family-bound woman and her lover, the reader learns in another trite story by Ulises Heureaux, the dictator's son, are due to meet a ghastly fate at the hands of her indignant husband, a train machinist. He has plotted to speed to a crash the train they have taken to Le Havre for a two-day holiday. By killing himself and the treacherous pair, he simultaneously avoids the shame that would weigh down on him and punishes his unfaithful wife. Perhaps these lamentable outcomes would have been avoided if the male characters in these stories had been aware that women were duplicitous. The words of one writer are unequivocal: "The moon is a sham: it does not have the shape which it shows us at present, nor does it travel in the direction that it appears to be traveling in, nor is the light it sends us hers. . . . Being feminine, being a woman, [the moon] is a liar: it looks at us sad, indifferent, or joyful, and its state is always the same, that of an immutable corpse!"[7]

Those women that did show their true colors, moreover, exhibited traits that were totally undesirable and performed actions that harmed innocent people. In another "local" tale, for example, the wife of the minister of the treasury pressures him to find jobs in government for her relatives: two fifteen-year-old sons, her father and grandfather, and fifteen cousins. She counters his reluctance by pointing out that a man who does not rule with his family is committing political suicide. Justifying her final request (to appoint their dog as doorman), she reminds her husband of the Roman emperor who appointed his horse to a senate seat. In a country notorious for nepotism, at the dawn of an era hopeful for integrity, blaming women for the practice was a wise move. A less directly relevant account of women's disturbing behavior tells of a society woman's habit of torturing oysters with lemon and fork before consuming them. The author, the woman's husband-to-be, suspects she would have liked to see their "faces" as they agonized in her hands.[8]

Impulsive perhaps because they were unintelligent, inexperienced, or naturally gullible, these "transparent" women only caused trouble for men. In one case, a young woman purposefully spreads rumors about another's virtue in order to provoke a breakup between the man she loves and his bride, the subject of the slander. The peasant kills his betrothed, her alleged lover, and himself—all because of a woman's reckless gossip. In another instance, a daydreaming wife reflects on her situation—her husband is passionless, practical; her children, demanding; and her servants, untrustworthy. Although she knows her husband would dismiss her concerns by comparing her circumstances to others' (less fortunate, one assumes), this incurable romantic ("*la novelesca*") imagines other times: "when men walked around with empty pockets, but a chest filled with an enormous heart, a heart where passion and rapture dwelled, and where common sense and reason, which now want to rule the world, didn't even have attic space." Another fanciful wife begins to imagine that her husband's visits to a brothel are sexually motivated simply because her friend has insinuated it. Written in epistolary form, the story concludes with a letter that explains that her husband and the madam were simply trying to arrange a marriage, an account of events the wife is apparently inclined to believe. In another story, an Italian nobleman, the Marqués de Vale Allegre, decides to marry the object of his affection, a lion tamer named Gilda, convinced as he is of her honorable parentage (*ascendencia digna*). A senator-friend warns him that "it was possible that beauty was the only atavistic bequest [Gilda has received from] Aphrodite." On the wedding night, Azís, Gilda's favorite lion, kills the groom when Gilda steps outside the tent. Faced with the horrific scene, she rushes to embrace her lover, then lowers her head against the lion's forehead, and stains herself with blood. If only women would stay still and keep quiet, if they did not transgress their station, these stories imply, reasonable men could continue going about their business undisturbed and be happy—in one case, alive.[9]

The fictional exchanges between a woman named Electricity and Thomas Edison best captured men's problematic associations with women. Electricity is introduced to the reader as a negative and a positive force, capable of both curing headaches and taking lives (through electrocution). Edison's relationship with her is, not surprisingly, conflictive—he accuses her of having passed through many (men's) hands—Italian, German, French—and resorts to caressing her with the purpose of "taming" her (*domarla*). It is with Edison, the author tells us, that

> this traitor has a frenzied love affair [*amores rabiosos*]. Notice that he treats her as a wretch, he makes her work from six to six as if she were black, exploits her, lives through her effort, and yet that shameless scoundrel does not rebel against her loved tyrant. For him only, she engages in obsequious debauchery, incredible weaknesses. She is a degraded and submissive slave.

In a moment of empowerment, Electricity charges Edison with trying to force her "to do something filthy," but he retorts she has no moral grounds to complain because she is a "flirt and an idler." The piece concludes by making fun of some of the applications of electricity (growing legumes in less time) and starkly stating: "Edison wanted a vulgarity, it's true, but the human species lives on vulgarities."[10]

Despite this allegory's enormous potential for psychoanalysis, it is more prudent to focus, for the purposes of this chapter, on the uniquely Dominican variants of eminently universal themes. Electricity possesses female character traits: she is disloyal and coquettish and must be *forced* to perform productive work. Even under a man's supervision, she only produces vulgarity. That man, however, is a foreigner, and for that reason, not a very reliable character himself. He treats her like an African slave, something the reader is expected to immediately reject as unthinkable, unless of course the woman is a shameless slut (the oversexed female). In that case, her unbecoming behavior strips her of any claim to respectable womanhood, and the reader can, if not justify, certainly suspend judgment on Edison's actions. Giving in to eminently national insecurities about race, gender, and the outside, the author chooses to disassociate from the unworthy turn of events, which he labels as "vulgar"—the product of the collaboration of a domineering foreign man and a weak racialized woman.

Fortunately for men, other stories collectively suggest, most women were plainly stupid and their actions were of no consequence. In one fanciful plot, two princes who are rivals for a princess's love consult a fairy for advice on how to discern her preference—the princess has apparently given both some hope. The fairy arranges for the princess's thoughts to be visible, and when the two young men return to the palace, they see coming out of the princess's head countless butterflies of all colors, "fluttering with lively charm," "swaying delicately [on flowers due to] their light weight." Restless, palpitating, inconstant, vivacious, fickle—such were a woman's thoughts. In another tale, supposedly illustrative of women's capacity for judgment, a woman allows a stranger into her home indefinitely. He mistreats her but always asks for forgiveness. One day, he announces his departure and explains he has never said he was there on a permanent basis. It was Love. "And Martha remained calm, mistress of her home, free of frights, fears, or apprehension, and devoted to the company of grave and excellent reflection." Still, the narrator tells the reader, she hopes Love will knock on her door again. In another victim-of-love parable, a woman stops a man on the street, spits in his face, and tells him she hates him. Realizing he is the wrong man, she apologizes but immediately reneges when she confirms that he, in fact, looks like "him." To close this segment on inane women, a prostitute dies at the hands of one of her clients, a young and inexperienced man who had fallen in love with her. He finds her door closed one day and forces it open—to discover her with another man. As she agonizes, she finds relief in thinking that he is doing this only because he loves her. Airheads, hopeless romantics, irrational lovers, tenderhearted tramps—these women were nothing to worry about.[11]

If these examples were discouraging, others served to establish that men's expectations were not unreasonable, and the outcome of their efforts held some promise. Olimpia, a princess, is almost perfect: she has a beautiful face, blond hair, and skin like ivory. Despite these conspicuously feminine qualities, she has no compassion, a feature of her personality that men approach as a challenge, in one case dying in an effort to provoke some emotion in her. There are other details that made her an anomaly of the female gender. She is amused by "satirical writing" that ridicules humanity and does not read romances. Her room has no flowers or birds—only mirrors. When her mother dies, she does not cry and instead falls mysteriously ill. The fairies the king consults indicate only that the use of a mirror, a handkerchief, and a pair of scissors are needed to break the spell. Doctors advise her to cut her hair so that her head will clear up, but she refuses. While the princess sleeps, however, her governess carries out the instructions. Only then does she cry, repenting for having been so cruel. Those tears redeem her, the author interjects for the benefit of the reader, and rid her of her sins. Conveniently, Olimpia is now perfect: beautiful, white, blond, *and* emotional. Conceivably, she also likes flowers and birds and loves humanity—a paradigm of womanhood.[12]

Another mechanism used to reassure men that everything was in order was the conviction that women were a known quantity. A Hindu tale of creation published at the time confirms this notion. The myth explained how Twashtri made the first woman after he had spent all of his creative material on the first man.

> He took from the moon its roundness, the undulating curves of the serpent, the graceful interweaving of a vine, the velvety softness of flowers, the lightness of a feather, the sweet look of a gazelle, the tears of clouds, the sweetness of honey, the cruelty of a tiger, the heat of fire, the coldness of snow, the chatter of a parrot, and the murmur of a dove.[13]

Regardless of whether there was indeed a Hindu legend that recounted this process or not, it is significant that a Dominican magazine saw this literary piece as interesting or useful to its readers. With two exceptions, women's physical attributes derived from the inanimate world, and their character traits, from animals. Women as nature motivated by instincts, to be exploited or domesticated by men—here lay an eminently turn-of-the-century Western European trope applied to inferior peoples.

In some exceptional stories, individual women acted on their own with the valor and clearheadedness characteristic of men. Margarita de Ruyssac, high nobility by birth, promises her mother she will marry the Count of Meridor. A friend of her brother falls in love with her and provokes the count to a duel; if he loses, he figures, he will at least die thinking of her. During the duel, the two adversaries do not seem to want to kill each other. At some point, the count tells his foe that he does not want to be haunted by the other's death when he marries Margarita, to which the unsolicited suitor responds with a deadly offensive, only to realize that "the count" is Margarita herself. Hopeless, Margarita's admirer buries his own sword in his chest so he can die with her as they kiss. Although the story line in this case parallels the others insofar as a woman is the cause of tragedy, including her own, remarkably, the real hero in this story was Margarita. The count disappeared from the plot, the smitten family friend ruined his own chances of quite literally "getting the girl," but Margarita was as good as any man in that she was noble enough to know what her duty was (to keep her promise even though she loved another) and saw the incident through to its logical conclusion.[14]

Another positive representation of women, not surprisingly, results from the intertwining of the destinies of woman / mother and fatherland (*patria*), a connection that works better in Spanish because the word "*patria*" is feminine. A short story about a moribund man and a baby who both await the stroke of twelve midnight to, respectively, depart this world and celebrate life, concludes with the author's words: "Yes, let us salute him [the baby, and by extension, his mother], may he be prosperous, fecund, full of light, but of that light that will illuminate the patriotism of those who rule our destinies, for the greatness of the Fatherland" (purposefully equivocal, implying both the baby's mother *and* the country). Holding that women are more virtuous than men, another writer labeled women "the heroines of the fatherland," intimating that for women the fatherland (country) was family and home. Because women were weak beings, he explained, they gravitated toward strength (protection—in the form of the state, one surmises), so that if the country collapsed, women, the keepers of home and family, would be eminently vulnerable—a veritable predicament. Despite the positive role-identification, it is clear, only males could make women great or effect their downfall.[15]

In contrast to the majority of women protagonists, men leads in all these stories are rational, responsible, and above their peers. In a first-person short reflection, the author bids a final good-bye to his lover, who "belongs to another." He laments man's cowardice in the face of "the despotic laws he himself composes to torment himself [monogamy? marital fidelity?]." Painfully conscious that he and his loved one have done the right thing, he resigns himself to loneliness. Another dutiful citizen, this one in an exotic land, is equally accepting of his fate. Ahmed and his love, Fátima, had been solidifying their relationship when Fátima was whisked away to the sultan's harem, "where innocence bows its forehead and dies between the lascivious and defiling arms of some crowned satyr." Ahmed, in desperation, "commits the sacrilegious act of professing a threat against the sacred life of the Son of the Prophet," for which faux pas he is found stabbed on the banks of the Tigris. Although the reader is called on to feel pity for Ahmed, his transgression against the state is undoubtedly worthy of the punishment he received—understandably, Ahmed's soul must find solace in wandering through the world searching for his beloved.[16]

As living vehicles of respectability, men thought of family and state first, as opposed to women, who behaved as if their actions had no consequences. In one story, a woman proposes to her rich and unattractive husband that he allow her to have an affair with a man who awaits her company outside the door. She will pretend to love her husband in public but secretly consume her passion with the other man. If her husband forces her to have sex with him, she threatens to find thousands of lovers. Although twenty-first-century readers are denied the denouement of this dilemma (the pages are missing), it seems that the husband was ready to accept this proposition for the sake of appearances (to save his manly honor). Likewise, the author of an op-ed-style piece vehemently appeals for a reprieve of the sentence for a Cuban woman "of modest extraction" who shot the father of her daughter, a high-society young man who did not legally acknowledge their baby. The mother, who lived in penury, ran into her former lover one day and shot him. Although the court sentenced her as lightly as it could, the article advocates a full pardon for "the unfortunate avenger of her honor." In both of these cases, men uphold notions of honor that hold society, and the state, together.[17]

There is only one exception to this pattern of men who do right by women, and women who are either demanding ingrates (which is bad) or accepting of their fate (which is good)—the amusing story of Teresa, who is "pretty as an angel and painted like a pig." Teresa directs her feminine charm, always in a most decorous manner, toward a group of artists at the seashore, who show their appreciation by giving her some of their paintings. On one occasion, she persuades each of them to fill in a part of the canvas she is working on—sea, clouds, waves, rocks, some nude female figures. The following year, she enters the painting in a competition and receives an honorable mention, primarily because the three men who contributed to her composition are part of the jury and cannot help but admire their own work. Although the woman in this story was as deceitful as others in this genre, and her only visible asset was her beauty, she is different from other female characters in that she manipulated men in a way that was intended to be funny and exposed what came across as a male flaw, vanity.[18]

There were other, more direct, ways to tell bourgeois women what their

LEFT: Ulises Heureaux Jr., the dictator's son. (Archivo General de la Nación, untitled photo index, photo 34, 2.) RIGHT: Young women of San Pedro de Macorís. (Unidentified magazine page in Archivo General de la Nación.)

station was and what society's expectations were for them. Like today, advertisements and advice columns emphasized appearance and health. Tocologic pills, for example, restored health lost "for reasons peculiar to [women's] organisms"—one assumes menstruation, pregnancy, menopause—which diminished the requisite fresh complexion, firm body tissue, and healthy countenance. The pills also "cured the most inveterate disorders"—one can only surmise what these were. It comes as no small comfort to some of us today that women were esteemed in this time period for the "soft roundness of their form." But "if nature, who does not always distribute favors according to human desire, denies this rotundity, or worse, replaces it by a superabundance of angles and impertinent bones, only the seamstress can calm the desperation of Eve's daughters," but happily, so can the application of the creams and lotions recommended. Other products augmented breasts and lightened skin color. Advice columns were for the most part "modern" in outlook, and so, if they did not value health over beauty, they at least made them synonymous. An article explained that in the past men and women wore garters below the knee for aesthetic reasons and to denote wealth through elaborate designs and their skillful execution. Recent scientific advances had shown that this practice could cause circulation problems, so now it was recommended that women place their garters seven to eight centimeters above the knee. Tight or heavy dresses, corsets, and narrow shoes, it was said, were shown to cut off circulation, cause indigestion, and prevent the development of muscles.[19]

In addition to achieving beauty and health, women were expected to excel in the more important function of managing households and raising children, for which men admired and became devoted to them. The following examples evoke similar efforts in this period in the United States to place women "on a pedestal," thus immobilizing them with adulatory praise. The editor of *La Miscelánea*, a short-lived triweekly magazine, wished to "see her [the generic woman] placed on a throne," from which he apparently expected her to teach her children "to have heart" and acquire "superficial traces or notions of arts, letters, and sciences, to guide conversations in her salons or to be able to understand the CONFERENCES and SOIREES that she attends!" One advice column told the story of a woman "not very young nor pretty, with an average education but intelligent, who loved her husband and knew how to admire his qualities and intelligence." She decided that her calling in life was to make the home a refuge for him and dedicated her time to preparing healthy and elaborate meals, to have in the house the magazines he liked, to smile when he got home from work, to not talk to him when he brought work home from the office, to keep the house clean. One day, he rewarded her efforts by telling her that her outstanding quality was "to find time for everything." Another writer stated categorically that women were only fulfilled when they discovered love. Their achievements resided in the home, where they functioned as the heart, and their husbands as the head. To form children's characters, in the opinion of the author, was a mission more worthy than men's accomplishments and certainly more admirable than that of famous women recognized in world history texts. As if to add legitimacy to Dominican values, *Renacimiento* published one short paragraph by U.S. president Theodore Roosevelt to the effect that men formed homes and brought the bread, while women supported men, raised children, and managed domestic aspects.[20]

Not all of the efforts to locate women on a plane agreeable to bourgeois male intentions were as transparent and as alien to twenty-first-century readers as the ones discussed above. There were very serious reflections on women's subordination, especially through the institution of marriage, that resonate even today because of the inevitably negotiated nature of unions between men and women worldwide and because of the consistently inflexible position of the Catholic Church with respect to civil divorce. Male and female writers lamented that, although the legal system gave women civil and political rights, they were incapable of exercising them because of the way they were educated both at home and in the schools. "Slavery" was not too strong a word to describe the relationship that existed in a sexual union, as the author called marriage. Another writer went further: not only had women not been taught that a man's psychology was a function of his physiology (that men's sexual organs governed their behavior) so that "matrimony . . . is a bag containing ninety-nine snakes and one eel," but in addition, divorce was not really an option because women's only "career" was marriage.

The debate over divorce must have been so significant that it prompted one woman to write a booklet entitled *La mujer: Lo que es y lo que debe ser el feminismo: Mi modo de pensar sobre el divorcio* (Woman: What feminism is and what it should be: My thoughts on divorce). The title of this publication, however, should not suggest that the author was not very much a woman of her time. She explained, for example, that working women should not be looked upon with suspicion, since a woman would never abandon her other duties, because equal rights "did not excuse her from what is natural law, reinforced by custom." The author was more than conciliatory; she believed that the development of women's intellect in childhood and puberty would allow them, as adults, to examine their marital problems and find a solution, thus guiding men, who like other human beings, after all, "have a heart and are [morally] upright." If divorce existed as a necessary contingency, as a way of avoiding other harmful paths (an abusive situation, an unhappy marriage), "[male] superiority would end and mutual respect would shine in the home." Nevertheless, she emphasized, marriage was a contract, and if broken, both partners should be able to enjoy their free will.[21]

Along the same lines, other authors advocated measures that ameliorated the situation of women. Latin American young women, one article lamented, became wives and mothers without adequate preparation. They indulged their children by allowing them to do whatever they wanted, and this lack of discipline resulted in a generation poorly equipped to lead the country responsibly. In contrast, both parents raised children in the United States, and women had some contact with the world outside the home through work. In a U.S. contest covered in a Dominican magazine, the winning entry to the question, "What should we do with our daughters?"

was highly praised: provide them with primary schooling, teach them domestic labors, teach them to save, explain to them that a hardworking husband is better than an elegant one, teach them to tend to gardens and flowers and to reject false appearances, instill in them that in choosing a husband morality is more important than wealth. A local female author added that women's calling extended beyond the strictly domestic and should reach out to things sublime, useful, and good—through the reading of history. Since women were physically limited to the domestic arena, a well-known Spanish writer argued, journalists had a special responsibility to bring the world to them. By reading the newspaper, women could experience "history" vicariously and acquire knowledge without compromising their virtue. Husbands should be grateful that their wives' imaginations were being stimulated in a controlled setting and not by activities women themselves devised in the isolation of the home.[22]

Unfortunately, and notwithstanding their limited scope, the lightweight misogyny of regular contributors counterbalanced the solemnity of these columns. One writer published a weekly listing of women who should not get married, among which were flirts, who "provoked men in a scandalous manner," and jealous women, who "imagined" their husbands were unfaithful. In Hungary, another columnist informed his reading public, bigamists were disciplined by forcing them to live in the same house "with all the women." This would be an even more terrible punishment, the writer added, if mothers-in-law were included in the package. Another commentator captured men's expectations of women best in his advice to newly married women, coined as the ten commandments: (1) to love her husband above all things; (2) not to promise love in vain; (3) to arrange celebrations for him; (4) to love him more than her father and mother; (5) not to torment him with demands, whims, and tantrums; (6) not to trick him; (7) not to nag him, nor spend money on frivolities; (8) not to speak behind his back, nor pretend a nervous attack, nor anything of the sort; (9) not to desire another other than her husband; and (10) not to covet others' luxuries, nor to stop to look at storefronts. These should be placed in the makeup drawer and read twelve times a day.[23] The facetious demands of these authors reminded readers of the aplomb and self-assurance that was synonymous with male privilege.

To be fair, men might really have feared the consequences of the empowerment of women: the loss of male privilege or equality—which, ironically, took on a ludicrous configuration. One journalist reported that there had been cases in Madrid of women killing their husbands for adultery. His voice thundered out of the newspaper's pages in the face of this injustice:

So be it: If a man whose honor is injured, who runs the risk, if the deceit continues, of educating another [man's] children, who is mocked in the most violent way possible given society's conventions, requests a jail sentence [for his cheating wife, one assumes], that breaks the deceitful heart of the woman who stole his hopes, happiness, and honor, what punishment should a woman receive who without losing her honor (a husband's infidelity lends a certain aura of victimization to the woman who far from losing her dignity is elevated) kills the husband because he doesn't love her as much as she wishes him to?

Another columnist notified Dominicans of scientific experiments, carried out in Denmark, that measured hair loss in men and women. Since women at present preserved their thick hairlines through old age, the writer figured, they would be able to grow mustaches in a hundred years. One detects a certain uneasiness with respect to what is understood as a threat to patriarchy.[24]

There were other, oblique, ways to place women in predetermined roles that were ancillary to men's actions. From the perspective of writers of this period, for example, men made the land produce—by penetrating virgin soils with piercing instruments, by irrigating land with their sweat and fertilizing it with other bodily fluids, by introducing seeds that would germinate in nature's womb. With a sensuality uncharacteristic of a persuasive piece, one journalist beseeched the reader in eloquent terms:

> May our poor agriculture rise from its prostration, let wise and advantageous measures come from the high spheres of power to encourage and stimulate those who are good; let every man be a farmer and every farmer an affectionate father to the soil; cultivating it and making it produce.... There they are, virgin and full of fertility, all across the territory of the republic, the lands that you seek to achieve your goals. Moisten the land with the sweat of your forehead, those of you that long for a better future, and you will have served the fatherland and yourselves.[25]

Vigorous men made feminized fields produce.

Curiously, the beautification of the urban core came to be described in feminine terms, as the transformations in the cityscape were ostensibly promoted precisely for the benefit of the young ladies of the upper class, who allegedly wished to stroll about and circulate with decorum. One newspaper article made the connection between the manipulation of the environment and women, reinforcing the nature-versus-culture dichotomy that subordinated them to men. Beauty in vegetation (without any purpose or practical application), the piece explained, was synonymous with femininity:

The cultivation of flowers is a very important part of the education of women. We think the teaching of floriculture should begin . . . in girls' schools, to direct them to love natural beauties and to obtain from that love sublime comparisons for life itself. We believe that a woman who does not enjoy flowers is a rarity, an untamed animal, an evil spell, whom we cannot approach without it causing us harm. The beauty of a woman and the beauty of a flower are complementary: one was created to be confused with the other.

In an article arguing for the utility of trees, the author explained that farmers consider trees their enemies because branches attract birds that eat their crops and because trees occupy land that could be used for planting. What they don't understand, the writer continues, is that trees produce rain, protect against cold winds that would delay vegetation, defend against warm winds that cause erosion, increase the production of dew, provide wood for the home, and produce leaves that fertilize the soil. Trees, like women, do not produce anything; but they are naturally good and can be used by men.[26]

The short stories, advice columns, advertisements, and opinion pieces I examined coincide in their representation of ideal gender roles: dutiful and selfless women should stand by their men, who toiled in government, agriculture, trade, and so on, thus strengthening the body politic. Under the watchful eye of attentive husbands or vigilant fathers, bourgeois women were entrusted with the task of raising the new generation of citizens. If not themselves naturally the vessels of rationality, responsibility, common sense, morality, and virtue, women could be shaped by male creative energies into useful vehicles for the transmission of certain national attributes—diligence, uprightness, selflessness. Implied in the characterizations of women, good and bad, deployed by these periodicals was an unavoidable message regarding the behavior that was conducive to the desired social order. For a bourgeois woman to hold the admiration of Dominican patriarchs, it was essential that she be obedient, patient, constant, virtuous, maternal. As these writings attest, enormous pressure to conform was applied to those who deviated.

Few did. Although the number of articles and advice columns directed at women would make one think the social order had been turned on its head, in-depth news coverage of middle-class women's activities in Santo Domingo and San Pedro de Macorís points to an idyllic conformity to the desired mold. Upper-class women gave "proof [of] their intelligence, capacity to work, and commitment" in the sewing, knitting, cross-stitching, and crocheting classes at the professional institute. Some organized cultural evenings in collaboration with the town council and were active in charitable activities. As Rhoda Reddock suggests for Trinidad, this was precisely the kind of work, unpaid and voluntary, that both eased women out of the home and raised their social status. Others served as ambassadors of goodwill in patriotic parades, inaugurations of city services, and advertising campaigns. In their public appearances, they exhibited the grace and modesty appropriate to their class and gender. A group appealed to the president of the town council, for example, to rectify an embarrassing situation for them—at the Parque Colón, where some ladies had strolled the previous Thursday, more than fifty dogs offended their sense of morality. Years later, women "exercised and amused [themselves]" in the carousel, where, the writer fantasized, ribbons games could be organized.[27]

Travelers' passing comments confirm the impression that gender roles, as envisioned by elite men, were firmly in place. Upper-class women could not be considered the companions of men by any stretch of the imagination. They spent the entire day lazing about the home, lying in hammocks, hardly ever attending public functions, except when accompanied by watchful fathers or husbands. Beautiful when they were young, most commentators remarked, they looked old before they were thirty. They overdressed, used too much makeup, and flirted in a way that was shocking to the more sedate American visitor. This turn of events would not have been surprising to a contemporary Dominican feminist, who pointed out that, as children, girls received dolls and stoves to play with, while boys got guns, bicycles, and books.[28]

THE POLITICAL USES OF PATRIARCHY

It would be a stretch to assert that male Dominican intellectuals and popular writers placed the future of the Dominican Republic in the hands of bourgeois women. Yet as biological and ideological reproducers of the collectivity and replicators of its culture, bourgeois women had an important role to play in the selection of appropriate political paths and the realignment of social forces. Their recruitment to the task of nation-building was consonant with the generalized desire to position the country auspiciously. Unlike their working-class sisters, upper- and middle-class women possessed the physical attributes and had access to the material wherewithal—education, money, property—that made possible the renovation of the Dominican "race." Although obliquely, political and literary figures at the turn of the nineteenth century recognized bourgeois women's value as transmitters of characteristics ascribed to their class.

The intelligentsia were incapable of conceiving of women as citizens, however. Liberals imagined citizens as individuals who owned property, were in charge of their households, labored in productive work, and participated in politics. The Napoleonic Code, which had ruled Dominican law since 1804 and continues to guide the legal system, considered women minors— single women with fathers or brothers and married women could not dispose of property, act as heads of household, establish separate residence, or be witnesses in court. It would have been rare at the beginning of the century for upper-class women to work outside the home for pay. The submission of the will of women to that of their husbands was enough at the time to place serious doubts on their capacity to act politically as independent agents— and they most certainly could not vote.

Outside citizenship, educated upper-class women resorted to a device common to early feminists in their efforts to infiltrate public life: they claimed a higher moral standing by virtue of their sex and treated it as a biological trait. Since "modernity, as envisioned by Latin American elites, was itself premised on the selective incorporation of women into public life," it was not a leap in logic to allow the input of women in progressive legislation that promoted the public welfare. Before long, as one might suspect, the inclusion of women's issues became a part of the discussion. In the Dominican Republic, the careful insertion of upper-class women in prescribed roles was one of the many negotiations in the shifting ground of progress.[29]

The need to reconceive the nation in order to bolster the state, however, made necessary the surveillance of precisely these moral and outspoken women as they began to operate in new circumstances in urban centers. One early example of the goings-on that elite men might have feared was the activism of teachers. Altagracia Henríquez, for example, refused to be demoted to school assistant and demanded back pay as director of the night school for young women. Cecilia Viguié protested being called back to the job or risk losing it after "twenty years of service to the republic" and under doctor's orders not to travel from Jamaica after surgery. Petronila Angélica Gómez requested that the amount usually paid for building rental be added to her monthly pay as director of the 27 de febrero school. The Bobadilla sisters called for increased pay for teaching more students. A group of fifteen women asked the San Pedro town council to allocate money to a girls' high school, which had been operating for several days as a corporation made up of all the students.[30] These women were not only educated but were also apparently aware of their rights and purposefully ignorant of their need for male patronage.

Almost as if to forestall the appearance of "unmanageable women" (with the will and the resources to contribute to the polity in their own right), writers in this period engaged in the ideological construction of women as good wives and mothers (and therefore not as students, workers, or citizens) and the deployment through literature of images of women as adversaries of men who, motivated by "irrationality and eros," subverted male agendas. Men, then, conceiving of themselves as symbols of "respectable manliness" and the only ones worthy of the task of state-building, were called upon to control bourgeois women so as to assure themselves of the continuity of their actions.[31]

The carefully prescribed roles for bourgeois women in building the Dominican nation serve as good examples of the political uses of patriarchy. At its most elementary, feminizing the nation has been used repeatedly to mobilize patriotic emotions on "her" behalf. The woman being represented as worthy of being saved from the invaders' violations, naturally, had to be faithful, motherly, chaste, and dutiful—in the Dominican Republic as well as in Europe. In the installation ceremonies for teachers, Ercilia Pepín, considered by many to be an early feminist, made the connection between women and *patria*: "The fatherland is a spacious home, and women are called to be educated to serve [it]." Apolinar Perdomo, a local poet, was less optimistic. His *patria* had been devastated "by error, egotism, ambition"—crimes committed by her own children. An "eternal *mater dolorosa*," her tears could purify the heart of her children, her divine light could once more illuminate the future. "Who would produce this miracle [in the *patria*]? Who would whisper to her the well-known: 'rise and walk'?" The poet's solution was a twentieth-century Juan Pablo Duarte, a heroic man who was worthy of her sacrifices. In another association between dedicated women and the fatherland, Arturo Logroño, an orator known for his defense of the island's autonomy, beseeched a group of students on Flag Day to love the flag as they did their mother, because the fatherland was their mother. He continued, "May the pledge that you make today, citizen of tomorrow, to that illustrious flag . . . , be a sacred promise that sprouts in your young hearts and produces for the fatherland, in the future, the healthy fruit of splendor and civilization." The role of gender "as a commodity in the spectacle of representation" could not come across as more real.[32]

Further imbuing politics with the rules of patriarchy, this iconography had to be made real. To belong to the nation, then, virtuous women had to be joined with respectable male citizens—quite literally and until recently, when a woman became entitled to retain her citizenship affiliation although married to a man from another country. As Reddock suggests for Trinidad, the monogamous, nuclear, property-holding family unit was essential to the plans of nationalist reformers. In the Dominican Republic, marrying "well" was without a doubt a probable course for upper- and middle-class women, and a possible occurrence for a number of working-class women (who might marry or settle into a permanent relationship with the paradigms of Dominicanness described earlier). But those who failed to do so—sexual workers, single mothers, economically independent women—fell per force outside the pale of Dominicanness. In order to maintain nationality within male elite boundaries, then, worthy men situated bourgeois women under their guardianship and dismissed working-class women as unimportant to nationbuilding. In denying women, even those of their own class, the capacity to promote the goal of national development on their own recognizance, bourgeois men in turn-of-the-century Santo Domingo effectively monopolized citizenship. Women, then, became symbolic of the limits of national difference between men.[33]

The process described above follows closely Doris Sommer's understanding of nationalist novels as reinforcing patriarchy at a critical moment in the formation of the Latin American republics. According to Sommer, the fictional stories that have served as the foundation for many a Latin American country expound as ideal a patriarchal and hierarchical family structure that is also presented as natural. In them, a hardworking male "People" and a fertile, untamed female "Land" are productively united until an illegitimate, usurping "Enemy" comes along, in the form of either class conflict or a foreign invasion. The favorable management of these threats, through misrepresentation or sublimation (as in *Enriquillo*, the Dominican example she offers), confirms that an auspicious future is achieved through properly constituted and harmonious households, such as the Dominican intelligentsia envisioned.[34]

The insidious manipulation of the roles of bourgeois women ultimately secured for white elite men their position at the helm of decision-making processes. At a turning point in Dominican history, when the most industrious and most inspired minds of the country believed that political, economic, and social change was indeed possible, limiting the courses of action to a few controlled alternatives became crucial. Targeting women, by definition responsible for passing on socially desired biological and cultural traits, seemed logical enough. Ironically, the instrumental role assigned to women in elite imaginings of the future pointed precisely to the limitations of their brand of citizenship, as the construction of national boundaries remained effectively a white male prerogative.

CHAPTER FIVE

Working People in the City

In their daily interactions with authorities and among themselves, working-class men and women worked out their own notions of citizenship in ways unsuspected by the formulators of progress. Because of the clash between the intelligentsia's illusory plans for a greater Dominican Republic in the new century and the day-to-day experiences of laboring men and women in the city, the working poor found themselves in constant conflict over the roles they were to play in urban centers. In his study of Trinidad's plantation society, David Trotman calls the conflict caused by the elite's political decisions and the reaction of the disenfranchised "the quarrel of the elite." This framework sheds light on the Dominican case as well, as it points to the capacity of nonelite men and women to have an impact on the future lawmaking and law enforcing of their "superiors" by behaving and acting in customary ways. As the "quarrel" evolved in Santo Domingo and San Pedro de Macorís, its terms changed, as I will show below, due to the insistence of working people on making governmental structures respond to the reality of their working lives.[1]

As was suggested in chapter 2, city officials generally treated the popular classes as one more element in their campaign to bring Santo Domingo up to the standards of urbanity that had reached them from more "civilized" countries. Based on this reasoning, the town council of Santo Domingo religiously noted violations to city ordinances and other occurrences under the supervision of the municipal government, thus making public a snapshot of the city and its dwellers. Similarly, public order officials in the capital and San Pedro made their rounds in troublesome neighborhoods at night, quieting down or picking up disturbers of the peace. State authorities also dealt with formal accusations from city residents for theft, insults, and beatings.

Through all this, newspaper articles and other writings singled out working people, because they did not conform to bourgeois patterns of comportment, and cast suspicion upon them, because they consorted openly with the feared "other" or were themselves the stereotypical immigrants who introduced disease into the island, engaged in illegal activities, and worked only to spend their wages elsewhere. Seemingly everywhere, the working class posed a threat to the renovation of the nation.

Working people in Santo Domingo and San Pedro, however, acted and re-acted to the complexities of the urban setting in a variety of ways, as this chapter and the next will demonstrate. That they operated with their own code of conduct and had their own expectations regarding fairness becomes clear after a careful reading of police reports and travelers' accounts. Working women, in that they faced particular circumstances by virtue of their class and gender, defined citizenship in the everyday world differently, not only from their bourgeois "superiors" but also from men in general. In either case, the fears of intellectuals and public officials were unfounded, and their mandates for social order may have served only to bolster their undisputed positions of power.

THE REGULATION OF URBAN
WORKING PEOPLE

The growth of the city alone must have been a bureaucrat's nightmare. As Santo Domingo's population swelled to over thirty thousand residents in the first decade of the century and San Pedro's reached almost fifteen thousand, so also grew markets dominated by petty traders, schools staffed irregularly by a new generation of female teachers, small businesses precariously owned by lesser entrepreneurs, rental property administered by tough slumlords, and sex provided by prostitutes in bordellos or part-time sexual workers operating independently. For municipal authorities intent on improving the quality of city life, these populations represented serious obstacles to their goals. They circulated freely around the city, presumably cared little about their personal appearance and hygiene, exhibited "scandalous" behavior, and thus strained the resources available to their superiors and public authorities to manage their existence.

The municipal government was, of course, relentless in its desire to control the activities of city residents. It expected that the enforcement of ordinances and the continued maintenance of the public peace would make Santo Domingo a safe and pleasant place to live in and visit. *Contravenciones*, simple violations of the law for which the infractors paid small fines, were published weekly in the *Boletín Municipal* or recorded in town council minutes. A sampling of these sources indicates that the situations the ayuntamiento dealt with were uncomplicated, despite official insistence on micromanaging them. About fifteen to twenty men and two to three women were fined monthly in Santo Domingo for a number of offenses that ranged from adulterating milk to resisting authority. In San Pedro, the ayuntamiento charged about ten to twenty men and four to eight women for similar offenses, although the incidence of "scandals" appears greater there.[2]

Several sources suggest that "crime," as the authorities defined it, was increasing in the Dominican Republic in this period. Juan I. Jiménez Grullón reports that 1,714 people were accused of 1,447 crimes in 1906; the numbers were 3,061 and 2,580, respectively, for 1910. My own unscientific count reveals that the number of petty crimes in the mid-1890s increased as well. Jiménez Grullón attributes the rise in criminality to the "social crisis" experienced during the Cáceres administration, and a similar case could be made for the last years of the Lilís dictatorship. Trotman, however, offers an alternative explanation (for Trinidad) that deserves consideration in the Dominican case. Departing from the premise that crime is socially constructed, he explains that in plantation Trinidad anything that did not approximate European white customs, practices, and behavior was suspect and ultimately labeled as deviant, if not illegal. Most of the activities of the nonwhite urban lower class, then, were persecuted when not prosecuted. As I show in the following paragraphs, municipal authorities in Santo Domingo and in San Pedro, in their effort to preserve the social order and to instruct the population on urbane comportment, cracked down on what *they* considered problematic or offensive conduct.[3]

The marked presence in Santo Domingo of working men and women and the increasing multiplicity of their economic roles were fated to become troublesome for government officials and the ideologues behind them because of two circumstances that are difficult to separate from one another: class and birthplace. The regulators of city life were likely to react, both discursively and practically, to a number of behaviors that working-class men and women exhibited both because of their socioeconomic status and their geographical origins. As a function of their constant need to work, the city's popular classes were uneducated, had limited aspirations, did not own substantial property, and behaved in uncultured ways—at least from the perspective of city officials. As recent migrants from surrounding rural areas, other islands, or European countries, they were also unfamiliar with city ways and especially with a strict application of urban codes and industrial discipline. As was the case in other islands, the figurative "nonwhite" status of the offenders was an aggravating circumstance.[4]

The nature of these offenses suggests a population perhaps not yet accustomed to urban patterns and certainly not materially equipped for some of the physical exigencies of life in the city. It should not have been a surprise that residents of working-class neighborhoods and recent migrants from rural areas kept animals in their yards, did not fence them in properly, abused them, and butchered them at home. These patterns must have corresponded to common practices in the countryside, where sanitary considerations were less pressing, population density did not have to be taken into account, and bourgeois sensitivities toward domesticated animals were not the rule. In addition, it is unlikely that people living in working-class districts could actually conform to city codes—they simply did not have the means. Building a fence or keeping an animal well fed and well trained required time and money that manual laborers did not have at their disposal. The activities of the working-class residents of Santo Domingo and San Pedro, then, could indicate either a different set of values and therefore resistance to impositions from above, or a desire to conform that was lost to the historical record because of their economic incapacity.[5]

There are other infractions, however, that illuminate the precise sources of noncompliance and, as such, point to a subaltern sense of entitlement distinct from elite definitions. A list of infringements that recall rural life, and therefore a radically different understanding of what was appropriate, would include burning trash in the yard or disposing of it in a place not designated for that purpose; riding on carts, driving a vehicle without headlights or without a license, or abandoning a cart on the road; having a "filthy sewer" or a "latrine in bad state"; and as already mentioned, failing to control animals. Even public drunkenness and disturbances of the peace, I would argue, were lesser offenses in the rural context, where the possibility of hurting others or causing property damage was diminished by the mere fact that the population was sparse and social pressure from friends and neighbors more effective. I am not arguing that recent migrants got in trouble because they were unaware that their surroundings demanded different patterns of behavior or because they were ignorant of the law. Rather, I am suggesting that the consequences of their actions were not that evident to them even in the new context, which remained unfamiliar only in form, since the urban location had not noticeably altered their existence. To working-class people, their city digs might just have evoked the transparency of function, the openness of domestic life, and the collective sense of purpose for which the rural areas were known.

This does not mean, of course, that public officials were tolerant of the antics of recent arrivals. To the contrary, they were suspicious of the motives of rural folk and took the animosity between city and countryside as a given. In a statement stripped of any sense of a cultural context, a municipal official in San Carlos, in the jurisdiction of Santo Domingo, proposed that wakes be issued licenses because they always ended up as dances. Whether he chose to feign ignorance of peasant funeral practices or was motivated only by the desire to generate revenue for the municipality, the end result of his statement was to point to what city folk would generally perceive as an atavism. In an article describing the fire that occurred in a sugar mill, the writer explained that not all the known information had been disseminated because the truth had still to emerge from the "astute and malicious" Dominican peasants— clearly the enemy and almost a separate segment of the population. Pedro Francisco Bonó, ever the defender of the oppressed, linked what he in- controvertibly labeled the propensity of the rural masses to support the party that opposed the city, or any party at all for that matter, to the abuses committed upon the countryside by city folk who denied the surrounding areas any benefits whatsoever. Given this hostility, urban law enforcers read deviations from city norms as direct challenges to their authority.[6]

Other contraventions suggest a bit more familiarity with city ways and a more deliberate effort to subvert bourgeois standards of fairness. Adulterat- ing milk, selling below the measure, or selling spoiled food; opening for business on a holiday or at other unauthorized times, or reselling coal before the stipulated time; making itinerant sales without a license—these infrac- tions point to a decided attempt to get an edge on the competitive capitalist economy. Whether the reasoning behind regulations made sense to small- time merchants operating for the first time in the marketplace or not, they undoubtedly chose to break the law with the intention of making more money—perhaps simply to make ends meet.

Although there is no indication that the authorities were moved by this common predicament, journalists appeared sympathetic to the plight of the working class. One article that reported the attempt of two young men to steal some items at the Vicini warehouse, putting lives at risk, considered them fully responsible for their actions but also attributed the crime to unfor- tunate circumstances, noting that the young men had lived "with no father but fate and no home but the abyss." Expressing equally middle-class values, another columnist bemoaned the necessity for all the members of an apoc- ryphal laboring family to work. Since salaries were so low, and the most basic need was nourishment, he explained, the wife had to abandon housework to become a laundress; the children, rather than go to school, were rented out to sell candy, fruit, or lottery tickets; and at times "the pitiful couple of old folk" (*el pobre par de viejos*—the grandparents) had to go out on the street to beg. Despite the formulaic nod to the woman's role within the house, the importance of education, and the stigma of assistance, or perhaps moved by these values, these writers were more understanding than city officials regarding the dire situation of working people. While the goal of police was simply to control the manifestations of poverty as they threatened the smooth operation of the city, the objective of journalists appears to have been exploring its causes as if it could be uprooted.[7]

The premise and desired outcome of both city officials and social critics remained nevertheless monolithically bourgeois. As everywhere else, the more physically exerting and directly manual the type of work required in a particular employment category, the less prestige the occupation carried with it. As Marisol de la Cadena shows for Peru, income had little to do with it, as some low-status jobs actually brought in plenty of money to those who performed them. In Santo Domingo, for example, the man in charge of the slaughterhouse made almost the same amount as the printer of the *Boletín Municipal*, and both made more than the highest-paid school principal at fifty-one pesos (see Table 4). The prestige any one of these occupations carried with it varied considerably, in large part because elites found it easy to take the mental leap required to equate low-status occupations with deficient morality and aberrant practices. Moreover, as Karin Rosemblatt demonstrates for Chile, virility went hand in hand with "regular" (read "industrial") work, and those who worked in nonsalaried occupations were considered dependent or feminized. Although the Dominican Republic was just beginning to industrialize, a similar bias existed for irregular work performed by the task and for multiple employers, such as would be the case for domestic work and other manual, unskilled occupations. Working-class people in Santo Domingo and San Pedro, because of the jobs they held, invariably invoked these negative associations.[8]

They were unlikely, moreover, to observe "proper decorum" in their exchanges with each other and with public officials—they would talk loudly, use "inappropriate" language, gesticulate in "vulgar" ways, and taunt each other, sober or drunk, at all hours of the day and night. Already, as detailed in chapter 2, municipal authorities had identified *bailes de cueros*, dances in which the drums were played, as undermining morality and cultured ways. Enrique Deschamps, in his inventory of the country's economic, cultural, and political capital, revealed the continued misgivings of the elite in this

TABLE 4

Salaries and Costs of Living in Santo Domingo,
ca. 1910

Monthly Salaries

municipal doctor for indigent	$55
school principal	$51 (maximum)
night pharmacist	$100
slaughterhouse attendant	$65
printing the *Boletín Municipal*	$60
cemetery watchman	$20
urban telephone director	$12
public clock	$12
janitor in municipal palace	$5
day laborer	$16.20 (maximum)

Expenses

"the most modest dwelling"	$10 a month
a room in a house	$3–5 a month
one plantain	$.01–.02 (compared to $.002 in the countryside)
a bottle of milk	$.08–.14 (compared to $.02–.06 in the countryside)
a pound of beef	$.12–.20 (compared to $.08–.10 in the countryside)

SOURCES: "Estado demostrativo de las operaciones verificadas en la tesorería del ayuntamiento de Santo Domingo durante el mes de junio de 1908," *Boletín Municipal* 19.361 (16 Mar. 1909); "Sesión del 11 de febrero de 1915," *Boletín Municipal* 23.453 (5 Mar. 1913); "El jornal y el costo de la vida," *Renacimiento* 1.5 (22 Apr. 1915).

respect. In his description of the refinement that had obtained at the games of San Andrés, he related their origin: the popular classes would soak the well-to-do with colored water on the street or through syringes strategically placed in front-door keyholes. In the early twentieth century, he was happy to report, "*bailes blancos*," in which the upper class dressed in white, only to be covered with colored confetti, or prearranged watering locations, where conceivably the quantity of water was controlled, were the norm. Likewise, carnival took on a very different tone over the years so as to delimit its most sordid aspects. Among the upper class,

> honorable matrons, ladies who are regularly models of propriety, and
> timid and naive girls, who without [the cover of their] masks observe
> public and privately irreproachable calm, good manners, and com-

posure, frequently become, by virtue of a simple mask, wonders of genial indiscretion and playfulness, ingeniously kidding around with everyone, insinuating the disclosure of others' love affairs, unknown or potential, and even stirring everybody's curiosity by exposing the loose ends of any one of the jams that any of us who go through life have more or less hidden, whether we admit to it or not.[9]

If this is what the upper class indulged in during festivities, one can only imagine their reaction to more overt ways of "kidding around" and the alarm this must have caused.

WORKING PEOPLE AT WORK

Just as officials sought to alter the public comportment of the population to match the elite's expectations of progress, working-class men and women, who either came from the surrounding countryside to look for work or found new tasks to perform within the changing cityscape, insisted on forging their livelihood around the new urban context. Ayuntamiento records show that men and women worked in a variety of occupations all around town, meeting the demands of the growing population and making money for themselves and their families. Men drove carts, carriages, boats, or ferries; made pottery, bread, cigars, jewelry, shoes, or clothes; played musical instruments; fixed mechanical appliances; tanned leather; sold liquor; cut hair; slaughtered animals; painted buildings; caught fish; built houses; served in the police force; ran all manner of businesses; and more. The skilled crafts were generally a monopoly of men—they worked as masons, blacksmiths, carpenters, and the like. Women appear conspicuously in ayuntamiento records and other sources as milk sellers, market vendors, itinerant dealers (the famous *marchantas*), laundresses, domestic servants, seamstresses, cooks, nurses, errand girls, small shop owners, midwives, tobacco workers, market administrators, wage workers in municipal agencies, healers, and teachers. In these roles, they engaged the state apparatus and interacted with their fellow citizens in an attempt to carve out space for themselves in a new environment.[10]

As most everywhere else, and with the notable exception of tobacco workers, occupations remained segregated by gender. Women entered the labor force by performing jobs that were an extension of their own home work and labored sporadically, when market forces facilitated access, and on an individual basis. In Santo Domingo, this meant domestic work in the homes of the well-to-do and laundering for anyone who could pay for it. Of the sixty-four women who requested medical assistance for themselves or their children from the municipal doctor in September 1909, twenty-seven listed "*quehaceres domésticos*" (domestic tasks) as their occupation, which suggests that they worked in their own homes and probably also in somebody else's. In addition, thirteen worked as laundresses or ironed clothes, five were cooks or candy makers, and one sold lottery tickets. There were fifty-one men who received medical assistance or were in charge of children who did. Their occupations were much more varied (baker, coachman, blacksmith, road-construction worker, tobacco worker, mason, carpenter, tailor, mechanic, store attendant) and were for the most part tasks for which they had trained. One noteworthy role reversal in these lists is the number of men who took their children to be examined by the municipal doctor or requested that he visit their home. Of the thirty-seven children whose parents are known, twenty-two were being taken care of by their fathers.[11]

Women monopolized domestic occupations, and explanations for this occurrence have stressed cultural practices rather than economic considerations. In a string of events familiar to Dominicans to this day, the "*chacha*" (for *muchacha*, girl) arrived at an urban well-to-do household from the countryside at a young age and was supposedly treated as if she were a member of the family. She was expected to perform all house chores, according to her age and ability, and received in turn room and board as well as an education. Conceivably, family and servant developed such bonds that the *chacha* catered to the family's food preferences, offered her opinion on family matters, kept family secrets, and eventually "grandmothered" the new generation, when she could no longer perform demanding physical labor. A romanticized account of such a relationship laments that, with modernization in the late twentieth century, this "warm and authentic human connection between individuals of separate social classes" has ceased to exist, although there are plenty of Dominicans who to this day have "*hijas de crianza*" ("daughters," insofar as they grow up in the household) whom they allegedly treat as part of the family. Marked by a touching personal story or not, domestic service required no training other than that which low-income young girls and women received by virtue of their class and sex.[12]

Like domestic servants, laundresses performed home work for other people. In the countryside, they washed clothes in streams and hung them on bushes and trees, but in the city, they made use of public wells or the Ozama River and used as drying surfaces what was available in those settings or piled up rocks in the client's yard. An idyllic description of the process in remote areas suggests the problems that would be faced in the city. According to the writer, washerwomen carried both their family's clothes and those that they washed for others to the river on their heads. The housewife who had contracted their services would provide the "*cuaba*" soap (made from a tree bark and still preferred, to the chagrin of laundromat operators), the cubed "*azul añil*" for whitening clothes, powdered starch, and the money to buy wood or coal with which to boil water. The water was boiled with the *azul añil* and guava branches and other aromatic herbs. Fists or rocks served to get the dirt out. As the clothes dried under the scorching sun, the laundresses bathed seminaked in the river. "The play in the clear waters of the river made the sweats of the body and the griefs of the soul evaporate. The clothes ended up smelling like a country breeze, and the colors of the fabrics shone impeccably. A bit of the fragrance and the light of the tropics went with every bundle of clean clothes."[13]

It is doubtful that washing clothes in the river was as pleasant a job as the author would have us believe. In the city, however, this physically demanding labor on the part of uneducated women was complicated by the public nature of the performance. The low esteem in which the occupation was held alone suggests that laundresses were considered loud, inappropriately dressed, and lacking in manners. Even the sympathetic voice of a poet who praised their hard work, resignation toward their lot, and dedication to their children referred to flying strips of fabric that constituted their dress, which, one can imagine, covered them minimally.[14] If, as the photographic record suggests, laundresses dipped not only the clothes but also themselves into the water, the sight would have been quite a scandal in the city.

Another group of "self-employed" women who extended their domestic activities into the marketplace were the "*marchantas*." The origin of this term is obscure, and in fact, I have heard it refer both to the specialized itinerant vendors who traveled through the city on a fixed route selling fruit, prepared food, household items, and the like and to the buyers of these products. In the latter representation, the housewives who were the steady clients of a traveling seller prepared tea, or brewed coffee, or served fresh water for their providers when they came by. In addition, women were well known for the aggressive skills they displayed in the market itself, where booths were assigned precisely to inject some order into a potentially chaotic arrangement, as well as to provide the municipal treasury with some income. As was the case for laundresses and domestic servants, ambulatory vendors or attendants of stands in the marketplace had entered the work force by merely expanding their sphere of action from the home to the street.[15]

Men dominated the trades, as already mentioned, but also the commercial sector, from the largest warehouses to the tiniest local store. Of approximately 455 businesses that required a license from the municipal government, 437 (96 percent) were owned by men and ran the gamut of specialties

TOP: Laundresses by the river. (Archivo General de la Nación, Colección ADAI, album 2, p. 24, photo 389.) BOTTOM: The Mercado del Ozama. (Enrique Deschamps, *La República Dominicana: Directorio y guía general* [Santiago de los Caballeros: Vda. de J. Cunill, Barcelona, n.d., ca. 1906–11], 52.) OPPOSITE: Artist's rendering of activity in the market square. (Samuel Hazard, *Santo Domingo, Past and Present; with a Glance at Hayti* [New York: Harper & Brothers, 1873].)

and volume of trade—notions store, corner store, stationery store, liquor store, tobacco shop, soap factory, pub, warehouse, coffeehouse, leather shop, pharmacy, perfumery, hardware store, investing firm, bakery, saddler, rum shop, billiards, silver shop, distillery, ice factory, match factory. There was plenty of room in Santo Domingo for the activities of merchants at the lower end of the scale, also denoted by the classification of the license as first, second, third, all the way down to eighth class, and one can safely assume that a fifth-class *pulpería* (local general store), of which there were many, was enough to barely make ends meet for its owner. As expected, the pubs, corner stores, liquor shops, and rum shops with low ratings (fourth to eighth class) concentrated in the working-class neighborhoods, while the more specialized stores were located in the business district where the bourgeoisie shopped.[16]

Only eighteen shops were the property of women in their own right or as a result of their husband's death, and they were usually small businesses— notions store, corner store, liquor shop, bakery. These women were better off than their patently working-class sisters, either because their husbands had bequeathed them the family business or because they themselves had proven able administrators. Several of these small-scale entrepreneurs were identified in municipal records as "*vda*" (for *viuda*, widow), and it is likely that the former means of acquisition was the case for them. Among them were a brick maker, a fireworks manufacturer, a market administrator, and a market co-owner, all of whom appeared to be outspoken defenders of their customary prerogatives. One can also find women who had clearly arrived at their métier on their own—for example, some "*señoritas*" (unmarried women) who made roof tiles ("*hacen lozas tejas*"), ran a passenger transport business between San Cristóbal, west of the capital, and Santo Domingo, and performed intelligence work for the U.S. occupation forces. The U.S. operative was, according to her superior, a heavy drinker, a good shot, and somewhat scandalous—"a gem, a diamond in the rough." She had been the lover of highly placed bureaucrats and so had been privy to important matters of state, and she was paid the highest salary in the secret service. Her superior also praised her for her loyalty and for "respecting him sexually."[17]

PROSTITUTION

An exclusively female occupation in this time period was sexual work. Prostitutes (*meretrices*) were frequently labeled as such in the record or can be identified by place of residence (Ponce, San Pedro Street, Misericordia Street, Barrio San Miguel, Barrio San Antón) and by circumstances (a man was in the room a woman rents, a man owed a woman money for services, a woman refused to live with a man "for a time"). One can also speculate that women who did not follow the rules of urbanity set by "their betters" were, if not part-time sexual workers, certainly considered "loose women" and treated with little respect and consideration. Behavior such as running dance halls, calling others names, drunkenness, and other implicative evidence (aliases such as "Caramelo" and "La Mulita" [the little mule] or simply being out late at night) irrevocably connected working-class women to sexual work in the minds of Santo Domingo's elite. That Fernando Victoria felt entitled to strike Francisca de los Santos (La Mulita) on the spot, because she insulted him from the street as he rode in a cart with his family, suggests an exercise of prerogative that is a function of privilege in the face of sordidness. In their actions and through their writings, government representatives and civic leaders repeatedly treated proletarian women as social pariahs.[18]

Prostitution was not a crime, however, and was only a problem from the perspective of authorities insofar as it impacted the social order and public hygiene. Liberals throughout Latin America—and the Dominican Republic was no exception—continued to try to reconcile their respect for individual and commercial liberty with the irrepressible desire of the state to make everyone conform to bourgeois rules of public morality. Repeatedly, the

Santo Domingo town council refused to address the issue directly or indirectly. In response to a citizen request in early 1915, the content of which has been lost to the historical record, the ayuntamiento stated that it felt that it did not have the "legal capacity" to regulate prostitution and remarked that the lots in question (*los aludidos terrenos*), presumably where prostitutes gathered, did not belong to the municipality. This call for help had followed the provincial governor's appeal that no licenses to operate be issued to those establishments frequented by prostitutes "or persons of loose living" (*personas de mal vivir*). The most the town council committed to was to "continue putting at [the governor's] disposition, every [time] that it was necessary, the municipal police corps to help him keep the [public] order."[19]

The municipality of Santo Domingo was equally slow to react to prostitution as a public health concern, contrary to the position taken by San Pedro's ayuntamiento. Two lone references to sanitation issues stand out. In 1909, the Santo Domingo town council took a cursory look at the prostitution code sent by the Dominican consul in Le Havre along with rat poison—a revealing association. Years later, it appointed a commission to inspect hospices with the sole purpose of determining if diseased prostitutes could be cared for there. It was only the occupation of the country by U.S. Marines that prompted the approval of a strict code of hygiene for the practice of sex as work.[20]

San Pedro, on the other hand, targeted prostitutes as early as 1913 on two fronts: as polluting the environment and threatening public health. In July of that year, nine prostitutes who must have rented rooms in a building ("*prostitutas vividoras de una cuartería*") were brought to court because their yards were dirty ("*por tener suciedades en el patio de la casa*"). Although it was the hygiene inspector who cited the violation, it was the provincial prefect who made the accusation, pointing unequivocally to the connection between sexual work and (moral) filth. The mayor, who regularly presided over the hearings, released the women, apparently only allowing the sanitation violation to stand and thus disallowing the connection between the moral worth of the women and their surroundings.

In the same vein, the public health inspector regularly made entries regarding the conditions of ships upon arrival and of the prostitutes who had registered with the authorities—his function was clearly to record any situation that might develop into a public health crisis, and he treated ships and women with equal objectivity. The municipal doctor was also attuned to this attitude. In an appeal for a stricter enforcement of hygienic procedures, disappointingly limited to clean instruments and towels, he insisted on following up on his patients:

What do you get from, for example, cauterizing, stuffing up with iodoformed gauze, [and] douching these wretches, when they spend the night in bars drinking alcohol and given over to their trade? Besides, it is a fact that: they do not show their [identity] cards nor do the men who attend those places ask for them, and if they do show them, it is the cards of those to whom the doctor has given a mark of [good] health.

The concern of authorities was undoubtedly controlling the spread of disease, and for that purpose, prostitutes had to undergo weekly examinations, and the doctor had to make notations along a classificatory axis: completely well; with chancres, gonorrhea, metritis, or other venereal conditions; menstruating; in bed with fever; in another part of the country; absent; living an honorable life.[21]

The public discourse against prostitution, then, was neither well developed nor widespread. An early example of it connected sexual work to the depravity that supported the tyrant Heureaux—gambling, begging, and vagrancy. Prostitution was characterized as a sanitary problem very late, and even then as a "legacy from fathers to sons, [that] contributed to mental degeneration and the physical eradication of our race," and not as a devastating affliction for poor women. Even when they were included in plans to improve society, working-class girls who grew up to be prostitutes were believed to have "run the risk of [moral] ruin" because the flamboyant fashions and catchy lifestyles of prostitutes caught their eye, and they endeavored to imitate them, and not because of need. The focus of attention, evidently, was not on the prostitutes themselves, who some understood as "wretched women that society itself often hurls to opprobrium," but rather on their effect on their social superiors—namely, "honest and honorable ladies" who went to church, parks, or commercial establishments and children who lived in decent neighborhoods. The movement of these "terrible and painful social sores" had to be controlled, and so the police should keep them "within the very limit that their moral perversion demands" (*en el justo límite a que su perversión las hace acreedoras*). In port cities, where this discourse originated, foreign women were suspected not only of carrying disease, as were men, but also of being "even more depraved and mired in the school of vice [than Dominican] whores, themselves already perverted and shameless."[22]

This brief look at prostitution provides a clear picture of what working-class women represented for public authorities and for the architects of the country's future. What was an occupation to poor women was a natural function for some elite men, a sign of national decay for reformers, a site of disease for the medical profession, and a public-order issue for the town council. As did bureaucrats' obsession to control city life, elite reactions to prostitution point more to bourgeois anxieties than they do to general and genuine concerns about the welfare of the country's inhabitants.[23]

SHAPING THE WORK SPACE

Working people chose to relate to their "superiors" in ways that impacted on the more practical aspects of their lives. As manual laborers and in all sorts of occupations, they struggled to support their families and obtain an advantage in the economic race. They "cheated" their customers or municipal authorities, as previously indicated, probably with a view to making ends meet. In addition, they occasionally solicited pay raises or organized to negotiate better working conditions. Frequently, almost customarily, individuals requested the municipality to lower the rate at which their business paid for its license. Although the outcome of few of these petitions is known, the mere intention behind them is telling: those who worked felt entitled to engage their government to obtain a better existence. They were drawing their own picture of what the state should do for its citizens and what their contribution was to city life.

Manual laborers who performed assorted tasks for employers on a temporary basis and wage workers employed by individuals or government agencies did not make much money. It is true that some municipal employees did relatively well in terms of salaries—the night pharmacist earned $100 a month, the municipal doctor $55, a school principal as much as $51, the police captain between $30 and $35, the laundresses at the leper hospital $25 to $30. But most were paid almost on par with, or well below, a day laborer— the man who cleaned floors at the town hall earned $5 a month, and the cleaning woman for the hospital $12, compared to a little over $16 for a journeyman, $22 for a schoolteacher, and between $14 and $18 for a teacher's aide. One suspects that many people worked, formally and informally, in the small enterprises with which the municipality contracted—manufacturer of uniforms for the municipal guard, band member, street sweeper, coachmen, painters, typographer (a woman), contractor (also a woman)—but there are no payrolls against which to check their activities and remuneration. In one particularly insidious instance, a number of policemen requested that, instead of increasing the amount paid to an outside service for the cleaning and pressing of their uniforms (no doubt, by women), their salaries be raised— they were certain "their" women would take on the job, surely without demanding payment.[24]

Logically, these men and women demanded pay raises or improved conditions of work. In the case of the hospital for lepers, the *guardián* (a word usually used to refer to a security guard, who would most likely be just another employee and male) would periodically refer to the town council a collective petition from the nurse and the women who washed, ironed, cooked, and ran errands, or did so when circumstances changed, such as occurred in 1905, when the number of patients was expected to rise. Other municipal employees wrote their own requests to the ayuntamiento—poor penmanship, colloquialisms, and grammatical errors included—asking for pay raises. Eustaquio Gómez, the assistant prefect in San Pedro, explained his predicament thus: "Finding myself somewhat behind, and without major resources, with a large family, I ask the [council] president along with the corporation [town council] to grant me an increase in salary of five pesos more, as it used to be in the past, to be able to live a bit more comfortably" (*para poderme desaogar un poco mejor*). With impeccable timing, these requests came in when budgets were about to be approved, and they were granted as often as not. In one instance, the police captain asked for an increase in salary, and the officers in the corps for a Christmas bonus; he obtained his pay raise, while the rank and file had to content themselves with the upcoming holiday cheer.[25]

Besides demanding better pay, skilled and unskilled workers required other work-related benefits from the town council, including at times a job itself. Juan Castell, a mason, had apparently been offered a lot in the cemetery as payment for a job but had to write to request it. Another mason, more savvy than Castell, saw an ad in the paper to build a sidewalk in downtown San Pedro and made a bid for the job. Unsolicited, a budding entrepreneur proposed the following deal to the ayuntamiento: he would provide up to eight hundred cartloads of stones at the current price, for twenty-five pesos a month; he would take the stones where they were needed and would continue to do so until he reached the money or the cartload limit. The man who ran errands for the leper hospital asked to stay there in his old age. The caretaker at the cemetery negotiated with the ayuntamiento regarding the depth of the graves and the charge per grave. After a detailed description of the fixed price obtained per "customer" (twenty cents for the hospice, no charge for the military or indigents), he proposed receiving fifty cents for a grave four and a half feet deep, rather than six feet deep. Later in the year, he wrote to the ayuntamiento to confirm that he was, in fact, the corporation's employee and not his brother, who was actually digging the graves after he himself had taken the key to the cemetery from him. In one unusual case, a worker asked that he be paid for the job he had done. He had worked for three weeks, from sunrise to sunset, he said, and was a family man who had not been able to support his household nor pay his hired hands. He had nothing else to sell, as he put it; he had simply run out of resources. Santo Domingo's and San Pedro's workers knew what was fair, it seems, even when the town councils were equivocal, and they had no qualms about asking for those things.[26]

Another outspoken group of petitioners to the ayuntamiento were those who requested that the classification of their business be downgraded so they might pay a smaller fee for the operating license. These appeals came equally from established businessmen and fledgling entrepreneurs. At the high end, for example, was a business in Industria Street in San Pedro that paid sixty pesos; at the low end, Felipe Rojas closed down his assorted-goods store and declared himself *bodegonero* (storehouse keeper) and itinerant salesman to clear some of the merchandise. Some merchants asserted they had made less money than the previous year or had lost money during the year and so should pay less. Others promised that they would not sell liquor, because apparently that operating license was more expensive and the profits not forthcoming. There were at least two cases, in my random sampling, of people who argued against the fairness of the classification scheme: Gregorio Brito alleged that his shoe workshop also served as an apprentice school, and for that reason he should not pay for a license; and the Martínez brothers protested their classification as a commercial agency because they rented bicycles. The latter cited the Santo Domingo patent regulations and the "most common" (*vulgarísimos*) legal principles to bolster their case. Both of these were direct challenges to the rationale behind the classificatory apparatus of the government.[27]

The first stirrings of class awareness are evident in this period in the city, although there is much debate regarding their significance. Several groups that identified themselves as "*gremios*" (guilds) made their concerns known to the Santo Domingo and San Pedro ayuntamientos. In the capital, butchers asked the town council to reconsider the seven-and-a-half-cent increase to the tax on an *arroba* (between twenty-four and thirty-six pounds) of meat and were able to get the supervisor appointed by the municipality to weigh in on the matter. In San Pedro, the bakers wanted to get more rolls out of a pound of bread, and the masons, commanded by the same Juan Castell above, wanted to be indemnified for some work that lay paralyzed at the cemetery.

The cart drivers agreed to fix prices for specific loads (e.g., four large sacks of rice, three barrels of cement, ten boxes of beer, twenty boards of pine-wood). But they also protested when the ayuntamiento required them to carry in their carts a plank to protect the sidewalks when they unloaded merchandise in the commercial district. They felt that it was a nuisance to carry the plank in the cart, especially when they needed it only for commercial clients, and suggested that the businesses they served buy the planks and store them. The coachmen in San Pedro, associated as the Liga de Obreros (Workers' League), opposed setting prices similar to those in the capital, because the maintenance costs for carriages and animals were very different. Their spokesperson proposed instead a system of rates per hour and per run, for errands and for pleasure drives, on workdays and holidays, day and night, within the city limits and out in the countryside. He worried that some men who were not qualified to drive a coach were giving a bad reputation to the "profession" and wanted the league to issue licenses to those who wanted to belong to the guild. In an appeal that must have struck a chord with council members, he denounced the practice on the part of these men of passing as coachmen, "in short, individuals who without a clue as to how to deal with decent people and above all with the fair sex violate as if without consequence the rules of morality and urbanity and the considerations which certain passengers are worthy of."

A group of thirty-eight merchants from San Pedro used a similar argument to prevent the ayuntamiento from passing a Sunday closing law that would be detrimental to the workers in the rural areas, they said, because articles in town were cheaper than those in company stores. They sought the support of the governor "so that [their] spirits, in the struggle for honest work, not fail and so that every passing day [they] might have the energy to contribute to getting this progressive country back on track."[28]

As Roberto Cassá points out, there was no homogeneity in the work sphere of the cities. A skilled-work sector based on individual initiative that functioned as a small-scale capitalist enterprise with connections to the merchants coexisted with a budding proletarian work force, both rural and urban. Workers did not coalesce as such, but identified sometimes with their occupation or their place of work. Their organizations—charitable and mutual-aid societies, educational associations, Odd Fellows' lodges, social clubs, and guilds—appear to the historian to have been motivated by the material and cultural poverty that marked the urban setting and by the precapitalist relations of production that predominated at the time. If there was class consciousness, in Marxist parlance, there was little political activity as such. In fact, the apparent identity of interest between labor, capital, and state that was evident in working-class manifestations in this period was the kind of negotiation that postponed class conflict rather than exacerbated it.[29]

Given this state of affairs, it is not surprising that, besides negotiating with the town council regarding functions and pay scales, some of these *gremios* developed agendas that brought them even closer to collaboration with the conformist state. The trajectory of the Sociedad de Obreros (Workers' Society) is a case in point. Beginning in 1901, they expressed their interest in renting a particular building, La Soledad, to be repaired at their cost, in which to hold night classes. The following month, a commission from the "representative corps of workers and artisans" reiterated their desire to renovate the locale but asked that they be exempted from rent payments for as long as the ayuntamiento thought reasonable. The town council approved the suspension of rent for two years for this "most noble purpose," but it is not known whether it was actually put in force, because in 1913 the building was used to store flammable materials. In 1915, the ayuntamiento granted the use of a school for night classes, probably to the same group again, this time called Porvenir Obrero (Working-Class Future). In San Pedro, the goal was the same: to establish a night school "that [would] respond in an effective way to the intellectual progress and culture of the working class of this population—with the purpose of forming, for the future, citizens [who are] conscious of their duties and rights." In August of 1913, an artisan organization with no name requested the use of the Instituto de Señoritas Anacaona Moscoso for their night classes. Other groups, the Club de Artesanos (Artisans' Club), for example, "always enthusiastic and attractive, headed by the progressive Mr. Agusto [sic] Júpiter," organized dances and other cultural and entertainment activities.[30]

Despite the attempts of the state to help reconcile the interests of capital with those of the working class, there were organizations that were outright anticapitalist. In a sympathetic accounting of one such meeting, a journalist for *Nuevo Réjimen* reported: "There we were, the workers, all of us intermingled, in an intimate and eloquent communion of ideas, in intimate contact, [having] broken forever the restrictions with which human foolishness separates classes and isolates races; there we were, the workers in agreement, to respond to a high motive of hope and popular enhancement." The danger, another writer minced no words, was a splinter organization that called itself Círculo Católico de Obreros (Catholic Circle of Workers). In one of the few mentions of Catholicism as a force in Dominican society, he warned that "the comrades of yesterday, turned into Judas," had set themselves aside from the workers who sought to improve their situation. Most of the workers were "dragged along by a Jesuitic frenzy, dominated by the false doctrines of Catholicism, preached to all and sundry by the swarm of bums who call themselves *ministers of the Lord* and who are not more than abject beings who live off the state budget and off the misnamed *alms of the faithful*." No sooner did laborers organize to improve their lot and discern their condition, the writer continued, "than immediately there appears the fatidic masked silhouette of the crows in cassocks, ready to disperse [the workers], for which evil effect they use with satanic astuteness illegal means." Despite the lack of measurable labor unrest, there were a few voices who nevertheless highlighted the tension between the interests of labor and the goals of capital.[31]

Not everyone, of course, believed that the welfare of the working class was being undermined by other social forces, least of all the church. The editor of *Nuevo Réjimen*, for example, categorically denied a few months later any need for worker activism. In his opinion, workers should unite to improve their situation. But it would be a mistake to adopt the label "working class" as necessarily opposed to the interests of the country. That workers were equal (to capitalists?) was evident when one remembered that public office had always been within their reach. In the countryside, however, the fear that workers would turn against capital seemed increasingly real. Even under Lilís, a fire at one of the sugar mills was not easily extinguished because four hundred laborers refused to put it out. The possibility for social unrest was always larger in the rural areas, but it was not unthinkable that it would spread to the cities, precisely because workers congregated there and their expectations had begun to grow.[32]

As is clear from the preceding, the working lives of the inhabitants of Santo Domingo and San Pedro did not exactly correspond to the images held by the intellectuals who patronized them through their writings or by the state officials who tried to intimidate them through the application of the law. Either because they were not accustomed to city ways or because they did not have the material means to comply, and probably because they had other ideas regarding what rules befitted their work contexts, recent and not-so-new urban residents evaded regulations or tried to bend the law to conform to their needs. In so doing, they "quarreled" with the elite, perhaps not acquiring a sense of class based on their actions, but at the very least actively developing a working version of citizenship.

CHAPTER SIX

Claiming Citizenship from Below

Working men and women in Santo Domingo and San Pedro de Macorís took on the attributes of citizens, most notably and not surprisingly, when they interacted with authorities over issues that the bourgeois intellectual and political apparatus recognized as important. As is true in modern market economies and liberal democracies, such as the Dominican Republic aspired to be, education, property, and personal reputation became clearly established as markers of status up and down the social scale. Men and women of the working class in the two cities under study engaged daily in a struggle to prove themselves in these arenas, to define what was culturally appropriate, sometimes literally fighting for what they felt they were entitled to. As they involved municipal officials in settling scores and establishing principles, they both challenged the judgment of their "superiors" and submitted to their authority. That they felt entitled to voice their opinion, sometimes quite violently, suggests that they had something at stake and that at some level participatory citizenship was becoming a natural course of action.

As individuals or collectively, the working people of the city requested or demanded, as the case might be—to cite varied examples—that a man be removed from a public post whom several neighbors had opposed three times already; that a specific person be named as grammar school teacher; that the ayuntamiento grant an exemption from the 4 percent tax on electric lighting; and that the local government contribute twenty pesos to bleach the church for the celebration of Corpus Christi. The reasons offered to convince the town council to act as requested were equally varied—everyone was satisfied with the man who was currently holding the job to which the unpopular candidate had been appointed; the teacher had been performing her duties without pay for months; poverty and a large family prevented the payment of the electric tax for the widow who requested it; the town council regularly contributed to the preparations for the Corpus Christi festival and so was expected to do the same this year. These petitions suggest that, rather than feeling helpless when confronted with the monolithic power of the state, men and women of the popular classes did not have any qualms about making their opinions known.

Although the activism of city residents is very much in line with the expectations of a bourgeois state apparatus, the enthusiasm with which working people engaged the municipal government was somewhat of an anomaly. One possible reading of this behavior is offered by David Trotman: "The law and legal institutions represented not only the state monopoly of the coercive agencies but insofar as the law was obeyed and the jurisdiction of the courts assented to—both by those who came before it and by those who agreed with its treatment of those who came before it—the law represented the extent of consent." But rather than bending to the will of their "superiors," I believe, the people who were affected by it were actually contesting it and shaping it on a daily basis. Urban dwellers in Santo Domingo did not behave like an amorphous mass that simply reacted to the modernizing project imposed from above. Rather, they used its framework to advance their agenda and to shape the role of government in their lives. In so doing, Santo Domingo's working class was forging citizenship.[1]

THE DEMAND FOR EDUCATION

City residents, acting either on their own or collectively, advocated one cause in particular with extraordinary determination, and that was education. The illiteracy rate in the Dominican Republic was between 70 and 90 percent for the population over ten years of age, and parents of all social classes were aware that the future of the country depended on an educated population. In Santo Domingo, the issue was relatively settled, and the ayuntamiento regularly assigned funds to teachers as a salary and to meet the expenses of running their schools. It was not unusual for teachers to ask the ayuntamiento to appoint them to a school, or to confer municipal status on the school they themselves had formed. Neither did teachers satisfy themselves with the meager amounts allotted to schools, as noted in chapter 4. In San Pedro, however, instructional matters were still being debated at the turn of the twentieth century, and citizens up and down the social scale joined in the discussion. José Francisco, who taught primary school, explained to the town council that the parents of the boys and girls under his supervision could not contribute to the maintenance of the school. He requested a monthly compensation so that "the noble and transcendental cause of education" would be well served.

El Eco de la Opinión, ever the supporter of progressive causes, congratulated Arturo Bermúdez and other "self-sacrificing gentlemen" for their "dignifying effort" in founding a school for poor children. Equally forceful was the author of an article that accused the members of the Sociedad Propagadora de la Instrucción (Society for the Dissemination of Education) of wanting education only for their own children and chastising them for asking the ayuntamiento to contribute to a school where poor children would not be admitted. Although the advocates of the school in question shared with him the rhetoric of a progressive education, saying that the school (significantly, named "Progreso") was the product of citizens (*la ciudadanía*), not of government or municipality, *El Eco* charged that the teachers who were members of the society distributed "the good salaries" among themselves and their relatives. It was the advocates of the society who said it, but both contenders would probably have agreed: "Only the ignorant or the vicious can whisper against the contributions destined to the support of schools. Only pathetic people want cheap teachers and methods of instruction at reduced prices."[2]

THE PRIVILEGING OF PROPERTY

The most recognizable way for city residents to gain a foothold on the citizenry front was, of course, to own property and treat it as a private asset. Liberals believed property grounded the interest of citizens in the functioning of the state, and the actions of working-class Dominicans confirmed this understanding. The historical record teems with references to conflicts over property, including evictions, attempts to safeguard valuable items, cases of theft, monetary claims, and the like. Although they may not have had much to keep safe, working-class urban Dominicans valued highly the sanctity of private property.

The municipal councils of Santo Domingo and San Pedro received many complaints throughout this period, against individuals and against the government, which rested on the inviolability of individual property. In one instance, the owner of a stall "absolutely refused any kind of arrangement" (although not specified, one assumes it involved vacating temporarily, or exchanging her house for another, or receiving compensation for her loss) to facilitate the repair of the street in which it was located. Another property owner demanded that the ayuntamiento repair her shed, which was damaged when an electric pole collapsed. This notion of being reimbursed for damages to valuable belongings was at play when Belisario García insisted on knowing whether the ayuntamiento would indemnify him for having cut down a coconut tree on his land. He interpreted this as a violation to his property, one that when performed to open the way to further urban settlement or because the trees obstructed traffic, was always reimbursed at the fixed price of ten pesos per plant, he said. A French baker cited encroachment of property rights as the reason he brought to the attention of the town council, and not his consul, the removal of a fence, a strip of land, an outhouse, and a palm tree from his property line. Finally, one homeowner sued his neighbor because (he believed) the neighbor had built a latrine less that six feet from his house. These apparently petty complaints to the town council indicate clearly that the people involved had a well-developed sense of what was theirs, what it was valued at, and who was responsible for replacing or repairing it if it was damaged.[3]

The highest form of private property was undoubtedly urban real estate that one could rent for profit. The men and women who owned houses or rooms that they rented to other people were a mixed group, as were the renters. In cases of eviction or demands for back rent, owners were seldom represented by an attorney or identified by anything other than name, but when they were, they empowered their legal representative to take any decisions he considered necessary and used the appellative "merchant" to refer to their trade. Landlords and landladies were likely to have one property, at most two, and charged between three and seven pesos monthly for a house, and from two to five pesos for a room. Contracts could be written or oral, and subletting was infrequent. Renters were for the most part individuals, and in a few cases families, of limited means, which I assume both because they found themselves in the predicament of being evicted from their dwellings and because their occupations, when listed, were usually "domestic servant" or coachman.

Both tenants and proprietors knew the law well. When problems arose, landlords and landladies took the issue directly to the *alcaldía*, the lowest municipal court of justice, which was presided over by the mayor. A few property owners, perhaps less familiar with the goings-on of the justice system, took their complaints to the police station and then were referred to the court. If the contract was written, and the tenant was late in making payments, he or she was expected to vacate the premises immediately, without advance warning. In the case of oral contracts, a two-month grace period was allowed, after which the owner could demand immediate eviction. Sometimes the tenant came up with a reason for not having vacated and proposed a payment plan, which was never accepted by the court. Usually the tenant did not attend the proceedings, and he or she was ordered to leave the rental space and pay the court costs. In one case, the tenant appeared in court and was granted the sixty-day grace period, but even though she promised to pay six months' worth of back rent that she owed, was ordered to vacate the property and pay the court costs.[4]

A few cases point to some revealing understandings on the part of the subalterns regarding what was at stake monetarily and what principle was going to safeguard it. The primacy of the law was one lesson quickly learned. Maray Berboda sued Guillermo Alberto so he would return to her some furniture he had seized. He stated that she owed him two pesos for rent, which she countered by saying that it was her concubine who had rented the room. She added, surprisingly, that even if she owed him money, the landlord had to proceed according to the law, an obvious reference to the modus operandi described above, a brave defense of her property and an unequivocal appeal to the power of the law. A similar conflict ensued between Beatriz Ganett and Tomás Thompson over a bed, which the defendant alleged he kept on her instructions to sell it for the six pesos she owed him for the room. In both cases, the judge ruled in favor of the two women.

In two other cases, the manipulations of the parties to make their oral or written words prevail suggest a thorough knowledge of the court system. Anastacia Medrano requested than Anita Gross vacate a room, which Anita, through Ricardo Gross (a relative?), alleged had been rented to her by Félix Medrano, and not by Anastacia. When a receipt for $3.50, signed by Félix, was presented as proof of the oral contract between him and Anita, Anastacia's case was thrown out, and she was saddled with the court costs. Eloísa Fridan asked that Sofía Melium be evicted from a house that they rented from the Wallá widow. Eloísa alleged that she had allowed Sofía to stay there for a few days and had even charged her rent, but now that she was about to move, she wanted to turn the house over to its owner. Sofía stated that both of them rented the house and so only the owner could evict her. Going strictly by the testimony of the two women, the judge ruled against Fridan, who was ordered to pay the court costs. These cases show that working-class men and women had their own notions about what was correct procedure and what mattered to them. The cases also point to their competence in working the system.[5]

Working people protected their belongings in life as well as in death. The procedures known as "*fijación de sellos*" (fixing of seals) and "*levantamiento de sellos*" (lifting of seals) were carried out when a person died and his or her belongings were thought to be of value to that person's descendants or other interested parties. Typically, the spouse of the deceased or a close relative requested the municipality to send the appropriate official, who in the presence of witnesses sealed any chests or rooms in the house that contained valuable goods. When they were opened, it was in the presence of the heirs, their attorneys, or any legal representative. For example, Anita Coen, a domestic worker, asked that seals be fixed in the house of her husband, Bruno Nivar, on 26 January 1910. The next day, she affixed her rudimentary signature to a statement alleging that two chests and two guitars had been transferred to Jacinto Gros's house. Simona Yepes, someone whom Anita apparently trusted, stated that nothing had been removed from the chests. At Anita's request, the seals were broken in the presence of five of the Nivar children (conceivably, they were also Anita's), and the contents of the house were inventoried (see Table 5). In another case, a man who was admitted to the old-age home had his house inventoried. The amount of furniture it contained and some of the objects listed (a strongbox, 281 hardcover books, and 2 bathtubs, all in good condition) indicate that his material life was well provided for.[6]

Accusations of theft are equally revealing. It was not uncommon for the crime to have been "solved" before the authorities were notified. In one such "report," Sirbano Camarena listed for police the items that had been removed from a chest in his bedroom: a mosquito net, cut cloth for a suit, a bedspread, a gold ring with a white stone, three silver forks, and a china jar. Indaleza Evangelista claimed to have found some of these objects in María Berroa's house. Several other people testified to the same effect. In another accusation, a familiar person allegedly went into an acquaintance's home, ate something, and then stole some money.

In most of these cases, people knew where to look for their lost items—pawn shops, the suspect's house or business—or had information on how to locate the guilty party. By the time they went to the police station and were referred to the municipal court, they could accuse the suspect directly and would offer information as to the reason for the crime. Guadalupe Polanco, for example, knew that Josefina Vivaraz had taken a bedspread from her house in payment of $1.50 she owed Vivaraz. On other occasions, more valuable things appeared in the black market, which made authorities suspect theft. Jacinto Tejo bought six initialed silver knives from a boy for a very low price, which should have clued him to the fact that the items were stolen; the police apprehended him. The unexpected also occurred, as when María del Amparo Reyes de Moreno saw María de los Santos, a former neighbor, wearing the dress that she had put out to dry two months before. For the most part, these cases of petty theft point to what was considered valuable for working people, not only in terms of monetary value but in terms of their wherewithal (see Table 6).[7]

TABLE 5
Contents of a House Where Seals Were Fixed,
ca. 1910

pool table with 22 cues and a stick holder	$150
pine table	$3
29 local chairs	$3
new cooking pot	$.60
2 small pine tables	$1.50
small counter	$4
4 pine benches	$1
5 drill jackets and 3 pairs of pants	$2
hat	$.50
4 pairs of eyeglasses	$.50
in the chests:	
a bill from the National Bank of Santo Domingo	$2
a pair of gold loops with green stones	$5
a contract to sell the pool table	
a tin box containing $1.62	

SOURCE: Archivo General de la Nación, Alcaldía de Santo Domingo, bundle 42, doc. 1, Bruno Nivar, 26 Jan. 1910.

A similar pattern was evident in demands for money or retribution. Both men and women, after attempting to obtain the money owed them through other means, resorted to the authorities to intervene. The amounts involved and the objects exchanged, as well as the timing of transactions, give an idea of what Santo Domingo's working population considered valuable—and what could reasonably be expected of them: $5.00 in back rent; $52.00 for domestic service for a year and a half; a cock; $7.40 in cash, $4.50 in meals, and two (lottery?) tickets on credit; "interest" on a loan; $10.00 in proceeds from a dance hall; a cart and a horse; a clock; $16.69 in meals and drinks. As in the theft cases above, it appears that it was not so much the monetary return that impelled the accusers to come forward but an intangible sense of value that was placed, not on a material object, but on the transaction that had occurred before it was lost. María Wilson sued Juan Nathaniel for $10.00 that she had lent him to repair a boat. When brought to court, Nathaniel quickly admitted he owed Wilson the money, and he was ordered to pay it and the court costs. In these and other cases of personal loans, defendants showed a healthy respect for the law, as did accusers by trusting that the authority of the law could help them obtain what they had all along known was their due.[8]

TABLE 6

Items Reclaimed by People Who Had Been Robbed,
1891–1897

---

pair of slippers
$1 in lieu of a blanket
several plantains
hen
knife
pocket watch
dog
clock
donkey
13 bags of coal
bedspread in lieu of $1.50
jewelry
7 jars of condensed milk, 2 large bottles of beer, 8 sardine tins, the plaid handkerchief
    in which everything was wrapped up
2 hens

SOURCE: Archivo General de la Nación, Alcaldía de Santo Domingo, bundle 1, [various dates] 1891, 1893–97.

A more transparent desire to preserve the principle behind lending money is evident in two cases brought by Ana Foy against two women, one for $1.37, another for $.75, for merchandise they had purchased on credit. It is true that any amount of money is worth a lot when means are scarce, as was probably true for many of these people. At the same time, it appears that to send the message that reneging on your debts is a serious offense was more important than the amount recovered. There are two instances of fraud in the cases I examined, and these involved large amounts or valuable items, at least from the perspective of those who labored to obtain them. In one case, a credit issued by the government was both sold to an individual (and subsequently to several others) and cashed by the original seller. The other case involved the deed for a shed, which Petronila Peguero had wanted to mortgage by sending her concubine, Angel Torres, to the house of Epifano Isambert, probably an independent businessman. Instead, Manuela Encarnación apparently intercepted the transaction and had the mortgage payment done in her name so as to claim the property. In both these instances, the injured parties intended not only to set the record straight but also to obtain the material advantage they should have gained.[9]

By engaging the municipal council over salaries, classification of businesses, appointment to public posts, contributions to community services, the founding of schools, and the like, and by rushing to the lowest state court to protect their property or affirm their rights against other city residents, Santo Domingo's and San Pedro's working class both gave expression to their notions of citizenship and asserted their right to do so. Acting precisely as the intelligentsia had envisioned an active citizenry would participate in government, they were invested in their surroundings, were outspoken about their needs and desires, and respected the authority of the law. Contrary to the elite's understanding that the successful establishment of a sense of common purpose originates in a national bourgeoisie, the Dominican case shows that an inchoate working class could express itself politically very effectively.[10]

WORKING-CLASS RESPECT

Working-class men and women established for themselves and municipal officials the parameters within which they could maintain their sense of worth and uphold their self-esteem. Ironically, evidence of this effort comes from the most common denunciation of working-class behavior, besides letting animals roam unsupervised: "*escándalo*," a disturbance of the peace that could include obscene words and gestures, personal insults, physical injury, and drunkenness. Any combination of these could occur between men, or between men and women, but it was not unusual to have two women brought to the *prefectura* (provincial seat) under these charges. A listing of the districts in which this occurred—the public market, La Misericordia, Ponce—and notations regarding the national origins of the perpetrators— *turcos, sirios, árabes, ingleses* (for West Indians), *franceses* (from the French islands), *haitianos*—typecast these cases as a working-class phenomenon that the police handled as routine. Working-class people, for their part, were concerned about maintaining their sense of self and community as much as authorities wanted to maintain the public order, and they took very seriously personal affronts and repeated provocation.

Ordinarily, night watchmen (*serenos*) or daytime police officers charged offenders with "inciting scandal" that "called public attention" to them and passed the cases on to the municipal lower court, which fined the guilty parties small amounts (a peso per infraction) or put them in jail (if insolvent or a repeat offender). Neither the frequency of these small explosions nor their routine treatment by police and courts is surprising—these were the years during which the city received an influx of immigrants who would fill the demand for labor in an expanding economy based on sugar and its ancillary economic activities. The men and women who yelled "unseemly words" at each other, danced "indecently," "took each other on," and organized dance halls in their houses had for the most part migrated from nearby islands and had settled in the southeastern part of the city and in other working-class neighborhoods. If not professional sexual workers, the women undoubtedly supplemented their income with the material benefits that accrued from casual or long-term associations with men.

From the perspective of public officials, the concentrated presence of these types of people multiplied the probability for social disorder. From the standpoint of working-class urban residents themselves, I would speculate, their circumstance made it all the more urgent to fiercely claim "habitable" space vis-à-vis their neighbors and public authorities. With so little to lose, as Lara Putnam points out in her case study of Limón, Costa Rica, both immigrants and locals felt compelled to safeguard their access to what they did possess by securing their social standing through any means necessary.

For the most part, authorities charged the offending men and women in the *alcaldía*, summarily stating the circumstances of the scandal. A typical case of disturbance of the peace would read like this: "In the San Miguel sector, at nine P.M., Manuela Marcano and María Olegaria verbally injured each other [*se injuriaron de palabra*], causing a great scandal." Another type of "scandal" occurred in dance halls, oftentimes specifically identified as taking place in the home of prostitutes or attended by them. Here, mostly men, but sometimes men and women, were cited for dancing "*indecorosamente*" (indecorously) and "causing disorder." Public drunkenness, of course, also posed problems for the authorities—in one instance, a drunk man tried to introduce himself into the house of a woman, and when caught, resisted arrest; another traversed the streets yelling obscenities, for which he too was arrested. In one case of what we would call indecent exposure, an American sailor "took out his virile member to urinate," disregarding the ladies that were walking leisurely down the dock. The scandal between Toasina Rodríguez and her daughter, Altagracia Cueva, alias "Talinga," "who disrespected [her mother], raising her hand against her," although it is as starkly described as the others, stands out because the additional detail shows that among "the lower classes" disrespect for elders was a major transgression.[11]

Insult cases in the Dominican Republic show patterns very similar to Putnam's observations for Limón. Extracting insightful details from her evidence, Putnam points to the precariousness of honor in a context of scarcity and therefore the viciousness with which reputation was defended. Street culture, as she describes it, demanded a constant reaffirmation of personal standing, upon which a great deal depended—for example, credit at the local store, a neighbor's help in times of illness, a little cash for an emergency purchase, and other small, material advantages. For men, a confrontational attitude was imperative to obtain on demand the "respect" they felt they deserved. For women, an impeccable reputation carried with it the necessary "decency" to operate successfully. The route to the desired outcome was also predetermined. Insults escalated from "verbal artistry" on the street and among friends to complaints at the police station between two parties, one of whom felt his or her honor had suffered a setback.

Notions of appropriate behavior, then, when invoking honor/respect/decency, did not emanate from the upper classes or from public officials and impose themselves violently on the popular classes but rather were shaped by a "language of argument" between equals at the top and at the bottom and between the self-proclaimed models of bourgeois values and their "inferiors." In complying with the norms imposed by authorities or negotiating their observance with peers, upper- and working-class men and women, recent immigrants and Dominicans alike, shaped the urban cultural milieu.[12]

The people who worked and lived in urban areas brought to the attention of public officials certain situations that they felt were problematic enough for the state apparatus to intervene. Working-class men and women referred to police headquarters conflicts that could be described as *escándalos*, that is, obnoxious behavior and coarse language meant to offend, although the public nature of the affront was not a prerequisite for the accusers to come forward. As opposed to the cases discussed above, in which authorities interfered in the name of law and order to contain a potentially obstreperous situation, the matters citizens brought to the police station and subsequently to the municipal court concerned ongoing assaults on a person's dignity or sense of worth. City residents from the lowest rungs of the social hierarchy asserted their claims to honorable status by challenging those who put it in doubt by word or deed. In so doing, they engaged in an eminently deliberate attempt to contribute, as did other ordinary citizens, to urban political culture.[13]

According to the women who accused men of offending them, the men had either slandered their character or directed vulgar language at them. In either case, the women appealed to their status as decent people, who were not the "witches" or "thieves" men had declared them to be, nor were they the kind of person to whom one could show such impudence. Ana Maria Dilson demanded that Roberto Foster reveal who had told him she was using witchcraft on him or be punished for having said this about her. Ermenegilda Urbais stated that Evangelista Sanbuá had "mistreated her in word and labeled her a thief." Francisca Salas complained that Manuel de Vargas had come to her house "to disrespect the decorum and decency of her person, through the effrontery of wanting to kiss her." María del Rosario Guerrero testified that for four days Alfredo Maduro "had been harassing her [*haciéndole algunos escándalos*], proffering indecorous and immoral words." Other women related having "dishonest words" directed at them or being, as one plaintiff put it, "injured with quite obscene expressions, disregarding her daintiness [*faltándole a su delicadeza*]."[14]

Insulted men, on the other hand, simply registered their complaints, in noticeably fewer numbers than women, generally without directly referring to what in their persons had been so egregiously injured. Their cases are one-liners that merely state the accused and the accusation thus: "Santiago Díaz complains at the police headquarters because Manuela Velázquez insulted him, promoting a great scandal." The same was true if the offending party was a man—a mere note is made of the unlawful activity. One exception to this stark recollection of events are instances in which a man's wife, partner, mother, or sister is the object of lewd comments. This was the case with Ignacio Billardea, whose wife was "referred to as shameless, vagabond, and the like" (*tratándola de sinvergüenza, vagabunda y demás por el estilo*) by Arquímedes Concha. The testimony of four women was taken, and all agreed on the chain of events. Juan Aber y Montilla also complained that two men had wronged his wife "with defamatory words." Since "both contenders exchanged insults and humiliations," the chief of police referred the matter to the *alcaldía*.[15]

Each lawsuit had its peculiarities. León Ciprián accused Feliz Brito of walking into his house and up to the bedroom while insulting his wife. Pedro Estrada filed a suit against Inés "*la inglesa*" (the Englishwoman, a West Indian) and Juliana Osoria, who had "proffered calumnious words against María Rivera, to whom commitments bound him at present." Silverio Otoño, accused Juana Francisca Fajardo of emitting "injurious phrases against [his] mother's conduct." The military commander of San Pedro wrote a personal note to the mayor of Santo Domingo because his sister was insulted publicly and violently by a man named Arroyo. The commander asked the mayor, as a courtesy, since they belonged to the same party, to make sure justice was applied, because he felt that the affront had been made on him directly and feared "that the efforts of the weak woman would face obstacles and might not be enough to defeat the machinations of her enemies."

Up and down the class ladder, men protected their honor in a singular way—when the insults referred to their own persons, they were hardly worth reporting; when the insults were directed at the women they were intimately in contact with (and especially in the case of wives or sexual partners, over whom they were expected to have control), they felt the record had to be set straight. Unlike the situation for women, who above all wanted to maintain intact their reputation as decent people, men measured their worth by their capacity to protect.[16]

The difference between the ways Dominican men and women defined challenges to their personal standing can be explained by calling upon Hispanic traditions. In Spain, the now conventional explanation asserts, claims to status require that women guard their sexual reputations and that men protect "their" women against such threats. According to this logic, arguments between men over women are really "about" men and their own status as a measure of power (rather than "about" women or the skills and talents that might make them desirable to men). Putnam, again, provides a clever alternative to this scheme, one that allows women to insert themselves as players, rather than bystanders, and that might well be applicable in the Dominican case. In Limón, she points out, women argued over their economic capacity, although the language used was that of "honor" or "reputation." Remarkably, Putnam asserts, there was never a doubt that it was the woman's standing that was at play, because "her" man's capacity to protect her from insult or harm did not come into the picture. In the Dominican Republic, as in Limón, women challenged being called names that they felt they did not deserve—thief, witch, shameless, vagabond, and the like—and did so on their own account.[17]

As was true for the *escándalos* brought to court by the police, insults between women were the most numerous of the complaints brought by individuals to the police station. Many of these came through as accusations of slander, although what was said or even suggested is impossible to know. A good number cite the archetypal "indecorous words and threats," "a thousand insults and slurs," "phrases that injured her daintiness and honor," and "inconsiderate insults"—which suggest again that working-class women wanted to maintain an honorable reputation, especially among themselves. These women, after all, knew each other, perhaps all too well, and it must have been important to establish claims to their place in the community. When Manuela Ortiz and Toribia González, for example, insulted Clara Batista as she sat on her doorstep at 3:00 P.M., and Clara responded, "reflecting variously on some of the slanders she had received," one can hardly assume that the three women did not know each other for some time, lived in the same vicinity, and interacted daily.

Likewise, the "bundle of objects" and the written note that Rosario Guerrero de Masió threw at Altagracia Lugo indicates that perhaps the two women had lived in the same house and that Altagracia was no longer welcome in it. If Felipa Estay could go into Cornelia Robinson's kitchen to take some equipment, against Robinson's will and amid "great scandal," she must have felt entitled to it, based on old acquaintance, some prior understanding, or just plain malice. When Irene Feliz put up a canvas divider in the room she shared with Susana López and threw a garbage can at her, she was breaking whatever arrangement bound the two women. In this highly charged atmosphere, where temporary and more permanent relationships conferred material advantages, and personal matters took on a public countenance by virtue of the proximity between neighbors and co-workers, it is not surprising that women vied for primacy by establishing their "rights" and letting their expectations be known.[18]

There are a few cases in which litigants desired a particular outcome beyond the cessation of the behavior that had prompted their complaint or a reprimand or fine from properly constituted authority. The two men who had dirty water thrown on them by the servant of Luisa Cambiaso vda. (widow) de Sturla as they conversed in front of her house surely wanted an apology, if not compensation. They probably felt like Brígida del Rosario, whose neighbor threw a rag full of muck in her yard, that the affront on their persons had to be rectified. Ezequiel Evangelista, on the other hand, hoped that by filing a complaint against Benito Creas with the police, the latter would stop mortifying him with witchcraft. Likewise, Gabriel Hermodisis was seeking some sort of police protection from the three men who stood watch over his house day and night. Another individual might have been hoping for the same result from his imputation—Feliz Figuereo, alarmed to find a satirical poster referring to him and his wife, suspected "the only enemy they had in the neighborhood, Marcos de Castro." Carolina Henry sued Francisco Penso so that he would immediately return his niece, María Hanley, the girl for whom Henry cared, or pay her two hundred pesos for the services she had rendered the infant for four years. Armed with a birth certificate, she sought to prove that she was the girl's godmother and adoptive mother, which she managed to do.

These incidents, which men and women thought important enough to be brought to the attention of the authorities, point to additional ways of claiming citizenship on the part of workers. Whether it was confirmation of a prior entitlement, corroboration of their sense of justice, support against what they considered strange comportment, or legal protection, working men and women were asking the government to side with them, to validate their "rights," although they may not have used that word.[19]

Another sense of the subaltern's expectation of fairness arises out of disagreements over partnering arrangements. There are numerous instances of discord among cohabiting couples, some because of jealousy, some reaching "scandal" level. For the most part, the exact causes of conflict are unknown, despite the fact that couples went to the police headquarters to "air" (*ventilar*) the matter. Usually the two parties could not reach conciliation, and the prefect submitted the file to the *alcaldía*, but all record of the outcome is lost. In one case, the prefect determined that the matter at hand was "purely a great scandal and immorality that existed between them," and he transferred the case to the municipal court, evidently not to mitigate the hostilities but to charge the couple.[20]

Women went to the police station to seek protection against men with whom they used to live. María Olivero Morales accused her concubine of threatening to beat her and of breaking a cot cover and other items—"all this because she refuse[d] to continue living for a time with him." Enemencio Martí was picked up when he tried to break into his concubine's dwelling. Felícita Fabián lived with Jesús Guerrero for eight years, but she "complains that she no longer wants to live with him because it is not advantageous to her [*no le conviene*] and he persists in going to her house to bother her." Two women in this group sought the equivalent of child support and custody. Petronila Noboa demanded that José Luis de Vargas provide a room where she and their two children could live. Agustina Cabral simply wanted her child back, a boy that her live-in partner had taken with him. One paternity case made it to my random sample: Margarita Peguero was pregnant, and Luis Pereira, the son of a music teacher, appeared to have been responsible for her disgrace.[21]

A particularly detailed case sheds light on gender relations at several levels. Manuel Ortiz, a coachman, was scheduled to be married to Lucila Abreu, who broke the engagement. He had given her thirty pesos to buy furniture, which she did, and now he wanted to give the furniture to Miguel A. Mota, from whom he had borrowed the money to buy it in the first place. The file that Ortiz submitted contained many letters from Abreu detailing, in bad calligraphy and worse orthography, the pieces she had bought and her thoughts and feelings—she is not embarrassed to be seen with him but rather afraid of suffering more; she goes to bed early at night and suffers without him; he must do what is necessary to get the house, since she has been evicted, and it is his duty to protect her; he must, please, send the white dress, which she hopes is pretty; he should write but should not come to see her when it is raining, because she prefers not to see him rather than to see him when he's sick. She calls him "Ortiz," "my adored," "sweet and adored Ortiz," "daddy" (*papacito*), "my life," "my soul," and refers to herself as "your unforgettable," "your adored," "yours until death," and "yours, who loves you." All this forgotten, she declared that some of the furniture belonged solely to her and that she was willing to return the rest if he paid her ninety-five pesos for having nursed him when he was sick. The court considered possession as equivalent to a deed, and as she did not claim all the pieces, she should turn over to him the ones to which she was not entitled. Ortiz would have to pay for the court costs. A few days later, Abreu sued Ortiz for ninety-five pesos or "the ring." He denied that she had contributed to his recovery the previous year, because he had been assisted by the Sociedad Benéfica Española (Spanish Beneficent Society) with money, a doctor, and medicines (for an injury or disease on his hand), and the court ruled against Abreu, finding her allegations unsustainable.[22]

I find this case revealing because it points to entitlements on the part of working-class men and women that are not usually so transparent. Ortiz, who was either a few social notches below Abreu or whose hand was mutilated (she wrote that she should be embarrassed to be seen with him but is not) had done what was within his means to get well and get married. Although it is not clear why Abreu broke the engagement, it appears that she had every intention of keeping the furniture—otherwise, Ortiz would not be suing. If we go by the letters that she wrote to him, she had much to lose by not getting married—in the midst of the girlish endearing terms and candid wishes for a beautiful dress and a house, she made a plea for marriage, probably because she had lost her virginity, and her position was severely compromised. Now that that option was no longer open, it is not inconceivable to think that Abreu wanted to find herself in an advantageous position economically. Ortiz, who despite his medical situation nonetheless had a job and could borrow a substantial amount, was leaving the engagement basically with only his pride hurt. Whether Abreu did or did not take care of him during his illness, she felt that she had (or was lying outright) and wanted monetary recognition of the fact, again, I suspect, to bolster her position as a single woman with lost virtue. Abreu's hopes and plans for a married future, the material possessions with which she intended to protect her now insecure position, and Ortiz's use of the medical and legal systems to remedy his own predicament are good examples of how working-class men and women worked the system differently in order to remain both economically competitive and socially active.

PHYSICAL VIOLENCE

Incidents that resulted in bodily injury followed a similar pattern in terms of the moral economy to which most accusing parties subscribed. These cases, which involved men, women, and children who either accidentally or deliberately injured the other party, were either reported by the authorities themselves or brought to the attention of the *alcaldía* when one of the participants wanted either retribution or protection from others. Most commonly, a police officer testified about an accident that involved an animal or some inanimate object, such as a cart, in which someone had been hurt, sometimes gravely, that the officer suspected was the result of negligence or some other aggravating circumstance, such as drunkenness. On other occasions, for example when Ansilia Angut blamed Ramón A. Quezada for gashing her when he waved his saber to scare some dogs away, the aggrieved obviously demanded some sort of retribution.[23]

Just a handful of cases involved men only, and these were either on-the-spot detentions by police when situations got out of hand or death threats in which deterrence was sought. In one particularly detailed civil action, fourteen-year-old baker Armando Zayas finished work in the house of José Parras and took off his clothes to take a bath in the patio, where the family moved about, instead of in a private place set aside for that purpose. Parras reprimanded him and also hit him in the head with a oboard, causing fractures. In a typical physical intimidation case, Caetano Arvino alerted police that a few days earlier Henrique Fuentes came to his house armed with a revolver and threatened him, causing a racket. Daniel Masturzi likewise complained that Antonio Masturzi had entered the house of Josefa Fernández vda. de Amblá and in her presence slapped Daniel in the face and grabbed him by his shirt collar. For the most part, then, man-on-man violence took on a very grave tone, perhaps precisely because bravado was an essential element of exchanges between men. In a nonincident between Frenchman José Diesch and a customs policeman, the latter explained that when he warned Diesch that he could not board the ship, the Frenchman "went off with threats and boasts, calling him a scoundrel and a suck-up, who did not carry out his duty." Had Suncal, the policeman, chosen to consider that his manhood was on the line, bodily injuries would have been the inevitable result.[24]

A surprising number of public briefs on violence and citizen denunciations of aggression involved children. With little provocation, men abused children. Elías Colón, for example, tore a boy's clothes in the market because the child had tried to recover from him some sweet potatoes the boy thought belonged to him. Nicolás Ortiz broke a board and some dolls that children were playing with on Comercio Street. Women and children, however, were not exempt from engaging in this type of behavior. Regis Vásquez filed a complaint against Josefa Rodríguez, who not only killed a chicken that had wandered onto her property but also beat up Vásquez's daughter, grabbing her by the throat and yelling insults and slurs at the girl when she came looking for the chicken. Cornelia Robinson denounced María Llepes because Llepes's son had mistreated Robinson's daughter. Francisca Generí's son beat Adolfo Vergez's son in the face. Short of a "culture of poverty" explanation, there is little one can say about these instances of violence based on the information given. Clearly these were disempowered people in many ways, and these outbursts could have been brief moments of self-assertion. Surely an even temper was not the most prized moral possession for the working class, and verbal explosions, although serious, were not frowned upon. When they escalated toward physical violence, of course, and especially if directed toward children, both authorities and citizens denounced their incidence.[25]

By far the most frequent acts of aggression occurred between men and women, usually on the part of men against women. Escolástica Peguero reported at the police station that Matías Cabelón entered her house at 3:00 A.M. on Sunday with the objective of raping her. Irene Feliz complained that Isaías Páez had broken a hanging lamp in the living area of the room she rented when she demanded that he return the peso she had given him to give to someone else, which he had spent himself. Ramón Santana, "after committing improper acts on the person of Miss Eliticia Pérez," hit her in the eye. Men were charged for having "damaged" (estropeado) their concubines. Men and women together were brought to the police station for scandals and brawls, in which fist punches (pescozones) and bites were liberally proffered. The list is long.[26]

Men in the Dominican Republic, as they did in Costa Rica, fought for "authority" in work contexts as well as in their relationships with women. Their encounters with other men were highly scripted and escalated according to predictable patterns. Although there was a cultural difference between West Indian men and Costa Rican men, the former being more given to teasing and mocking that might or might not end in physical violence, the "crescendo of verbal insult, injured honor, threat, and fatal challenge" was the same for both. Likewise, men's aggression against women, Putnam argues, was predicated on the woman's refusal to submit to male authority. Patriarchy, as in the Dominican case, was a powerful force.[27]

Needless to say, women also were responsible for some of these acts of violence. María Nula, for example, broke the forehead of Silvestre Escalante (alias "Prieto," jet black) during a fight at 1:00 A.M. the night before she was charged. Mrs. Din bit Wenceslao Méndez on his right side because he hurt

Mrs. Metí with the cart he drove. And Catalina Saldaña was the person charged in a brawl with her paramour, Manuel de Jesús Romano, not the other way around. These instances of violence are clearly those between lovers or prostitutes and their clients, and one can only guess what provoked them. In attempting to reconstruct what mattered to the working class, how they carved out the space of citizenship, it is telling that both men and women went to the police station expecting some sort of intervention— protection, retribution, or simply validation of their claims.[28]

It was not at all unusual for women to abuse other women. Unlike the altercations between men, fights between women seemed to be the result of long-term animosities that exploded unexpectedly and for no apparent reason. Flora Peláez testified that two other women had beat up her daughter and thrown rocks at her from their yard to hers. Similarly, four women beat up another with sticks and fists at 5:30 P.M. in the patio of Santa Clara convent. María García beat up Marte de la Rosa's concubine, putting her into a coma. One can assume that women who engaged in this type of behavior had relinquished expectations of living out the bourgeois life of small talk and niceties. Instead, they worked hard, held on to "their" men as long as it seemed advantageous, raised their children as best they could, and more or less actively pursued their interests as the sands shifted.[29]

THE GENDER AND RACE OF
THE WORKING CLASS

Dominican elite thinkers and city officials saw in the working class a problem insofar as the latter refused on a daily basis to conform to the rules of high culture that were the mainstay of modern urban centers. The kind of work they carried out was low status because it required manual labor and its performance brought little prestige. In the impermanence and inconsistency of their labor, they did not approximate the image of the manly, hardworking male breadwinner that the country needed. Their behavior during "downtime" clashed with the civility and other social conventions that urban life required as a rule. Clearly, the wage workers, the working poor, and unsupervised women had not embraced the ideals essential for the regeneration of the country.

There was a gender gap in the way that the elites viewed the subalterns and also in the manner that the latter shaped urban politics and thus entered that arena as citizens in their own right. Men who did not have a steady job, whose occupation was not formalized, who did not exert patriarchal authority over their family—these men were outside citizenship, in the sense that the state took no account of their economic activity. As Karin Rosemblatt shows for Chile, unorganized workers were excluded from state welfare benefits and depended on charity, like women.[30] A similar process took place in the Dominican Republic, as only educated Dominican men were expected to contribute to the construction of the nation. Wage workers and immigrants had to demonstrate literacy and cultural competency before they entered the category of citizens. Women, on the other hand, were embraced as, at the very least, nation-builders precisely when they remained dependent and as such subjected to men's projects. Self-reliant women, both bourgeois and working class, heightened fears of an unmanageable social order, precisely the kind of situation with which the nascent state did not want to be faced. Understood this way, those in power prevailed in "the struggle for cultural hegemony," for the definition of civilization and morality, for the significance of citizenship. But as detailed above, working men and women advanced their notions of citizenship despite elite efforts to control their actions—in ways familiar to them, men established their authority daily on the street, and women protected their "honor" fiercely when it was challenged.

Working women especially were far from the model envisioned by the intelligentsia, and I will argue that this occurred because they stood not only for their class and for their gender but also for a particularly noxious trait: race. Class was a troubling element in the constitution of working women. They certainly did not conform to the paradigm of the dutiful and selfless wife or daughter usually pictured next to "her" man, who in turn toiled in government, agriculture, or trade, thus strengthening the body politic. Laboring women had no attentive husbands or vigilant fathers who would guide their progress toward rationality, responsibility, and morality—the virtues necessary for civic rebirth. More probably, they were mixed-race, uneducated women who, as a function of their jobs, constantly interacted with immigrants and other "lowlife." Working-class women, then, did not possess the desired attributes for the task of nation-building and could not be trusted to act for the benefit of the country. They required the supervision, even persecution, of public authorities.

Their gender also stigmatized the seamstresses, laundresses, domestic servants, and itinerant sellers of food or small wares who worked the city streets and thus were the urban female complements to the hardworking, productive Dominican male. By virtue of their economic functions, they should have shared the emblems of nationality with their iconic working-class male counterparts: the capacity to work, the transparent honesty, the unwavering commitment to build a better future, and so on. As a function of their limited sphere of action, one could even argue, working-class women may have stood a better chance of preserving Dominican values because, unlike men, they stayed in the home plane, consorted only with "their own," and returned to the hearth with the products of their labor. When they did not, however, they instantly evoked the dangers of contagion from outside sources. Insofar as they were not men (who lose nothing when they engage in any kind of intercourse with outsiders, because they cannot unequivocally pass on socially valued attributes), working-class women were the likely culprits (or victims, depending on the slant) of association with the feared outsider—Haitians or West Indian immigrants. Laundresses who moved freely about city and suburbs, prostitutes who offered their services to all men alike, and domestic servants who went in and out of private homes became a problematic population by virtue of their occupation and gender. As such, they were denied citizenship by the formulators of the national project.

Working-class women were marginalized as well because of their marital status. To belong to the nation, virtuous women had to be joined with respectable male citizens—quite literally, at the time, since it is a recent development for a woman to be allowed to retain her citizenship affiliation when married to a man from a country other than her own. Marrying "well" was without a doubt the most probable course for Dominican upper- and middle-class women and even possible for many working-class women (who might marry or settle into a permanent relationship with the paradigms of Dominicanness described earlier). But those who failed to do so—sexual workers, single mothers, economically independent women—fell per force outside the pale of nationhood. Working women had shown themselves to be economically self-sufficient and sexually freer than their bourgeois sisters and so functioned outside conventional patterns and behaved in socially abhorrent ways.

Working-class women, finally, found themselves racialized by the discourse that surrounded their persons and regulated their lives. It is probable that the prostitutes, the door-to-door vendors, the lottery-ticket sellers, or the laundresses who traversed the city were mixed race, as were their male counterparts. Studies on the racial composition of the country at the time, and even today, suggest that the bourgeois ladies who were considered feminine, gracious, and honorable were probably women of color as well, although they were regarded as white. Both working-class men and bourgeois women, however, were spared the burden of race, which was reserved for working-class women. Urban female workers were saddled with negative

CONCLUSION

T he discourse of progress, carefully crafted by Dominican intellectuals to address the country's circumstances and their own anxieties, captured the moment of hope and fear that they lived. As the unfolding of international events would prove, not only the Dominican Republic but every country in Latin America would need to lay out the nature of their claims to nationhood, given the context of growing imperialism on the part of the United States and of the eugenics movement in their own immediate surroundings. The obvious intentions of the North American giant provided a powerful incentive for the Dominican intelligentsia to align itself with its Hispanic roots, claiming whiteness and cultural proximity to Europe and juxtaposing its experience to that of the nearby islands, which they labeled as black, African, and pagan. Their proclaimed superiority did not actually prevent U.S. interference in Dominican internal affairs, as American intervention in the area was widespread and inexorable. Yet it provided a sense of self-worth that was imperative for a reemerging nation— had it been allowed to pursue the course it had fitfully traced for itself, the Dominican Republic might have achieved its own and, ironically, American goals for the hemisphere.

The timing of the discourse of nationalism was significant also because the Dominican Republic, like other national entities in the Americas, was hoping to enter the ranks of the industrial world on an equal footing precisely when a people's worth was increasingly measured by their propinquity to Western standards of production, spirituality, and physique. As Dominicans themselves were well aware, they had had a less than illustrious political and economic trajectory, a circumstance that did not reflect well on their aspirations. Although many at the time pointed to the current racial makeup of the population to make dismal predictions about the future, the political elite concentrated on the genetic pool that was available among the already mixed population and the potential traits immigrants could bring to the country. This was not an entirely biological calculation—Nancy Leys Stepan detects in similar efforts in the region advances toward "a biopolitical homogeneity"—but it undoubtedly privileged white, bourgeois, male concepts of merit and awarded them extraordinary weight in the international scale.[1] If Dominicans had left much to be desired in the past, now would be the time to rectify that situation through the adoption of the work habits and the technological advances of Western Europe and the United States and the infusion into the Dominican "race" of white immigrant blood.

Reality being the spoilsport that it is, it interfered with reformers' plans to turn around the course of Dominican development, and the intelligentsia squarely faced, and lamented the presence of, undesirable elements in precisely the population most likely to benefit from the opening up of social, political, and economic opportunities—the residents of urban centers. It was in the cities that the national attributes that would enhance the potential of the country were to be found—expanding economies, educational institutions, cultural activities, newspapers, organizations. But if the desired traits did not come together in an archetypical rural figure as was the case in Cuba and Puerto Rico, neither were they recognized piecemeal in the city's most visible social groups—immigrants from the West Indies and some Haitians, bourgeois women, and working-class men and women. The elite promptly exercised their mental adroitness to fit these groups into the national project—bourgeois women as the keepers of biological and cultural assets to be passed on to the next generation under the vigilance of "their" men; immigrants as the suspect "others" against whom Dominicans could define themselves culturally; and the working class as the experimental matter intended to be transformed, at least figuratively, from dependent, uncultured, and colored to manly, refined, and white.

The intelligentsia's notions of the requirements to belong to the nation might have been dictated by Liberal ideas that traveled from Europe to the Americas and sometimes comfortably settled here. Its recipients, however, did not know to conform to these "superior" forms of political participation, economic progress, and social uplifting and, in fact, found their own ways to construct their own notions of citizenship on a daily basis. Bourgeois women who worked insisted on getting enough resources to, say, run the school they were assigned to. West Indians and other foreigners complained about their neighbors, requested town lots, argued over taxes, and resisted authority, as did Dominican nationals. "Lower-class" men and women defended their honor and asserted their right to be heard in court with equal force, and in some instances, organized more formally to make representations to the government. These "marginal" groups did not vote, own property, or hold on to a steady job, but they found a way outside the conventional Liberal track to impact the processes that affected their daily lives. In doing so, they forged citizenship on a daily basis.

Despite the high hopes and devoted efforts of the forward-looking intelligentsia and the everyday input from their subalterns, this period ended inauspiciously with the invasion by forces of the United States in 1916 and the occupation of the island by the Marine Corps until 1924. The United States had gradually interfered more and more with the country's fiscal policies throughout this period and, by extension, had much to say about economic and political matters. At the moment of crisis, when a rebellion challenged the results of elections in 1915, the United States intervened in favor of the winner, who preferred to resign rather than serve as an accessory to a U.S. invasion. With a view to preserving power in Dominican hands, the legislature selected as president Francisco Henríquez y Carvajal, one of the most prolific writers of the period and an outspoken political critic. Returning from self-imposed exile in Cuba, Henríquez y Carvajal tried as best he could to cooperate with the invader, but when the United States demanded absolute control of the treasury, it had to obtain it by force.

The discourse of progress did not die with the possibility of self-government in 1916. On the contrary, the occupying forces took advantage of the groundwork laid by the Dominican intelligentsia and fully capitalized the sugar industry, overtook *terrenos comuneros*, proletarianized the rural population, established an American-based public school system, built roads, supervised elections, and trained a professional army. Rafael Leonidas Trujillo, who led the country from 1930 to 1961, continued on this path and added a dose of political repression and persecution to the mix of economic and social modernization. Ironically, the candid discussions regarding the potential of Dominicans to arrive at the highest levels of political participation and economic progress that had taken place at the turn of the century gave way to the ruthless institution of the more material and more individualistic aspects of the discourse of progress. The input of flesh-and-blood citizens, perhaps only a function of the imperfect nature of development in previous years, became totally irrelevant.

The construction of citizenship is, fortunately, an ongoing process that serves a particular population's needs at specific moments in the course of history. This statement is not meant to justify the appropriation of the national character by such infamous figures as Trujillo and after him Joaquín

NOTES

ABBREVIATIONS

AGN: Archivo General de la Nación
AlcSPdM: Alcaldía de San Pedro de Macorís
AlcStoDgo: Alcaldía de Santo Domingo
AytoSPdM: Ayuntamiento de San Pedro de Macorís
AytoStoDgo: Ayuntamiento de Santo Domingo
Boletín: *Boletín Municipal*
Cuna: *Cuna de América*
Eco: *El Eco de la Opinión*
Gaceta: *Gaceta Oficial*

PREFACE

1   For a rundown on the historiography on nationalism see Lloyd Kramer, *Nationalism: Political Cultures in Europe and America, 1775–1865* (New York: Twayne, 1998), 2–3. Nicola Miller, *In the Shadow of the State: Intellectuals and the Quest for National Identity in Twentieth-Century Spanish America* (London: Verso, 1999), 36; Jeffrey Lesser, *Welcoming the Undesirables: Brazil and the Jewish Question* (Berkeley: University of California Press, 1995), 4; and Benedict Anderson, *Imagined Communities: Reflections on the Origin and Spread of Nationalism*, rev. ed. (London: Verso, 1991), 86, 115, 118, address the question of elite inclusion of the popular classes in the national project. For some thoughtful comments on the process of self-representation, see David McCrone, *The Sociology of Nationalism: Tomorrow's Ancestors* (New York: Routledge, 1998), 102; Sarah Radcliffe and Sallie Westwood, *Remaking the Nation: Place, Identity and Politics in Latin America* (London: Routledge, 1996), 19; Kramer, *Nationalism*, 537–38; Ada Ferrer, *Insurgent Cuba: Race, Nation, and Revolution, 1868–1898* (Chapel Hill: University of North Carolina Press, 1999), 9; and Mabel Moraña, "Ilustración y delirio en la construcción nacional, o las fronteras de *La Ciudad Letrada*," *Latin American Literary Review* 25.50 (1997): 32.

2   Florencia E. Mallon, *Peasant and Nation: The Making of Postcolonial Mexico and Peru* (Los Angeles: University of California Press, 1995), 6, 9.

3 Gail Hershatter, *Dangerous Pleasures: Prostitution and Modernity in Twentieth-Century Shanghai* (Berkeley: University of California Press, 1997).

4 See Radcliffe and Westwood, *Remaking the Nation*, 2, 13, 15, which introduces also the concept of the decentered self, to juxtapose it to the notion of an elite-centered idea of the nation-state. The quote is on page 20.

5 The last set of ideas in this paragraph comes from Anderson, *Imagined Communities*, 6; O. Nigel Bolland, "Creolization and Creole Societies: A Cultural Nationalist View of Caribbean Social History," in *Intellectuals in the Twentieth-Century Caribbean*, vol. 1, *Spectre of the New Class: The Commonwealth Caribbean*, ed. Alistair Hennessy (London: Macmillan, 1992), 52; Lloyd Kramer, "Historical Narratives and the Meaning of Nationalism," *Journal of the History of Ideas* 58 (1997): 526; Miller, *In the Shadow*, 32; Kramer, *Nationalism*, 9–10; McCrone, *Sociology of Nationalism*, 103; Natividad Gutiérrez, *Nationalist Myths and Ethnic Identities: Indigenous Intellectuals and the Mexican State* (Lincoln: University of Nebraska Press, 1999), 2.

6 Elizabeth Dore, "One Step Forward, Two Steps Back: Gender and the State in the Long Nineteenth Century," in *Hidden Histories of Gender and the State in Latin America*, ed. Elizabeth Dore and Maxine Molyneux (Durham: Duke University Press, 2000), 8, summarizing Philip Corrigan and Derek Sayer's argument in *The Great Arch: English State Formation as Cultural Revolution*; Greg Grandin, *The Blood of Guatemala: A History of Race and Nation* (Durham: Duke University Press, 2000), 14. The quotes are from Mallon, *Peasant and Nation*, 7, 9.

7 A compilation of the "watershed events" brand of nationalist historiography can be found in Frank Moya Pons, "Modernización y cambios en la República Dominicana," in *Ensayos sobre cultura dominicana*, ed. Bernardo Vega et al., 4th ed. (Santo Domingo: Fundación Cultural Dominicana, Museo del Hombre Dominicano, 1996), 236–45. See also Pedro Troncoso Sánchez, *Evolución de la idea nacional* (Santo Domingo: Museo del Hombre Dominicano, 1974), 19. In addition, Roberto Cassá and Genaro Rodríguez examine the foundations of nationality in the sixteenth century in "Algunos procesos formativos de la identidad nacional dominicana," *Estudios Sociales* 25.88 (1992): 69.

8 Danilo de los Santos, "El Cibao y la sociedad nacional: Un enfoque parcial de las manifestaciones culturales entre 1840–1900," *Eme Eme* 10.56 (1981): 20–25; José Joaquín Hungría Morell, "Influencia de algunos factores geográfico-históricos en la integración de la dominicanidad," *Eme Eme* 14.79 (1985): 39–47; Harry Hoetink, " 'Escasez' laboral e inmigración en la República Dominicana, 1875–1930," in *Santo Domingo y el Caribe: Ensayos sobre cultura y sociedad* (Santo Domingo: Fundación Cultural Dominicana, 1994), 103; Lauren Derby, "Haitians, Magic, and Money: Raza and Society in the Haitian-Dominican Borderlands, 1900 to 1937," *Comparative Studies in Society and History* 36.3 (July 1994): 488–526. Derby, of course, falls squarely into the group of historians who argue that Dominicans, high and low, defined themselves vis-à-vis Haitians.

9 Josefina Zaiter, "La identidad como fenómeno psico-social," *Ciencia y Sociedad* 12.4 (1987): 489; Ramonina Brea, "La cultura nacional: Encuentros y desencuentros," *Ciencia y Sociedad* 10.1 (1985): 45; Manuel Cruz Méndez, *Cultura e identidad dominicana: Una visión histórico-antropológica* (Santo Domingo: Editora Universitaria UASD, 1998), 4; Manuel Núñez, *El ocaso de la nación dominicana* (Santo Domingo: Editora Alfa y Omega, 1990), 26, 223; Carlos Esteban Deive, *Identidad y racismo en la República*

Dominicana (Santo Domingo: Ayuntamiento del Distrito Nacional, Junta Municipal de Cultura, 1999), 14; Franklyn J. Franco [Franklin J. Franco Pichardo], *Cultura, política e ideología* (Santo Domingo: Editora Nacional, 1974), 51; Jesús Tellerías, "Algunos aspectos teóricos-metodológicos del problema de la identidad cultural a propósito de la dominicanidad," *Eme Eme* 14.79 (1985), 105; Pedro San Miguel, *La isla imaginada: Historia, identidad y utopía en La Española* (San Juan and Santo Domingo: Editorial Isla Negra and Ediciones La Trinitaria, 1997), 83; Harry Hoetink, *The Dominican People, 1850–1900: Notes for a Historical Sociology*, trans. Stephen K. Ault (Baltimore: Johns Hopkins University Press, 1982), 185–90.

10   Frank Moya Pons, "Los historiadores y la percepción de la nacionalidad," in *El pasado dominicano* (Santo Domingo: Fundación J. A. Caro Alvarez, 1986), 258–59, 262.

11   Juan I. Jiménez Grullón, *Sociología política dominicana, 1844–1966*, 2nd ed., vol. 2 (1898–1924) (Santo Domingo: Editora Alfa y Omega, 1978), 22, 231. Jiménez Grullón differs from Juan Bosch, one of the most prolific and respected literary and historical writers of the second half of the twentieth century, in that the latter does not recognize the existence of a bourgeoisie until the Trujillato (1930–61). See especially Roberto Cassá, "El racismo en la ideología de la clase dominante dominicana," *Ciencia* 3.1 (1976): 66–67, 73, for a brilliant critique of Trujillo's strain of nationalism and the pitfalls of the search for a national bourgeoisie in the early twentieth century.

12   Andrés L. Mateo, *Mito y cultura en la era de Trujillo* (Santo Domingo: Librería La Trinitaria e Instituto del Libro, 1993), 69; Ramonina Brea, *Ensayo sobre la formación del estado capitalista en la República Dominicana y Haití* (Santo Domingo: Editora Taller, 1983), 173, 175; Ernesto Sagás, *Race and Politics in the Dominican Republic* (Gainesville: University Press of Florida, 2000), 5; Harry Hoetink, "Ideología, intelectuales, identidad: La República Dominicana, 1880–1980," in *Santo Domingo y el Caribe*, 116; Raymundo González, "Ideología del progreso y campesinado en la República Dominicana en el siglo XIX," *Ecos* 1.2 (1993): 35.

13   Pedro San Miguel, "La ciudadanía de Calibán: Poder y discursiva campesinista en la República Dominicana durante la era de Trujillo," *Revista Mexicana del Caribe* 4.8 (1999): 6–30, and *El pasado relegado* (Santo Domingo: La Trinitaria, 1999), 177–82; Richard Lee Turits, *Foundations of Despotism: Peasants, the Trujillo Regime, and Modernity in Dominican History* (Stanford: Stanford University Press, 2003), 1–2, 9, 13, 66. Diógenes Céspedes, "El efecto Rodó: Nacionalismo idealista vs. nacionalismo práctico: Los intelectuales antes y bajo Trujillo," in *Los orígenes de la ideología trujillista*, ed. Céspedes (Santo Domingo: Colección de la Biblioteca Nacional Pedro Henríquez Ureña, 2002), 147–222, addresses the earlier period.

14   The wording here comes from Miller, *In the Shadow*, 33; and Kramer, *Nationalism*, 6.

15   Kramer, *Nationalism*, 8, citing Stuart Hall, and "Historical Narratives," 543.

16   My notion is a combination of Michiel Baud's "corporate elite," in Harry Hoetink, "Ideología, intelectuales, identidad," in *Santo Domingo y el Caribe*, 116, and Angel Rama's "*letrados*" in *The Lettered City*, trans. John Charles Chasteen (Durham: Duke University Press, 1996).

17   In adopting this usage, I am following Gayatri Chakravorty Spivak's lead in "Subaltern Studies: Deconstructing Historiography," in *Writings in South Asian History and Society: Subaltern Studies IV*, ed. Ranajit Guha (Delhi: Oxford University Press, 1985), 337–38. For a discussion of the impact of subaltern studies on Latin American historiography, see Florencia E. Mallon, "The Promise and Dilemma of Subaltern Stud-

ies: Perspectives from Latin American History," *American Historical Review* 99.5 (1994): 1491–1515.

18 Hershatter, *Dangerous Pleasures*, 24; Mallon, "The Promise," 1498; Ileana Rodríguez, ed., *The Latin American Subaltern Studies Reader* (Durham: Duke University Press, 2001), 9.

INTRODUCTION

1 The most succinct exposition of the so-called discourse of progress can be found in Raymundo González, *Bonó, un intelectual de los pobres* (Santo Domingo: Editora Buho, 1994), especially 31, 34, 38, 64, 132–34. Recently published, Raymundo González et al., eds., *Política, identidad y pensamiento social en la República Dominicana (siglos XIX y XX)* (Madrid: Ediciones Doce Calles, Academia de Ciencias Dominicana, 1999) is the best analysis of these issues across time.

2 Following a similar logic, Ernesto Sagás, *Race and Politics in the Dominican Republic* (Gainesville: University Press of Florida, 2000), 37, argues that the traits that came to symbolize the national character were embodied in the figure of the peasant from the Cibao, who, conceivably untouched by modernization, produced for subsistence and for regional consumption.

3 Angel Rama, *The Lettered City*, trans. John Charles Chasteen (Durham: Duke University Press, 1996), 77, 78, 80, 88, 96–97.

4 Julio Ramos, *Divergent Modernities: Culture and Politics in Nineteenth-Century Latin America* (Durham: Duke University Press, 2001), ix, xlii; Pedro San Miguel, "Intelectuales, sociedad y poder en las Antillas hispanohablantes," *Revista Mexicana del Caribe* 6.11 (2001): 245; Silvia Alvarez-Curbelo, *Un país del porvenir: El afán de modernidad en Puerto Rico (siglo XIX)* (San Juan: Ediciones Callejón, 2001), 50–51; Nicola Miller, *In the Shadow of the State: Intellectuals and the Quest for National Identity in Twentieth-Century Spanish America* (London: Verso, 1999), 6. See Tulio M. Cestero, *La sangre: Una vida bajo la tiranía*, 2nd ed. (Ciudad Trujillo: Librería Dominicana, 1955), 180, 204, a period novel that illustrates the dilemmas of the intellectual in the tumultuous years following the death of Lilís.

5 Miller, *In the Shadow*, 3, 5–6, 12; Michiel Baud, "Ideología y campesinado: El pensamiento de José Ramón López," *Estudios Sociales* 19.64 (1986): 77; Harry Hoetink, "Ideología, intelectuales, identidad: La República Dominicana, 1880–1980," in *Santo Domingo y el Caribe: Ensayos sobre cultura y sociedad* (Santo Domingo: Fundación Cultural Dominicana, 1994), 116; Benedict Anderson, *Imagined Communities: Reflections on the Origin and Spread of Nationalism*, rev. ed. (London: Verso, 1991), 44–45.

6 E. M. (Eugenio María) de Hostos, "Quisqueya, su sociedad y algunos de sus hijos," *Eco* 701 (19 Nov. 1892); "Asociaciones existentes en el país," *Renacimiento* 1.1 (7 Dec. 1915); Valentina Peguero and Danilo de los Santos, *Visión general de la historia dominicana* (Stevens Point, Wisc.: William T. Lawlor Publications, 1989), 262–78.

7 An in-depth investigation of the public lives of the authors and editors cited in this article, carried out by renowned historian Roberto Cassá, in the author's possession, shows that literati and political thinkers, if not one and the same, certainly moved in the same circles of Dominican high society.

8 The use of the press to disseminate particular ideas and images since the inception of printing and to this day has been well documented for the United States and Western

Europe. Following are some examples that address the representation of women only: Gloria Y. Gadsden, "The Male Voice in Women's Magazines," *Gender Issues* 18 (2000): 49–58; Mary Ellen Zuckerman, *A History of Popular Women's Magazines in the United States, 1792–1995* (Westport, Conn.: Greenwood Press, 1998); David T. J. Doughan, "Periodicals by, for, and about women in Britain," *Women's Studies International Forum* 10 (1987): 261–73; Francesca M. Cancian and Steven L. Gordon, "Changing Emotion Norms in Marriage: Love and Anger in U.S. Women's Magazines since 1900," *Gender & Society* 2 (1988): 308–42; Penny Tinkler, *Constructing Girlhood: Popular Magazines for Girls Growing Up in England, 1920–1950* (London: Taylor and Francis, 1995); Nancy Burkhalter, "Women's Magazines and the Suffrage Movement: Did They Help or Hinder the Cause?" *Journal of American Culture* 19 (1996): 13–25; and Laura L. Behling, "'The Woman at the Wheel': Marketing Ideal Womanhood, 1915–1934," *Journal of American Culture* 20 (1997): 13–30. Similar work has been done for the Third World, but the effort has not been consistently sustained. See, for example, Seminar on Women and Culture in Latin America, "Toward a History of Women's Periodicals in Latin America: Introduction," in *Women, Culture, and Politics in Latin America*, ed. Emilie Bergmann et al. (Berkeley: University of California Press, 1990), 173-82; Johanna Mendelson, "The Feminine Press: The View of Women in the Colonial Journals of Spanish America, 1790–1810," in *Latin American Women: Historical Perspectives*, ed. Asunción Lavrin (Westport, Conn.: Greenwood Press, 1978), 173–98; June E. Hahner, "The Nineteenth-Century Feminist Press and Women's Rights in Brazil," ibid., 254–86; Jean Franco, *Plotting Women: Gender and Representation in Mexico* (New York: Columbia University Press, 1989), 79–102; and Gail Minault, "Urdu Women's Magazines in the Early Twentieth Century," *Manushi* 48 (1988): 2–9. For a fact-filled paragraph on the printed word and its users in the Dominican Republic, see José Luis Sáez, S.J., *Apuntes para la historia de la cultura dominicana* (Santo Domingo: Centro Juan Montalvo, S.J., 1997), 54.

9   The wording in this paragraph comes out of José Luis Romero, *Latinoamérica: Las ciudades y las ideas* (Mexico City: Siglo Veintiuno, 1976), 295, 297. I have put together the biographical sketches that follow from an assortment of sources, especially Donald E. Herdeck, ed., *Spanish Language Literature from the Caribbean*, vol. 4 of *Caribbean Writers: A Bio-Bibliographical-Critical Encyclopedia* (Washington, D.C.: Three Continents Press, 1979); and "Escritores dominicanos," <http://www.escritoresdominicanos .com/narradores.html> (accessed 25 Feb. 2005). A more formal treatment of these thinkers can be found in Franklin J. Franco Pichardo, *El pensamiento dominicano, 1780– 1940: Contribución a su estudio* (Santo Domingo: Editora Universitaria UASD, 2001), especially chapters 21–25.

10   The classic tale of the rise of nation-states is, of course, based on the experience of European countries with strong bourgeoisies, to which the Latin American cases cannot conform. I found useful the conversations around these models in Partha Chatterjee, *Nationalist Thought and the Colonial World: A Derivative Discourse?* (Minneapolis: University of Minnesota Press, 1986); Ernest Gellner, *Nations and Nationalism* (Ithaca: Cornell University Press, 1983); E. J. Hobsbawm, *Nations and Nationalism since 1780: Programme, Myth, Reality* (Cambridge: Cambridge University Press, 1990); Lloyd Kramer, *Nationalism: Political Cultures in Europe and America, 1775–1865* (New York: Twayne, 1998); José Oviedo, "Cultura y nación: La búsqueda de la identidad," *Ciencia y Sociedad* 10.1 (1985): 35–36; Jesús Tellerías, "Algunos aspectos teóricos-

metodológicos del problema de la identidad cultural a propósito de la domini-canidad," *Eme Eme* 14.79 (1985): 116–17; Ramonina Brea, "La cultura nacional: Encuentros y desencuentros," *Ciencia y Sociedad* 10.1 (1985): 45–46; Hugo Tolentino Dipp, "La raza y la cultura en la idea de lo nacional de Américo Lugo," *¡Ahora!* 239 (10 June 1968): 64; and Roberto Cassá, "El racismo en la ideología de la clase dominante dominicana," *Ciencia* 3.1 (1976): 66–67, which all refer to the absence of a middle class in the Dominican Republic as an obstacle to the modernizing project. Miller, *In the Shadow*, 4, 15, 16, 29–30, explains the appeal Gramsci's notion of pe-ripheral states had for many Latin American scholars in the 1970s. Even in the early twentieth century, writers had doubts regarding the usefulness of an intellectual class removed from society. In an apocryphal anecdote, José Ramón López relates that an American acquaintance questioned the respect paid a man who was shabbily dressed. López explained that he was a poet (an intellectual), to which the American replied that it was surprising he did not first cover his necessities before he set out to write verses. López agreed, and he wondered how, given this state of affairs, the Dominican Republic had managed to maintain its independence, its sovereignty, and even the welfare of its people; see "La caña de azúcar en San Pedro de Macorís, desde el bosque virgen hasta el mercado, 1907," *Ciencia* 2.3 (1975): 126.

11 Miller, *In the Shadow*, 6, 15, 19, 41, 95; Alan Knight, "Racism, Revolution, and *Indi-genismo*," in *The Idea of Race in Latin America*, ed. Richard Graham (Austin: University of Texas Press, 1990), 83; Rama, *Lettered City*, 85; Cassá, "El racismo," 66–67. Pedro Henríquez Ureña, in an essay entitled "Literatura Pura," asserts that literati from 1890 to 1920 removed themselves from the political realm, but because they couldn't support themselves by their literary writings alone, they worked as journalists, teach-ers, or both; see Rama, *Lettered City*, 77. Pedro San Miguel, on the other hand, categorically states that intellectuals entered politics because they craved power; see "Intelectuales, sociedad y poder." The last quote is from Miller, *In the Shadow*, 19 (citing Antonio Gramsci).

12 Rama, *Lettered City*, 74, reflects on the motives of the *letrados*. A precise description of the goals of the Liberal state appears in Maxine Molyneux, "Twentieth-Century State Formations in Latin America," in *Hidden Histories of Gender and the State in Latin America*, ed. Elizabeth Dore and Maxine Molyneux (Durham: Duke University Press, 2000), 42.

13 In Roberto Cassá's words, "The 'Azul' program had as one of its decisive components the establishment of institutions and juridical and political practices that matched those . . . [of] developed capitalist countries" (*Historia social y económica de la República Dominicana*, vol. 2 [Santo Domingo: Editora Alfa y Omega, 1992], 161, 165).

14 AGN, AytoStoDgo, bundle "nuevo" 2842, "El que no sabe cultivar las artes, debe trabajar con la azada," 10 June 1915; Freddy Peralta, "La sociedad dominicana vista por Pedro Francisco Bonó," *Eme Eme* 5.29 (1977): 18; Diógenes Céspedes, *Salomé Ureña y Hostos* (Santo Domingo: Biblioteca Nacional Pedro Henríquez Ureña, 2002), 20, 22; Cassá, "El racismo," 63, 66–67.

15 Pedro Francisco Bonó, "Opiniones de un dominicano," *El Eco del Pueblo*, 13 Jan. 1884, in *Papeles de Pedro F. Bonó: Para la historia de las ideas políticas en Santo Domingo*, ed. Emilio Rodríguez Demorizi (Barcelona: Gráficas M. Pareja, 1980), 274–75, 276, 280, 291; "Apuntes sobre las clases trabajadoras dominicanas," *La Voz de Santiago*, 23 Oct. 1881, ibid., 191, 226; "Privilegiomanía," *El Porvenir*, 6 Mar. 1880, ibid., 252; Pedro San

Miguel, *La isla imaginada: Historia, identidad y utopía en La Española* (San Juan and Santo Domingo: Editorial Isla Negra and Ediciones La Trinitaria, 1997), 89.

16 "La elección presidencial," *Eco* 686 (30 June [July] 1892).

17 Roberto Cassá, *Movimiento obrero y lucha socialista en la República Dominicana (orígenes hasta 1960)* (Santo Domingo: Fundación Cultural Dominicana, 1990), 57; Nelson Ramón Carreño Rodríguez, "Una introducción y una conclusión general del estudio sobre la agricultura en República Dominicana de 1875 a 1925," *Eme Eme* 11.62 (1982): 13; José del Castillo, "Azúcar y braceros: Historia de un problema," *Eme Eme* 10.58 (1982): 7; María Elena Muñoz, *Las relaciones domínico-haitianas: Geopolítica y migración* (Santo Domingo: Editora Alfa y Omega, 1995), 76–77; José del Castillo, *La inmigración de braceros azucareros en la República dominicana, 1900–1930* (Santo Domingo: Cuadernos del Centro Dominicano de Investigaciones Antropológicas, UASD, no. 7, 1978), 23–24; Frank Moya Pons, "Modernización y cambios en la República Dominicana," in *Ensayos sobre cultura dominicana*, ed. Bernardo Vega et al., 4th ed. (Santo Domingo: Fundación Cultural Dominicana, Museo del Hombre Dominicano, 1996), 216–19.

18 For a good summary of the events narrated in this paragraph and the next, see chapters 20 and 21 in Cassá, *Historia social*; and chapters 32 and 33 in Frank Moya Pons, *Manual de historia dominicana*, 9th ed. (Santo Domingo: Caribbean Publishers, 1992).

19 The Dominican press criticized U.S. pressure severely; see Dominicano [pseud.], "Por la juventud," *Nuevo Réjimen* (6 Jan. 1901); Perroquet [pseud.], "Menestra," *Nuevo Réjimen* (9 Jan. 1901); and "Este es el momento," *Nuevo Réjimen* (25 Mar. 1901).

20 José del Castillo, "Las emigraciones y su aporte a la cultura dominicana (finales del siglo XIX y principios del XX)," *Eme Eme* 8.45 (1979): 8; Wilfredo Lozano, *La dominación imperialista en la República Dominicana, 1900–1930: Estudio de la primera ocupación norteamericana de Santo Domingo* (Santo Domingo: Editora de la Universidad Autónoma de Santo Domingo, 1976), 113; Oviedo, "Cultura y nación," 34; "16 de agosto," *Gaceta* 11.524 (15 Aug. 1884). The quote is from "Pacto fundamental de la sociedad 'Liga de ciudadanos,'" *Nuevo Réjimen* (12 Sept. 1899).

21 *Caudillismo* refers to the personalistic rule of local, regional, and national charismatic leaders, admired for their physical attributes and military skills, and backed by their followers because of their capacity to deliver material rewards or government sinecures. Peguero and De los Santos, *Visión general*, 287; Sagás, *Race and Politics*, 39; Cassá, *Historia social*, 192. The last quote is from Peguero and De los Santos, *Visión general*, 330. For theoretical explorations of *caudillismo*, see Franco Pichardo, *El pensamiento dominicano*, 274–75; and Jonathan Hartlyn, *The Struggle for Democratic Politics in the Dominican Republic* (Chapel Hill: University of North Carolina Press, 1998), 5, 23, 32.

22 See Moya Pons, *Manual de historia*, 462.

23 For a comment on the significance of color in the development of nationhood, see Pedro San Miguel, "Discurso racial e identidad nacional en la República Dominicana," *Op. Cit.* 7 (1992): 69–120; and Harry Hoetink, *The Dominican People, 1850–1900: Notes for a Historical Sociology*, trans. Stephen K. Ault (Baltimore: Johns Hopkins University Press, 1982), 165–92.

24 Miller, *In the Shadow*, 34–35.

25 Kramer, *Nationalism*, 11, explains Eric Hobsbawm and Terence Ranger's notion of the invented tradition. The quote is in Rodolfo Domingo Cambiaso, *Bosquejo sobre la historia* (Santo Domingo: Imp. La Cuna de América, 1913), 30, 34–35.

26 This is consistent with what Rama, *Lettered City*, 92–94, suggests.

27 For a rundown on these views, see Danilo de los Santos, "Reflexiones sobre la identidad nacional y cultural de los dominicanos," *Eme Eme* 8.47 (1980): 5; Carlos Dobal, "Hispanidad y dominicanidad," *Eme Eme* 12.71 (1984): 90; San Miguel, *La isla imaginada*, 89; Pedro Troncoso Sánchez, *Evolución de la idea nacional* (Santo Domingo: Museo del Hombre Dominicano, 1974), 1–2; De los Santos, "Reflexiones," 5; Roberto Cassá and Genaro Rodríguez, "Algunos procesos formativos de la identidad nacional dominicana," *Estudios Sociales* 25.88 (1992): 96; and Frank Moya Pons, "Etnicidad, identidad nacional y migración," in *El pasado dominicano* (Santo Domingo: Fundación J. A. Caro Alvarez, 1986), 243.

28 The Trujillista discourse can be found in Ramón Marrero Aristy, *La República Dominicana: Origen y destino del pueblo cristiano más antiguo de América* (Ciudad Trujillo: Editora del Caribe, [1956?]). Raymundo González, "Peña Batlle y su concepto histórico de la nación dominicana," *Ecos* 2.3 (1994): 48; and Oviedo, "Cultura y nación," 40, explain its implications. For the Brazilian variant under Getulio Vargas, see Nancy Leys Stepan, *The Hour of Eugenics* (Ithaca: Cornell University Press, 1991), 164. The idea of an "official nationalist" discourse comes from Anderson, *Imagined Communities*, 118.

29 Florencia E. Mallon, *Peasant and Nation: The Making of Postcolonial Mexico and Peru* (Los Angeles: University of California Press, 1995), 4.

30 Brea, "La cultura nacional," 45; Manuel Cruz Méndez, *Cultura e identidad dominicana: Una visión histórico-antropológica* (Santo Domingo: Editora Universitaria UASD, 1998), 4; Louis A. Pérez Jr., *On Becoming Cuban: Identity, Nationality, and Culture* (New York: Ecco Press, HarperCollins, 1999), 94.

31 Rafael Abreu Licariac, "Unión y solidaridad latinoamericana," *Cuna* 3.21 (7 Dec. 1913).

32 Luis E. Garrido, "Trabajad!," *Nuevo Réjimen* (1 Oct. 1899).

33 Jafet D. Hernández, "Discurso," *Cuna* 3.10 (14 Sept. 1913).

34 The first quote appears in "Correspondencia del interior," *Eco* 692 (10 Sept. 1892). Other ideas in this paragraph can be found in Fra Diavolo [pseud.], "Realidades," *Nuevo Réjimen* (19 May 1901); "Fragmento de la memoria que al ciudadano presidente de la República, General Ramón Cáceres, presenta el ciudadano Ministro de Relaciones Exteriores Licenciado Emiliano Tejera—1907," in Emiliano Tejera, *Antología*, selección, prólogo y notas de Manuel Arturo Peña Batlle (Ciudad Trujillo: Librería Dominicana, 1951), 182; "Nuestras aspiraciones," *Eco* 680 (18 June 1892); Ada Ferrer, *Insurgent Cuba: Race, Nation, and Revolution, 1868–1898* (Chapel Hill: University of North Carolina Press, 1999), 191.

35 Miriam Fernández Sosa, "Construyendo la nación: Proyectos e ideologías en Cuba, 1899–1909," in *La nación soñada: Cuba, Puerto Rico y Filipinas ante el 98*, Actas del Congreso Internacional celebrado en Aranjuez del 24 al 28 de abril de 1995 (Aranjuez: Doce Calles, 1995), 128–29; Ferrer, *Insurgent Cuba*, 192.

36 "Como fue hecha la primer [*sic*] mujer," *Renacimiento* 1.4 (7 Apr. 1915); "¿Qué haremos con nuestras hijas?" *Renacimiento* 1.16 (15 Oct. 1915); "Organicemos," *Eco* 465 (13 Oct. 1888); "Pensamientos agrícolas," *Renacimiento* 1.2 (2 Mar. 1915); "Discurso leido por el doctor Alfredo Baquerizo Moreno, de la Universidad de Guayaquil, en inauguración de año escolar 1915–16," *Renacimiento* 1.13 (1 Sept. 1915).

37 Alejandro de la Fuente, "Race, National Discourse, and Politics in Cuba: An Overview," *Latin American Perspectives* 25.3 (1998): 43–69.

38 "El 6 de diciembre 1492–1892," *Eco* 604 (10 Dec. 1892).

39 "Rumores," *Eco* 659 (23 Jan. 1892); "Sociedad Literaria Hispano-Americana," *Eco* 679 (11 June 1892); Fran. X del Castillo Márquez, "Alma dominicana," *Mireya* 1.33 (10 Dec. 1911); "Centro Español (San P. de Macorís)," *Renacimiento* 1.14 (15 Sept. 1915); "De Puerto Rico," *Renacimiento* 1.2 (2 Mar. 1915). The last quote is in an editorial, "Ideal latinoamericano," *Mireya* 1.33 (10 Dec. 1911). These currents are clearly inspired by the writings of Cuban José Martí and Argentine José Enrique Rodó, both widely read in the Dominican milieu.

40 Félix Montes, "El árbol de la libertad," *Renacimiento* 1.5 (22 Apr. 1915).

41 As used in the preface, note 17, "subalterns" refers to those social groups that were denied representation as citizens in the national discourse, both because they were excluded from participation in political and social intercourse and because they were considered incapable of possessing the attributes that defined the national character.

42 Juan Bosch, *La mañosa*, 27th ed. (1936; Santo Domingo: Editora Alfa y Omega, 2001); Ramón Emilio Jiménez, *Savia dominicana* (Santiago: Editorial El Diario, n.d.); Juan I. Jiménez Grullón, *Sociología política dominicana, 1844–1966*, 2nd ed., vol. 2 (1898–1924) (Santo Domingo: Editora Alfa y Omega, 1978), 327; Andrés L. Mateo, *Mito y cultura en la era de Trujillo* (Santo Domingo: Librería La Trinitaria e Instituto del Libro, 1993), 74; Richard Lee Turits, *Foundations of Despotism: Peasants, the Trujillo Regime, and Modernity in Dominican History* (Stanford: Stanford University Press, 2003); Pedro San Miguel, "La ciudadanía de Calibán: Poder y discursiva campesinista en la República Dominicana durante la era de Trujillo," *Revista Mexicana del Caribe* 4.8 (1999): 6–30.

43 For examples from Latin America, see Aviva Chomsky, "Laborers and Smallholders in Costa Rica's Mining Communities, 1900–1940," in *Identity and Struggle at the Margins of the Nation-State*, ed. Aldo Lauria-Santiago and Aviva Chomsky (Durham: Duke University Press, 1998), 174; Lillian Guerra, *Popular Expression and National Identity in Puerto Rico: The Struggle for Self, Community and Nation* (Gainesville: University Press of Florida, 1998), 14, 82, 98, 57; Greg Grandin, *The Blood of Guatemala: A History of Race and Nation* (Durham: Duke University Press, 2000), 193; Patrick Bryan, "La cuestión obrera en la industria azucarera de la República Dominicana," *Eme Eme* 7.41 (1979): 68–69; and "Correspondencia del interior," *Eco* 673 (30 Apr. 1892). Sagás, *Race and Politics*, 37, believes the *cibaeño* (from the Cibao) peasant encapsulated "a culturally and racially homogenous society, safe from modernization." Baud, "Ideología y campesinado," 64, on the other hand, asserts there is no single prototype.

44 Stepan, *Hour of Eugenics*, 18, 59, 105.

45 For instances of these occurrences in Latin American history, see Marisol de la Cadena, "The Political Tensions of Representations and Misrepresentations: Intellectuals and Mestizas in Cuzco (1919–1990)," *Journal of Latin American Anthropology* 2.1 (1996): 117–18, 138; Grandin, *Blood of Guatemala*, 140; Alejandro de la Fuente, "Negros electores: Desigualdad y políticas raciales en Cuba, 1900–1930," in *La nación soñada*, 166, and "Race, National Discourse, and Politics"; Florencia E. Mallon, "The Promise and Dilemma of Subaltern Studies: Perspectives from Latin American History," *American Historical Review* 99.5 (1994): 1494; Silvia M. Arrom and Servando Ortoll, eds., *Riots in the Cities: Popular Politics and the Urban Poor in Latin America 1765–1910* (Wilmington, Del.: Scholarly Resources, 1996), 5, 8–9; Ferrer, *Insurgent Cuba*, 37, 40, 42; Guerra, *Popular Expression*, 9.

CHAPTER I

1 Enrique Deschamps, *La República Dominicana: Directorio y guía general* (Santiago de los Caballeros: Vda. de J. Cunill, Barcelona, n.d., ca. 1906–11), 283; "Nuestro modo de ser económico, y sus resultantes," *Eco* 694 (24 Sept. 1892); J. R. [José Ramón] Abad, "La reforma del ganado en Santo Domingo," *Revista de Agricultura* 3.2 (May 1907); AGN, AytoSPdM, bundle 5516, doc. 336, 17 Dec. 1904; "Un poco de doctrina," *Eco* 699 (5 Nov. 1892); Raymundo González, "Ideología del progreso y campesinado en la República Dominicana en el siglo XIX," *Ecos* 1.2 (1993): 34; "Apacibilidad de las cosas," *Eco* 686 (30 June [July] 1892); untitled, *Eco* 687 (6 Aug. 1892); "Memoria que al presidente de la república presenta el secretario de estado en los despachos de Justicia e Instrucción Pública," *Gaceta* 15.711 (7 Apr. 1888); Américo Lugo, *Historia de Santo Domingo: Desde el 1556 hasta 1608*, prólogo de Manuel Arturo Peña Batlle (Ciudad Trujillo: Editorial Librería Dominicana, 1952), xvi.

2 "La vecina República Dominicana," *Eco* 695 (1 Oct. 1892); "Inserciones," *Gaceta* 11.499 (16 Feb. 1884); "El doctor Gabriel Giménez," *Eco* 658 (16 Jan. 1892); "Sobre el cultivo del arroz," *Renacimiento* 1.9 (1 July 1915); Lugo, *Historia de Santo Domingo*, xviii. Decades later, Ramón Marrero Aristy, *La República Dominicana: Origen y destino del pueblo cristiano más antiguo de América* (Ciudad Trujillo: Editora del Caribe, [1956?]), 16, voiced the same opinion.

3 Otto Schoenrich, *Santo Domingo: Un país con futuro* (1918; reprint, Santo Domingo: Editora de Santo Domingo, 1977), 152–53; Bernardo Vega, *Los primeros turistas en Santo Domingo*, selección, prólogo y notas de Bernardo Vega (Santo Domingo: Fundación Cultura Dominicana, 1991), 55–56, 81, 109, 172; Randolph Keim, *Santo Domingo, pinceladas y apuntes de un viaje* (1870; Santo Domingo: Editora Santo Domingo, 1978), 248, 249.

4 José Ramón López, "La paz en la República Dominicana: Contribución al estudio de la sociología nacional" (1915), in *Ensayos y artículos* (Santo Domingo: Ediciones de la Fundación Corripio, 1991), 167; "El objetivo político de los haitianos y cuál deberá ser el nuestro," *Eco* 683 (9 July 1892). Bonó is cited in Danilo de los Santos, "El Cibao y la sociedad nacional: Un enfoque parcial de las manifestaciones culturales entre 1840–1900," *Eme Eme* 10.56 (1981): 16.

5 López, "La paz en la República," in *Ensayos y artículos*, 138; Ernesto Sagás, *Race and Politics in the Dominican Republic* (Gainesville: University Press of Florida, 2000), 38; Carlos Esteban Deive, *Identidad y racismo en la República Dominicana* (Santo Domingo: Ayuntamiento del Distrito Nacional, Junta Municipal de Cultura, 1999), 29.

6 Lugo, *Historia de Santo Domingo*, xvi; Pedro Francisco Bonó, "Apuntes sobre las clases trabajadoras dominicanas," *La Voz de Santiago*, 23 Oct. 1881, in *Papeles de Pedro F. Bonó: Para la historia de las ideas políticas en Santo Domingo*, ed. Emilio Rodríguez Demorizi (Barcelona: Gráficas M. Pareja, 1980), 192, 241; Fco. [Francisco] E. Moscoso Puello, "Ideas—para Evelina," *Cuna* 3.8 (31 Aug. 1913); E. M. [Eugenio María] de Hostos, "Quisqueya, su sociedad y algunos de sus hijos," *Eco* 701 (19 Nov. 1892). Michiel Baud, "Ideología y campesinado: El pensamiento de José Ramón López," *Estudios Sociales* 19.64 (1986): 72, quotes López.

7 Franklin J. Franco Pichardo, *Sobre racismo y antihaitianismo (y otros ensayos)* (Santo Domingo: Impresora Vidal, 1997), 148–49, citing Américo Lugo; "El proyecto de la reforma arancelaria," *La Producción Nacional* 1.8 (25 May 1901); "Memoria que al

presidente de la república presenta el secretario de estado en los despachos de lo Interior y Policía," *Gaceta* 15.712 (14 Apr. 1888); Francisco J. Peynado, "Estudio político y plan de reformas para la República Dominicana," 14 July 1902, in *Por el establecimiento del gobierno civil en la República Dominicana* (Santo Domingo: Imp. La Cuna de América, Viuda de Roques & Ca., 1913), 11; Andrés Julio Montolio, "De la guerra," *Cuna* 1.6 (10 May 1903); José Ramón López, "La alimentación y las razas," in *Ensayos y artículos*, 22–23, 39.

8 José Ramón López, "La caña de azúcar en San Pedro de Macorís, desde el bosque virgen hasta el mercado, 1907," *Ciencia* 2.3 (1975): 132; Francisco Henríquez y Carvajal, "Diarias," *El Liberal*, 26 Oct. 1900, in *Cayacoa y Cotubanama: Artículos publicados en La Lucha y en El Liberal: La cuestión palpitante, Improvement, Diarias y otros trabajos de actualidad sobre cuestiones políticas y económicas* (Santo Domingo: Publicaciones ONAP, 1985), 248.

9 Untitled, *Revista de Agricultura* 8.5 (Aug. 1913): 523.

10 AGN, AytoSPdM, bundle "nuevo" 5562, doc. 101, 26 Oct. 1885; bundle "nuevo" 5594, [doc. no. missing], 4 Sept. 1888; "Núm. 3522—Ley sobre crianza de animales domésticos de pasto 21 mayo 1895," in *Colección de Leyes, Decretos y Resoluciones emanados de los poderes legislativo y ejecutivo de la República Dominicana* (Santo Domingo: Imprenta del Listín Diario, 1929), 459; AGN, AytoStoDgo, bundle "nuevo" 3289, "Actas de las sesiones del Honorable Ayuntamiento de la Común de San Carlos," 7 Sept. 1906; bundle "nuevo" 2837, 3 Aug. 1900; Ayuntamiento de la común de Santo Domingo, *Recopilación de resoluciones, ordenanzas, y reglamentos municipales* (Santo Domingo: Imp. de J. R. Vda. García, 1920), 23; "Aclimatación del ganado del norte en — [page torn]," *Revista de Agricultura* 7.2 (May 1911); "Cabras," *Renacimiento* 1.7 (26 May 1915); José Ramón Abad, *La República Dominicana: Reseña general geográfico estadística* (1888; reprint, Santo Domingo: Sociedad Dominicana de Bibliófilos, 1993), 294. The quote is from J. R. [José Ramón] Abad, "La reforma de ganado en Santo Domingo," *Revista de Agricultura* 3.7 (Oct. 1907). In the words of Emiliano Tejera, "the revolutionary and the pig are the two enemies of the country" (quoted in González, "Ideología del progreso," 35).

11 José del Castillo, *La inmigración de braceros azucareros en la República dominicana, 1900–1930* (Santo Domingo: Cuadernos del Centro Dominicano de Investigaciones Antropológicas, UASD, no. 7, 1978), 25, 27, 28; Pedro Francisco Bonó, "Cuestiones sociales y agrícolas, por solicitud del presidente de la república," *El Porvenir*, 12 Dec. 1880, in Rodríguez Demorizi, *Papeles*, 264, and "Privilegiomanía," *El Porvenir*, 6 Mar. 1880, ibid., 252.

12 "Vías de comunicación," *Revista de Agricultura* 7.2 (May 1911); Bonó, "Apuntes sobre las clases," 206; Francisco J. Peynado, "Por la inmigración: Estudio de las reformas que es necesario emprender para atraer inmigrantes á la República Dominicana," Apr. 1909, in *Por el establecimiento*, 51.

13 The first quote is in "Cervecería," *Eco* 666 (12 Mar. 1892). Other examples of this perceived need are in "Lo mejor que puede hacerse," *Eco* 670 (9 Apr. 1892); "Meetings de hacendados," *Eco* 67 (3 Sept. 1880); and "Sociedad Agrícola Dominicana: Estatutos generales," *Eco* 71 (1 Oct. 1880). The longer quote is in "La sociedad agrícola," *Eco* 70 (24 Sept. 1880).

14 Juan Elías Moscoso Jr., "Tiranía y libertad," *Nuevo Réjimen* (12 Sept. 1899); R. J. Castillo, "Obras y no palabras," *Nuevo Réjimen* (28 Apr. 1901).

15 Luis F. Mejía, *De Lilís a Trujillo: Historia contemporánea de la República Dominicana* (Santo Domingo: Editora de Santo Domingo, Sociedad Dominicana de Bibliófilos, 1993), n.p.

16 R. J. Castillo, "Obras y no palabras."

17 Moscoso Jr., "Tiranía y libertad"; López, "La paz en la República," in *Ensayos y artículos*, 148. Bonó and Lugo also claimed that institutional inviolability was the basis of political stability; see Pedro San Miguel, *La isla imaginada: Historia, identidad y utopía en La Española* (San Juan and Santo Domingo: Editorial Isla Negra and Ediciones La Trinitaria, 1997), 76–80; and Franco Pichardo, *Sobre racismo*, 148. For the other views expressed in this paragraph, see Patriota [pseud.], "Cosas serias," *Nuevo Réjimen* (17 Mar. 1901); and "Mensaje del ciudadano presidente del honorable Congreso Nacional, en contestación al del Ciudadano Presidente de la república de fecha 27 de febrero de 1908," *Gaceta* 25.1904 (27 June 1908).

18 Franklin J. Franco Pichardo, *El pensamiento dominicano, 1780–1940: Contribución a su estudio* (Santo Domingo: Editora Universitaria UASD, 2001), 242–43; Mejía, *De Lilís a Trujillo*, 50–51.

19 Fco. [Francisco] E. Moscoso Puello, "Ideas—para Evelina," *Cuna* 3.9 (7 Sept. 1913). In Cuba, the national budget functioned, in Alejandro de la Fuente's words, as the principal economic sector of the country; see "Negros electores: Desigualdad y políticas raciales en Cuba, 1900–1930," in *La nación soñada: Cuba, Puerto Rico y Filipinas ante el 98*, Actas del Congreso Internacional celebrado en Aranjuez del 24 al 28 de abril de 1995 (Aranjuez: Doce Calles, 1995), 169.

20 Arístides García Mella, "Física gubernativa," *Cuna* 1.22 (30 Aug. 1903).

21 Marrero Aristy, *La República*, 48. The poem is by Juan Antonio Alix:

> . . . persona de alto rango
> que le gusta mucho el mango
> porque es una fruta grata.
> Pero treparse en la mata
> y verse en los cogollitos
> y en aprietos infinitos . . .
> como eso es tan peligroso
> él encuentra más sabroso
> coger los mangos bajitos.

22 Andrés Julio Montolio, "De la guerra," *Cuna* 1.11 (13 June 1903); Pedro Francisco Bonó, "Opiniones de un dominicano," *El Eco del Pueblo*, 13 Jan. 1884, in Rodríguez Demorizi, *Papeles*, 274–75; R. J. Castillo, "Los unos y los otros," *Nuevo Réjimen* (24 Feb. 1901); L. J. Bobea, "Cuento," *Mireya* 1.4 (16 Oct. 1910).

23 "Memoria que al presidente de la república presenta el secretario de estado en los despachos de lo Interior y Policía," *Gaceta* 11.506 (12 Apr. 1884); Peynado, "Por la inmigración," in *Por el establecimiento*, 6; López, "La paz en la República," in *Ensayos y artículos*, 143, 149; Peynado, "Estudio político," in *Por el establecimiento*, 8–9; Baud, "Ideología y campesinado," 75; Arístides García Mella, "Los cambios de gobierno o Los gatos ministeriales," *Cuna* 1.25 (20 Sept. 1903); R. J. Castillo, "Contradicciones," *Nuevo Réjimen* (26 May 1901).

24 Henríquez y Carvajal, "De política," *La Lucha*, 8 June 1900, in *Cayacoa y Cotubanama*, 74; "Festividad nacional," *Gaceta* 11.525 (23 Aug. 1884); Lugo, *Historia de Santo Do-*

mingo, xx; editorial, *Gaceta* 15.706 (3 Mar. 1888); R. J. Castillo, "Obras y no palabras," *Nuevo Réjimen* (28 Apr. 1901).

25 A very sophisticated treatment of this flow of ideas at the end of the nineteenth century can be found in Daniel T. Rodgers, *Atlantic Crossings: Social Politics in a Progressive Age* (Cambridge: The Belknap Press of Harvard University Press, 1998).

26 Víctor José Castellanos E., "Aporte jurídico a la integración de la dominicanidad," *Eme Eme* 13.78 (1985): 98. Peña Batlle sees in the French influence an element alien to the more congruous Hispanic legacy; see Raymundo González, "Peña Batlle y su concepto histórico de la nación dominicana," *Ecos* 2.3 (1994): 11–54.

27 One could say that the objectives remain unchanged. Note the vehemence with which the Dominican presidency's website defends what it calls the country's Magna Carta: "The Constitution is imposed on everything and everyone. Nothing or no one, neither on behalf of any one or anything can transgress it, without the risk of inflicting harmful or tragic consequences for the nation and its inhabitants" ("Presidencia de la República Dominicana," <http://www.presidencia.gov.do/ingles/juridica/constituciondominicana.htm>).

28 Américo Lugo, *A punto largo* (Santo Domingo: Imp. La Cuna de América, 1901), 220.

29 Henríquez y Carvajal, "La cuestión palpitante: Datos-reflecciones," *La Lucha*, 24 Apr. 1900, in *Cayacoa y Cotubanama*, 30; "El artículo del licenciado Américo Lugo," *La Lucha*, 20 Apr. 1900, in ibid., 19–20; Luis C. del Castillo, "Medios adecuados para conservar el desarrollo del Nacionalismo en la República," in *Tópicos nacionales: Trabajo premiado en los juegos florales provenzales de San Pedro de Macorís por el club "Dos de julio"* (Santo Domingo: Imp. La Cuna de América, 1920), 10; "Fibras y cañas," *Revista de Agricultura* 3.4 (July 1907); "Discurso leido por el doctor Alfredo Baquerizo Moreno, de la Universidad de Guayaquil, en inauguración de año escolar 1915–16," *Renacimiento* 1.13 (1 Sept. 1915).

30 The quote is in R. J. Castillo, "La escuela vieja," *Nuevo Réjimen* (14 July 1901). There are countless articles that establish links among public schooling, political freedoms, social tranquility, the moral worth of individuals, the right to work, and more. For a sampling, see Jaime Martí Miquel, "De la instrucción pública," *Nuevo Réjimen* (16 Jan. 1901); "Correspondencia del interior," *Eco* 678 (4 June 1892); Eurípides Roques, "Algunos artículos: La reforma social," *Nuevo Réjimen* (11 Oct. 1899); and "El camino del porvenir," *Cuna* 1.6 (19 July 1903). Another example of the political role of education can be found in Mexico; see Alan Knight, "Racism, Revolution, and *Indigenismo*," in *The Idea of Race in Latin America*, ed. Richard Graham (Austin: University of Texas Press, 1990), 82.

31 R. J. Castillo, "La nueva escuela," *Nuevo Réjimen* (30 June 1901). The United States, not surprisingly, was also much admired, precisely because of the connection between education and prosperity, meaning power. See "El camino del porvenir," *Cuna* 1.6 (19 July 1903).

32 AGN, AytoSPdM, bundle 5516, doc. 336, 17 Dec. 1904; "La muerte de Porfirio Díaz," *Renacimiento* 1.14 (15 Sept. 1915); "La gran lisiada," *Eco* 687 (6 Aug. 1892).

33 R. J. Castillo, "La nueva escuela"; "Perdónalos, Señor! [*sic*]—por un imparcial," *Nuevo Réjimen* (7 July 1901); "Conversaciones con un niño," *Eco* 666 (12 Mar. 1892); Lugo, *A punto largo*, 221–22; Salustio [pseud.], "Palique," *Nuevo Réjimen* (4 Aug. 1901).

34 "Núm. 393—Ley sobre la represión del ocio y la vagancia," *Colección de Leyes*, 114.

35 Ibid.

36 "Cosas pequeñas," *Renacimiento* 1.11 (1 Aug. 1915). It is worth noting that in Spanish, "fortune" (*fortuna*) is a feminine noun, and "work" (*trabajo*) is masculine.

37 "Correspondencia," *Eco* 669 (2 Apr. 1892).

38 Henríquez y Carvajal, "Varios puntos," *La Lucha*, 18 May 1900, in *Cayacoa y Cotubanama*, 49; José R. López, "Moralejas—a la plebe de la prensa," *Blanco y Negro* 4.182 (17 Mar. 1912); "Mirar a través de un prisma," *Eco* 688 (13 Aug. 1892); Lugo, *A punto largo*, 202; "El periodismo de 'El Reporter,'" *Nuevo Réjimen* (27 Sept. 1899); "Cuestión de hacienda," *Eco* 70 (24 Sept. 1880); "El nuevo réjimen," *Nuevo Réjimen* (7 Feb. 1901). The quote is in A. Arredondo Miura, "El periodismo y el periodista," *Nuevo Réjimen* (29 Oct. 1899).

39 "La barra," *Eco* 66 (27 Aug. 1880); "En Macorís del este," *Eco* 685 (23 June [July] 1892).

40 Fran. X del Castillo Márquez, "Páginas americanistas," *Mireya* 3.50 (22 Sept. 1912).

41 "Estado," *Eco* 72 (8 Oct. 1880); "El libre cambio," *Eco* 687 (6 Aug. 1892); "Malos cálculos," *Eco* 692 (10 Sept. 1892); "Sociedad agrícola e industrial," *Eco* 68 (10 Sept. 1880); "La sociedad agrícola," *Eco* 70 (24 Sept. 1880); "Males graves," *Eco* 242 (15 Feb. 1884); "Asociación," *Eco* 428 (21 Jan. 1888).

42 "Pensamientos agrícolas," *Renacimiento* 1.2 (2 March 1915); "Lo mejor que puede hacerse," *Eco* 670 (9 Apr. 1892); "Esperemos y tengamos confianza," *Eco* 671 (16 Apr. 1892); "Sobre el cultivo del arroz," *Renacimiento* 1.9 (1 July 1915); "Haciendas de caña—Santa Elena," *Eco* 40 (16 Feb. 1880); and "El libre cambio," *Eco* 687 (6 Aug. 1892).

43 Nelson Ramón Carreño Rodríguez, "Una introducción y una conclusión general del estudio sobre la agricultura en República Dominicana de 1875 a 1925," *Eme Eme* 11.62 (1982): 7; Wilfredo Lozano, *La dominación imperialista en la República Dominicana, 1900–1930: Estudio de la primera ocupación norteamericana de Santo Domingo* (Santo Domingo: Editora de la Universidad Autónoma de Santo Domingo, 1976), 105; Roberto Cassá, *Historia social y económica de la República Dominicana*, vol. 2 (Santo Domingo: Editora Alfa y Omega, 1992), 128; Bruce Calder, "El azúcar y la sociedad dominicana durante la ocupación americana," *Eme Eme* 12.69 (1983): 107; Roberto Cassá, *Movimiento obrero y lucha socialista en la República Dominicana (orígenes hasta 1960)* (Santo Domingo: Fundación Cultural Dominicana, 1990), 49; Freddy Peralta, "La sociedad dominicana vista por Pedro Francisco Bonó," *Eme Eme* 5.29 (1977): 18; Cyrus Veeser, *A World Safe for Capitalism: Dollar Diplomacy and America's Rise to Global Power* (New York: Columbia University Press, 2002), 49.

44 E. M. Hostos, "Falsa alarma," *Eco* 272 (25 Sept. 1884); these suspicions are also reiterated in "Males graves," *Eco* 242 (15 Feb. 1884); "Memoria que al presidente de la república presenta el secretario de estado en los despachos de Fomento y Obras Públicas," *Gaceta* 15.713 (21 Apr. 1888); Abad, *La República*, 262; J. del Castillo, *La inmigración de braceros*, 24; Harry Hoetink, *Santo Domingo y el Caribe: Ensayos sobre cultura y sociedad* (Santo Domingo: Fundación Cultural Dominicana, 1994), 98, 110; "Tratado de reciprocidad comercial con los Estados Unidos," *La Producción Nacional* 1.1 (1 Feb. 1901); María Elena Muñoz, *Las relaciones domínico-haitianas: Geopolítica y migración* (Santo Domingo: Editora Alfa y Omega, 1995), 78; Calder, "El azúcar," 100, 115. The quote is from "El jornal y el costo de la vida," *Renacimiento* 1.5 (22 Apr. 1915).

45 "Memoria que al presidente de la república presenta el secretario de estado en los despachos de lo Interior y Policía," *Gaceta* 11.506 (12 Apr. 1884); "Mensaje del ciuda-

dano presidente del honorable congreso nacional, en contestación al del Ciudadano Presidente de la república de fecha 27 de febrero de 1908," *Gaceta* 25.1904 (27 June 1908); "El Congreso Nacional en nombre de la república," *Gaceta* 11.532 (11 Oct. 1884); "La ley del porvenir," *Eco* 673 (30 Apr. 1892); "El Congreso Nacional en nombre de la república," *Gaceta* 11.531 (4 Oct. 1884); AGN, AytoSPdM, bundle "nuevo" 5562, doc. 32, 4 Apr. 1885; Henríquez y Carvajal, "Sobre aranceles," *La Lucha*, 18 May 1900, in *Cayacoa y Cotubanama*, 56; "Lo mejor que puede hacerse," *Eco* 670 (9 Apr. 1892). The last quote is in "Una fuente de riquezas," *Renacimiento* 1.4 (7 Apr. 1915).

46   AGN, AytoSPdM, bundle "nuevo" 5534, doc. 547, 15 Nov. 1906; bundle "nuevo" 5594, 26 Feb. 1888; bundle "nuevo" 5503, doc. 42, 13 Feb. 1893, docs. 51, 53, 54, 22 Feb. 1893; "Asunto serio," *Nuevo Réjimen* (19 May 1901); "En el ingenio 'La Fe,' " *Eco* 660 (30 Jan. 1892).

47   "Este es el momento," *La Producción Nacional* 1.4 (25 Mar. 1901); "Poder Ejecutivo: Documentos anexos a la memoria del ministro de lo Interior y Policía: Gobernación civil y militar de la provincia de Santo Domingo," *Gaceta* 15.720 (9 June 1888); "Memoria que el gobernador de la provincia de Santo Domingo presenta al ciudadano ministro de lo Interior y Policía," *Gaceta* 27.1338 (14 Apr. 1900). The two quotes appear in *Revista de Agricultura* (1905): 2; and "Juntas de agricultura," *Eco* 56 (11 June 1880).

48   "Inauguración de la granja-escuela en San Cristóbal," *Revista de Agricultura* 7.1 (Apr. 1911).

49   "Escuelas de agricultura," *La Producción Nacional* 1.6 (25 Apr. 1901).

50   "Prosperidad," *Eco* 430 (4 Feb. 1888).

51   González, "Ideología del progreso," 32, 39; Cyrus Veeser, *A World Safe for Capitalism: Dollar Diplomacy and America's Rise to Global Power* (New York: Columbia University Press, 2002), 63; L. C. del Castillo, "Medios adecuados," 25.

52   Baud, "Ideología y campesinado," 70–72; Patrick Bryan, "La cuestión obrera en la industria azucarera de la República Dominicana," *Eme Eme* 7.41 (1979): 58, 61; "Sociedad Agrícola Dominicana: Estatutos generales," *Eco* 71 (1 Oct. 1880); "La sociedad agrícola," *Eco* 70 (24 Sept. 1880). The quote is from "Palabras pronunciadas por el ciudadano general Ramón Cáceres, presidente de la república ante la asamblea nacional en el acto de prestar juramento," *Gaceta* 25.1906 (4 July 1908).

53   Florencio Fernández, "Temas sociales: De la soberanía del pueblo," *Renacimiento* 1.2 (2 Mar. 1915); López, "La paz en la República," in *Ensayos y artículos*, 155; Adán Reyes, "Por el pueblo," *Nuevo Réjimen* (12 Nov. 1899); Bonó, "Apuntes sobre las clases," 226. The quotation is in F. Velázquez Hernández, "Por el pueblo," *Nuevo Réjimen* (29 Oct. 1899).

54   Franco Pichardo, *Sobre racismo*, 154. The first quote is from Henríquez y Carvajal, "De política," *La Lucha*, 8 June 1900, in *Cayacoa y Cotubanama*, 74; the others, from Henríquez y Carvajal, "Diarias," *El Liberal*, 26 Oct. 1900, ibid., 246.

55   "Deberes recíprocos," *Eco* 705 (17 Dec. 1892); F. Pi y Margall, "El estado," *Nuevo Réjimen* (17 Feb. 1901); Lugo, *A punto largo*, 200; Perroquet [pseud.], "Menestra," *Nuevo Réjimen* (9 Jan. 1901); "La exposición de los pueblos," *Eco* 458 (25 Aug. 1888); "El último mensaje," *Eco* 65 (19 Aug. 1880); R. J. Castillo, editorial, *Nuevo Réjimen* (16 Sept. 1899); "Palabras pronunciadas por el ciudadano general Ramón Cáceres," *Gaceta* 25.1906 (4 July 1908).

56 "Bien por el ayuntamiento de esta capital," *Eco* 669 (2 Apr. 1892); "El último mensaje," *Eco* 65 (19 Aug. 1880); "El gobierno constitucional," *Eco* 66 (27 Aug. 1880); "Sobre los nuevos ministros," *Nuevo Réjimen* (6 Jan. 1901); Lugo, *A punto largo,* 204, 207–8. The quote is in Rafael J. Castillo, "Reedifiquemos," *Nuevo Réjimen* (13 Feb. 1901).

57 Lugo, *A punto largo,* especially 204; editorial, *Gaceta* 55.706 (3 Mar. 1888); "Convención," *Eco* 693 (17 Sept. 1892); "Saludo patriótico," *Cuna* 1.18 (2 Aug. 1903).

58 Henríquez y Carvajal, "Diarias," 246–47.

59 "La elección presidencial," *Eco* 680 (18 June 1892).

60 Rodgers, *Atlantic Crossings,* 101.

61 Ibid., 79–80.

62 "Ruinas," *Eco* 69 (17 Sept. 1880).

63 Rodgers, *Atlantic Crossings,* 3, 22–23, 25, 31.

64 Henríquez y Carvajal, "La cuestión palpitante: Datos-reflecciones," *La Lucha,* 24 Apr. 1900, in *Cayacoa y Cotubanama,* 26; Frank Moya Pons, "Modernización, industrialización y cambios en el siglo XX," in *El pasado dominicano* (Santo Domingo: Fundación J. A. Caro Alvarez, 1986), 207, and "Dominican Republic," in *Latin American Urbanization: Historical Profiles of Major Cities,* ed. Gerald Michael Greenfield (Westport, Conn.: Greenwood Press, 1994), 195.

CHAPTER 2

1 Jaime de Jesús Domínguez, *La dictadura de Heureaux* (Santo Domingo: Editorial Universitaria, 1986), 211, and entire chapter entitled "Las ciudades" (The cities).

2 Jorge Lizardi Pollock, "Espacio, memoria y ciudadanías: La arquitectura y la representación de las identidades nacionales en la Ciudad de México, 1863–1910" (Ph.D. diss., University of Puerto Rico, 2002), 3–5.

3 Rafael J. Castillo, *Revista Ciencias, Artes y Letras* 17, 19, and 20 (1897), in José Ramón López, *Ensayos y artículos* (Santo Domingo: Ediciones de la Fundación Corripio, 1991), 391; Pedro Francisco Bonó, "Opiniones de un dominicano," *El Eco del Pueblo,* 13 Jan. 1884, in *Papeles de Pedro F. Bonó: Para la historia de las ideas políticas en Santo Domingo,* ed. Emilio Rodríguez Demorizi (Barcelona: Gráficas M. Pareja, 1980), 286–89.

4 Roberto Cassá, *Historia social y económica de la República Dominicana,* vol. 2 (Santo Domingo: Editora Alfa y Omega, 1992), 149–50; José Luis Romero, *Latinoamérica: Las ciudades y las ideas* (Mexico City: Siglo Veintiuno, 1976), 262, 300, and chapter 6, "Las ciudades burguesas" (bourgeois cities).

5 Lizardi Pollock, *Espacio, memoria y ciudadanías,* especially chapter 3, "El orden de la memoria: Espacio público y poder en la Ciudad de México" (The order of memory: Public space and power in Mexico City); Daniel T. Rodgers, *Atlantic Crossings: Social Politics in a Progressive Age* (Cambridge: The Belknap Press of Harvard University Press, 1998), 112–14, 160–62, 318. The quote is on page 112.

6 Fernando Escalante Gonzalbo, *Ciudadanos imaginarios: Memorial de los afanes y desventuras de la virtud y apología del vicio triunfante en la República Mexicana—Tratado de moral pública* (Mexico City: El Colegio de México, Centro de Estudios Sociológicos, 1992), 32, 51; Leopoldo Artiles Gil, *El nuevo rol de la ciudadanía* (Santo Domingo: Pontificia Universidad Católica Madre y Maestra, Centro Universitario de Estudios Políticos y

Sociales, Grupo de Acción por la Democracia, 1996), 11–12, 23–24. Mark Thurner, *From Two Republics to One Divided: Contradictions of Postcolonial Nationmaking in Andean Peru* (Durham: Duke University Press, 1997), 17, describes the "unitary civil model of liberal nationhood."

7 Manuel Arturo Peña Batlle, *Constitución política y reformas constitucionales, 1844–1942,* 3rd ed., 2 vols. (Santo Domingo: Publicaciones ONAP, 1995); "El Congreso Nacional: En nombre de la república," *Gaceta* 8.356 (9 Apr. 1881); Sarah Radcliffe and Sallie Westwood, *Remaking the Nation: Place, Identity and Politics in Latin America* (London: Routledge, 1996), 48–49; Thurner, *From Two Republics,* 12, extending Benedict Anderson's notable thoughts on "imagined communities." For a review of the distrustful opinion of the elite regarding their subordinates, see note 1 in chapter 1, especially Américo Lugo, *Historia de Santo Domingo: Desde el 1556 hasta 1608,* prólogo de Manuel Arturo Peña Batlle (Ciudad Trujillo: Editorial Librería Dominicana, 1952), xvi. Romero, *Latinoamérica: Las ciudades,* 274, lays out the argument for subaltern agency.

8 Pedro Francisco Bonó, "Privilegiomanía," *El Porvenir,* 6 Mar. 1880, in Rodríguez Demorizi, *Papeles,* 251–52, and "Opiniones," ibid., 280, 286; "Párrafos patrióticos," *Cuna* 1.19 (9 Aug. 1903).

9 Bonó, "Opiniones," 284–85.

10 Thurner, *From Two Republics,* 35. The most notable example of this phenomenon occurred in Peru. The law of 1828, which privatized land, prohibited people who could not read in Spanish from alienating land. A distinction was thus created between *sujetos tributarios* (tributary subjects, as were Indians under Spanish rule) and propertied *ciudadanos* (citizens).

11 Francisco Henríquez y Carvajal, "Diarias," *El Liberal,* 9 Nov. 1900, *Cayacoa y Cotubanama: Artículos publicados en La Lucha y en El Liberal. La cuestión palpitante, Improvement, Diarias y otros trabajos de actualidad sobre cuestiones políticas y económicas* (Santo Domingo: Publicaciones ONAP, 1985), 261.

12 As Escalante Gonzalbo, *Ciudadanos imaginarios,* 43, reminds the reader, the understanding of the exercise of power as the eternal tug between the sovereign rights of people and the disciplinary capabilities of the state is Foucault's own contribution. See also pages 36–38.

13 Mabel Moraña, "Ilustración y delirio en la construcción nacional, o las fronteras de *La Ciudad Letrada*," *Latin American Literary Review* 25.50 (1997): 32, 35, 40; Angel Rama, *The Lettered City,* trans. John Charles Chasteen (Durham: Duke University Press, 1996), 82; Elizabeth Dore, "One Step Forward, Two Steps Back: Gender and the State in the Long Nineteenth Century," in *Hidden Histories of Gender and the State in Latin America,* ed. Elizabeth Dore and Maxine Molyneux (Durham: Duke University Press, 2000), 7. The cautionary sentence regarding the formation of citizens can be found in Escalante Gonzalbo, *Ciudadanos imaginarios,* 41.

14 Bernardo Vega, *Los primeros turistas en Santo Domingo,* selección, prólogo y notas de Bernardo Vega (Santo Domingo: Fundación Cultural Dominicana, 1991), 68–69, 75; "El ayuntamiento de Santo Domingo (anuncio de resolución)," *Boletín* 16.274 (7 Dec. 1906); AGN, AytoStoDgo, bundle "nuevo" 3289, 15 May 1908; bundle "nuevo" 2842, 5 June 1915.

15 Secretaría de Estado de Fomento y Obras Públicas, *Reseña de la República Dominicana* (Santo Domingo: Imp. La Cuna de América, 1906), 99; Otto Schoenrich, *Santo Domingo: Un país con futuro* (1918; reprint, Santo Domingo: Editora de Santo Do-

mingo, 1977), 145–46; *Censo de la ciudad de Sto. Dgo. al 20-XI-1908* [Santo Domingo?: El ayuntamiento de Santo Domingo?, 1909?]; *El ayuntamiento de Santo Domingo* (n.p., 1909), first page of photocopy; F. E. Moscoso Puello, *Navarijo* (Ciudad Trujillo: Editora Montalvo, 1956), 19, 30–31; Francisco M. Veloz, *La Misericordia y sus contornos (1894–1916)* (Santo Domingo: Editora Arte y Cine, 1967), 226, 229; Luis E. Alemar, *La ciudad de Santo Domingo (Santo Domingo, Ciudad Trujillo)* (n.d.; reprint, Santo Domingo: Editora de Santo Domingo, 1943), 250–60.

16   On the growth of the capital city, see Frank Moya Pons, "Dominican Republic," in *Latin American Urbanization: Historical Profiles of Major Cities*, ed. Gerald Michael Greenfield (Westport, Conn.: Greenwood Press, 1994), 205; José Ramón Báez López Penha, *Por qué Santo Domingo es así* (Santo Domingo: Banco Nacional de la Vivienda, 1992); José del Castillo, *La inmigración de braceros azucareros en la República Dominicana, 1900–1930* (Santo Domingo: Cuadernos del Centro Dominicano de Investigaciones Antropológicas, UASD, no. 7, 1978), 29. For other details included in this paragraph, see *Censo de la ciudad de Sto. Dgo.*, 7; Secretaría de Estado de Fomento, *Reseña*, 99; Enrique Deschamps, *La República Dominicana: Directorio y guía general* (Santiago de los Caballeros: Vda. de J. Cunill, Barcelona, n.d., ca. 1906–11), 106–7; Schoenrich, *Santo Domingo*, 145–46; assorted advertisements, *Eco* 660 (30 Jan. 1892); Myrna de Peña, *Desde la zona colonial: La perpetua novedad de su pasado* (Santo Domingo: Banco Central de la República Dominicana, 1996), 21–23, 111–13; León David, "La ciudad de Santo Domingo en algunos escritores de principios de siglo," in Comisión Municipal para la Conmemoración del V Centenario de la ciudad de Santo Domingo, *La ciudad de Santo Domingo en la literatura: Ponencias presentadas ante el primer foro de la literatura sobre la ciudad de Santo Domingo, 25 al 26 de octubre de 1996* (Santo Domingo: Ayuntamiento del Distrito Nacional, 1997), 209, 213.

17   Samuel Hazard, *Santo Domingo, su pasado y presente* (1873; reprint, Santo Domingo: Editora de Santo Domingo, 1974), 217, 223–24; David, "La ciudad de Santo Domingo," 217; Carlos Esteban Deive, "La herencia africana en la cultura dominicana actual," in *Ensayos sobre cultura dominicana*, ed. Bernardo Vega et al., 4th ed. (Santo Domingo: Fundación Cultural Dominicana, Museo del Hombre Dominicano, 1996), 114.

18   Luis Emilio Gómez Alfau, *Ayer o el Santo Domingo de hace 50 años* (Ciudad Trujillo: Pol Hermanos, 1944), 124; Schoenrich, *Santo Domingo*, 219; Moya Pons, "Dominican Republic," 193, 208; Moscoso Puello, *Navarijo*, 8–9, 54; Carmenchu Brusiloff and Juan Alfredo Biaggi, *Santo Domingo, llave de las Indias occidentales* (Santo Domingo: Imprenta Vallejo Hnos., n.d.), 43; Alemar, *La ciudad de Santo Domingo*, 111, 176.

19   Alemar, *La ciudad de Santo Domingo*, 167–68, 242–50; Brusiloff and Biaggi, *Santo Domingo*, 44–45.

20   Brusiloff and Biaggi, *Santo Domingo*, 36; Moscoso Puello, *Navarijo*, 54; Peña, *Desde la zona colonial*, 84; Alemar, *La ciudad de Santo Domingo*, 250–60.

21   Gómez Alfau, *Ayer*, 124; Veloz, *Misericordia*, 97.

22   Moya Pons, "Dominican Republic," 205; Deschamps, *La República Dominicana*, 172; *Eco* 245 (9 Mar. 1884); *Album del cincuentenario de San Pedro de Macorís, 1882–1932* (San Pedro de Macorís: Comité Directivo Pro-Celebración del Cincuentenario del Distrito Marítimo de San Pedro de Macorís, 1993); AGN, AytoSPdM, bundle "nuevo" 5503, doc. 225, 29 Oct. 1893; José R. López, "San Pedro de Macorís," *Cuna* 4.25 (1 Oct.1915).

23   Deschamps, *La República Dominicana*, 172, offers population figures. For a sampling of requests for lots in San Pedro, see AGN, AytoSPdM, bundle "nuevo" 5503, doc. 61, 16 Mar. 1893; doc. 63, 21 Mar. 1893; doc. 251, 24 Nov. 1893; doc. 227, 3 Nov. 1893; bundle "nuevo" 5534, doc. 525, 1 Nov. 1906; doc. 344, 22 June 1906; doc. 492, 11 Oct. 1906; bundle 5559, doc. 469, 26 June, 1 Aug. 1913; bundle "nuevo" 5562, doc. 39, 11 May 1885; doc. 58, 10 Aug. 1885; bundle "nuevo" 5594, 12 June, 18 Sept., 22 Nov., 27 Dec. 1888.

24   "Panorama semanal," *Cuna* 3.10 (14 Sept. 1913); AGN, AytoSPdM, bundle "nuevo" 5533, doc. 640, 9 Oct. 1914; bundle 5559, doc. 498, 6 July 1913; doc. 597, 13 Aug. 1913; doc. 845, 30 Nov. 1913; bundle "nuevo" 5551, doc. 146, 13 Sept. 1897; bundle "nuevo" 5563, doc. 34, 5 Jan. 1914; doc. 597, 18 Sept. 1914; doc. 403, [n.d.] 1914; doc. 439, 18 May 1914; doc. 587, 14 Sept. 1914; doc. 334, 30 Mar. 1914; doc. 383, 20 Apr. 1914; doc. 839, 28 Dec. 1914; doc. 766, 30 Nov. 1914.

25   "Correspondencia del interior," *Eco* 680 (18 June 1892); *Renacimiento* 1.11 (1 Aug. 1915); AGN, AytoSPdM, bundle "nuevo" 5563, doc. 347, 3 Apr. 1914.

26   AGN, AytoSPdM, bundle "nuevo" 5563, doc. 640, 9 Oct. 1914; doc. 658, 18 Oct. 1914; doc. 612, 26 Sept. 1914; doc. 505, 15 July 1914; doc. 597, 18 Sept. 1914; doc. 585, 14 Sept. 1914; doc. 483, 20 June 1914; doc. 33, 5 Jan. 1914; bundle 5516, doc. 214, 22 Aug. 1904; doc. 43, 25 Mar. 1904.

27   Rodgers, *Atlantic Crossings*, 159, calls municipalization "the first transatlantic project." For a sampling of these efforts in Santo Domingo, see Ayuntamiento de la Común de Santo Domingo, *Recopilación de resoluciones, ordenanzas, y reglamentos municipales* (Santo Domingo: Imp. de J. R. Vda. García, 1920). For San Pedro, see assorted minutes of the regular and extraordinary meetings and the correspondence of the town council in AGN, AytoSPdM, bundle "nuevo" 5555 (1887), bundle "nuevo" 5503 (1893), bundle "nuevo" 5551 (1897), bundle "nuevo" 5545 (1906), and bundle "nuevo" 5599 (1909).

28   See all of *Boletín* 6 (1899); "Acta de la sesión ordinaria del día 7 de julio de 1903," *Boletín* 13.210 (20 Aug. 1903); "Acta de la sesión ordinaria del día 30 de diciembre de 1904," *Boletín* 16.235 (27 Feb. 1905); AGN, AytoSPdM, bundle 5516, doc. 197, 6 Aug. 1904; AGN, AytoStoDgo, bundle "nuevo" 3289, "Actas de las sesiones del Honorable ayuntamiento de la Común de San Carlos," 20 Mar., 30 Mar., 9 Sept., 14 Sept. 1906, 15 Oct., 27 Nov. 1906, 21 Feb., 28 Feb. 1908; bundle "nuevo" 5551, doc. 59, 1 Apr. 1897; and AGN, AlcStoDgo, 1 Apr., 8 Apr. 1897. For comparative perspectives, see Juanita de Barros, *Order and Place in a Colonial City: Patterns of Struggle and Resistance in Georgetown, British Guiana, 1889–1924* (Montreal: McGill-Queen's University Press, 2002); Teresa A. Meade, *"Civilizing" Rio: Reform and Resistance in a Brazilian City, 1889–1930* (University Park: Pennsylvania State University Press, 1997); Michael Johns, *The City of Mexico in the Age of Díaz* (Austin: University of Texas Press, 1997); Arturo Almandoz, ed., *Planning Latin America's Capital Cities, 1850–1950* (London: Routledge, 2002); Ronn Pineo and James A. Baer, eds., *Cities of Hope: People, Protests, and Progress in Urbanizing Latin America, 1870–1930* (Boulder, Colo.: Westview Press, 1998); and Gilbert M. Joseph and Mark D. Szuchman, eds., *I Saw a City Invincible: Urban Portraits of Latin America* (Wilmington, Del.: SR Books, 1996).

29   AGN, AytoStoDgo, bundle "nuevo" 3289, "Actas de las sesiones del Honorable ayuntamiento de la Común de San Carlos," 15 Oct. 1906; bundle "nuevo" 3321, "Sesión de 21 noviembre 1909"; bundle "nuevo" 2830, doc. 13, "Relativo al remate

del ramo de mercado de la playa del río Ozama durante el año 1888," 12 Dec. 1888; bundle "nuevo" 2833, doc. 2, "Relativo a varias minutas de oficios dirigidos por la corporación," 22 Nov. 1890; bundle "nuevo" 2833, doc. 16, "Relativo a arrendamiento de terrenos," 23 Nov., 30 Dec. 1890; bundle "nuevo" 3289, "Actas de las sesiones del Honorable Ayuntamiento de la Común de San Carlos," 25 May 1906; "El ayuntamiento constitucional de Santo Domingo," *Boletín* 6.136 (1 Oct. 1899).

30   "El ayuntamiento de Santo Domingo," *Boletín* 23.465 (30 Sept. 1913); 16.243 (27 July 1905); Arístides Inchaústegui, *Altar de la Patria* (Santo Domingo: N.p., 1976), 7–8; "Memoria que al ciudadano presidente de la república presenta el secretario de estado en los despachos de lo Interior y Policía: 27 de febrero de 1900," *Gaceta* 27.1333 (10 Mar. 1900); "Acta de la sesión ordinaria del día 2 de diciembre de 1902," *Boletín* 13.199 (16 Jan. 1903); "Ayuntamiento constitucional de Santo Domingo," *Boletín* 6.168 (5 Sept. 1901); "Acta de la sesión extraordinaria del día 2 de mayo de 1903," *Boletín* 13.207 (7 July 1903); "Los animales," *Eco* 35 (10 Jan. 1880); AGN, AytoStoDgo, bundle "nuevo" 3289, 14 Feb. 1908, "Actas de las sesiones del Honorable Ayuntamiento de la Común de San Carlos," 13 Nov. 1908; bundle "nuevo" 3413, 7 Jan. 1913; AGN, AytoSPdM, bundle "nuevo" 5503, doc. 48, 18 Jan. 1893; "Ley de crianza," *Revista de Agricultura* 7.2 (May 1911). The cow incident can be reconstructed through AGN, AytoSPdM, bundle "nuevo" 5594, 15 Aug., 16 Aug., 2 Sept., 22 Sept. 1888.

31   "Bien por el ayuntamiento de esta capital," *Eco* 669 (2 Apr. 1892); "El virus vacuno," *Eco* 673 (10 Apr. 1892); "Preservativos contra el crup," *Eco* 688 (13 Aug. 1892); "(Resolución) del ayuntamiento de Santo Domingo," *Boletín* 19.359 (27 Feb. 1909); *Memoria presentada por el Sr. F. Baehr, presidente del ayuntamiento de Santo Doningo [sic], capital de la República, al nuevo personal que regirá en el bienio de 1908 a 1909* (Santo Domingo: Impprenta [sic] de J. R. Vda. García, 1908), 17; Báez López Penha, *Por qué Santo Domingo es así*, 95–96; "El ayuntamiento de Santo Domingo (anuncio de resolución)," *Boletín* 16.260 (5 July 1906); "Sesión del día 20 de mayo de 1913," *Boletín* 23.460 (8 July 1913); "El parque," *Eco* 40 (16 Feb. 1880); "Ornato público," *Eco* 57 (18 June 1880); AGN, AytoStoDgo, bundle "nuevo" 3289, 3 July 1906; bundle "nuevo" 3431, "Acuerdos y resoluciones del ayuntamiento de Santo Domingo," 1915.

32   C. T. Wayo, "Cosas," *Eco* 39 (7 Feb. 1880); AGN, AytoSPdM, bundle "nuevo" 5551, doc. 16, 25 Jan. 1897; AGN, AytoStoDgo, bundle "nuevo" 3289, 31 July 1906. The quote is in "Ornato público," *Eco* 57 (18 June 1880).

33   "Ley sobre policía urbana y rural," *Gaceta* 25.1932 (3 Oct. 1908); "Anexos a la memoria del secretario de estado de lo interior y policía: Número 1," *Gaceta* 29.2285 (6 Apr. 1912). The "*bailes de cueros*" reference is in AGN, AytoStoDgo, bundle "nuevo" 2824, doc. 49, Oct. 1884. The "*plenas*" discussion can be found in AGN, AytoSPdM, bundle "nuevo" 5503, doc. 50, 20 Feb. 1893. I should note that the speaker does not directly name the objects of his concern.

34   "Poder Ejecutivo: Documentos anexos a la memoria del ministro de lo interior y policía: Gobernación civil y militar de la provincia de Santo Domingo," *Gaceta* 15.720 (9 June 1888); "Memoria que el gobernador de la provincia de Santo Domingo presenta al ciudadano ministro de lo Interior y Policía," *Gaceta* 27.1338 (14 Apr. 1900); "Anexos a la memoria del secretario de estado de lo interior y policía: Número 1," *Gaceta* 29.2285 (6 Apr. 1912); AGN, AytoSPdM, bundle "nuevo" 5563, doc. 224, 19 Feb. 1914; "El ayuntamiento constitucional de Santo Domingo," *Boletín* 6.120 (27 Jan. 1899); "(Resolución) del ayuntamiento de Santo Domingo," *Boletín* 19.359

(27 Feb. 1909); AGN, AytoStoDgo, bundle "nuevo" 2830, doc. 12, "Relativo a varias comunicaciones de la prefectura municipal," 8 Nov. 1888; bundle "nuevo" 2833, doc. 9, "Relativo al Gobernador Civil de la Provincia," 9 Apr. 1890; bundle "nuevo" 3289, "Actas de las sesiones del Honorable Ayuntamiento de la Común de San Carlos," 24 July 1906.

35 "Proyecto de ley de policía urbana y rural," *Gaceta* 25.1881 (8 Apr. 1908); "El Senado Consultor: Previas las tres lecturas constitucionales, en nombre de la República Dominicana ha dado la siguiente Ley sobre policía urbana y rural," *Gaceta* 19.913 (20 Feb. 1892); "Poder legislativo—Reproducción—El congreso nacional en nombre de la república—(Ley sobre Guardia Republicana)," *Gaceta* 25.1935 (14 Oct. 1908); Roberto Cassá, *Movimiento obrero y lucha socialista en la República Dominicana (orígenes hasta 1960)* (Santo Domingo: Fundación Cultural Dominicana, 1990), 49. The quotation is in *Memoria presentada por el Sr. F. Baehr*, 11.

36 "Núm. 5126—Ley de Sanidad—G.O. Núm. 2314 del 17 de julio de 1912," "Núm. 5189: Ley de organización comunal—G.O. Núm. 2365 del 15 de enero 1913," "G.O. Núm. 2368 del 25 de enero 1913," "G.O. Núm. 2374 del 15 de febrero 1913," *Colección de Leyes, Decretos y Resoluciones emanados de los poderes legislativo y ejecutivo de la República Dominicana* (Santo Domingo: Imprenta del Listín Diario, 1929), 12–13, 164.

37 Marisol de la Cadena, *Indigenous Mestizos: The Politics of Race and Culture in Cuzco, Peru, 1919–1991* (Durham: Duke University Press, 2000), 68–69; Armando de Ramón, "Suburbios y arrabales en un área metropolitana: El caso de Santiago de Chile, 1872–1932," in *Ensayos histórico-sociales sobre la urbanización en América Latina*, ed. Jorge E. Hardoy, Richard M. Morse, and Richard P. Schaedel (Buenos Aires: SIAP, 1968), 113, 115, 116, 122, 126; Jorge L. Lizardi Pollock, "Disciplina popular y orden espacial: Una aproximación teórica," *Historia y Sociedad* 11 (1999): 114, 127, 137, expanding on David Sibley's "geographies of exclusion"; Greg Grandin, *The Blood of Guatemala: A History of Race and Nation* (Durham: Duke University Press, 2000), 97–98, based on Nancy Leys Stepan's work on the eugenics movement.

38 Lizardi Pollock, "Disciplina popular," 126, 132, 135; Jorge Cela, Isis Duarte, and Carmen Julia Gómez, *Población, crecimiento urbano y barrios marginados en Santo Domingo* (Santo Domingo: Fundación Friedrich Ebert, 1988), 33–34.

39 Silvia M. Arrom and Servando Ortoll, eds., *Riots in the Cities: Popular Politics and the Urban Poor in Latin America, 1765–1910* (Wilmington, Del.: Scholarly Resources, 1996), 7; Lizardi Pollock, "Disciplina popular," 126, 132.

40 Cela et al., *Población, crecimiento urbano*, 7 (citing Lucien Lefebvre), 8, 12; Lizardi Pollock, "Disciplina popular," 115 (citing Michel de Certeau), 123, 124; Néstor García Canclini, *Imaginarios urbanos* (Buenos Aires: Editorial Universitaria de Buenos Aires, 1997), 69 (citing Gino Germani), 72 (citing Antonio Mela); Rama, *Lettered City*, 68. Rama makes the point that, although the Liberal state relied on repression, at least in the cities, workers reaped the benefits of industrialization and increased trade.

41 Rodgers, *Atlantic Crossings*, 158.

CHAPTER 3

1 E. M. [Eugenio María de] Hostos, "Centro de inmigración y colonias agrícolas," March 1885, in *Hostos en Santo Domingo*, ed. Emilio Rodríguez Demorizi, vol. 1 (Ciudad Trujillo: Imp. J. R. Vda. García Sucs., 1939), 181, 182, and "Inmigración II,"

Nuevo Réjimen (19 Nov. 1899); José del Castillo, "Las emigraciones y su aporte a la cultura dominicana (finales del siglo XIX y principios del XX)," *Eme Eme* 8.45 (1979): 11 (quoting an article in *El Dominicano*), 13, 14.

2 E. M. de Hostos, "Inmigración," *Nuevo Réjimen* (15 Nov. 1899); J. del Castillo, "Las emigraciones," 14; E. M. de Hostos, "Inmigración y colonización," in Rodríguez Demorizi, *Hostos en Santo Domingo*, 1:91; "Memoria que el gobernador de la provincia de Santo Domingo presenta al ciudadano ministro de lo Interior y Policía," *Gaceta* 27.1388 (14 Apr. 1900); *Revista de Agricultura* (1909); "Mensaje que el presidente de la república presenta al congreso nacional en su legislatura ordinaria de este año," *Gaceta* 32.2691 (8 Mar. 1916).

3 Francisco J. Peynado, "Por la inmigración: Estudio de las reformas que es necesario emprender para atraer inmigrantes á la República Dominicana, Abril 1909," in *Por el establecimiento del gobierno civil en la República Dominicana* (Santo Domingo: Imp. La Cuna de América, Viuda de Roques & Ca., 1913), 24, 25–26, 46.

4 *Revista de Agricultura* (1909): 75; José Ramón Abad, *La República Dominicana: Reseña general geográfico estadística* (1888; reprint, Santo Domingo: Sociedad Dominicana de Bibliófilos, 1993), 273; "La vecina República Dominicana," *Eco* 695 (1 Oct. 1892), citing an article in *Le Peuple*.

5 "Sobre inmigración" and "Oficial: Secretaría de Estado de Justicia, Fomento e Instrucción Pública: Bases para los contratos con los inmigrantes canarios que vengan a la República Dominicana," *Eco* 274 (9 Oct. 1884); "Poder ejecutivo—Secretaría de estado de Justicia, Fomento e Instrucción Pública," *Gaceta* 11.533 (18 Oct. 1884); "Núm. 4627: Resolución del PE que reglamenta la inmigración.—G.O. Núm. 1634 del 11 de noviembre 1905," in *Colección de Leyes, Decretos y Resoluciones emanados de los poderes legislativo y ejecutivo de la República Dominicana* (Santo Domingo: Imprenta del Listín Diario, 1929), 190; "Núm. 5074: Ley de inmigración.—G.O. Núm. 2295 del 11 de mayo 1912," ibid., 59. The longer quote is in *Revista de Agricultura* (1909): 75.

6 "Inmigración," *Eco* 73 (15 Oct. 1880); "Cuestión inmigración," *Eco* 240 (1 Feb. 1884); "El Congreso Nacional en Nombre de la República," *Gaceta* 11.517 (28 June 1884); "Crónica," *Eco* 668 (26 Mar. 1892); "Acta de la sesión ordinaria del día 25 de julio de 1899," *Boletín* 6.141 (12 Dec. 1899); AGN, AytoSPdM, bundle "nuevo" 5503, 28 Apr. 1893; "Mensaje del ciudadano presidente del honorable congreso nacional, en contestación al del Ciudadano Presidente de la república de fecha 27 de febrero de 1908," *Gaceta* 25.1904 (27 June 1908); AGN, AytoStoDgo, bundle "nuevo" 2837, 6 Aug. 1908.

7 "Evolución económica," *Eco* 432 (18 Feb. 1888); E. M. de Hostos, "Quisqueya, su sociedad y algunos de sus hijos [cont.]," *Eco* 701 (19 Nov. 1892); José del Castillo, *La inmigración de braceros azucareros en la República Dominicana, 1900–1930* (Santo Domingo: Cuadernos del Centro Dominicano de Investigaciones Antropológicas, UASD, no. 7, 1978), 8, 11, 19–20, and "Las inmigraciones y su aporte a la cultura dominicana (finales del siglo XIX y principios del XX)," in *Ensayos sobre cultura dominicana*, ed. Bernardo Vega et al., 4th ed. (Santo Domingo: Fundación Cultural Dominicana, Museo del Hombre Dominicano, 1996), 196–201, 204, 208–9; Orlando Inoa, *Los árabes en Santo Domingo* (Santo Domingo: Editora Amigo del Hogar, 1991), 42, 44; J. del Castillo, "Las emigraciones," 25–32.

8 Orlando Inoa, *Azúcar: Arabes, cocolos y haitianos* (Santo Domingo: Editora Cole y FLACSO, 1999), 98, 103–4; J. del Castillo, *La inmigración de braceros*, 37, 41–42, 46; Pedro Mir, "Carta anti-prólogo," in Julio César Mota Acosta, *Los cocolos en Santo*

Domingo: Carta anti-prólogo de Pedro Mir (Santo Domingo: Editorial La Gaviota, 1977), vii; Mota Acosta, *Los cocolos*, 14–15, 17, 20; Manuel Cruz Méndez, *Cultura e identidad dominicana: Una visión histórico-antropológica* (Santo Domingo: Editora Universitaria UASD, 1998), 118–19.

9 Inoa, *Azúcar*, 109, 111–12, 196; J. del Castillo, *La inmigración de braceros*, 40–41, 42, and "Las emigraciones," 33; "Cuestión inmigración: Acuerdo," *Eco* 236 (4 Jan. 1884); Patrick Bryan, "La cuestión obrera en la industria azucarera de la República Dominicana," *Eme Eme* 7.41 (1979): 73.

10 Inoa, *Azúcar*, 101; José del Castillo, "Consuelo: Biografía de un pequeño gigante," *Inazúcar* 6.31 (1981): 37–38; William L. Bass, *Reciprocidad: Exposición presentada al gobierno de la República Dominicana por William L. Bass* (Santo Domingo: Imp. La Cuna de América, 1902), 80, 82; José Ramón López, "La caña de azúcar en San Pedro de Macorís, desde el bosque virgen hasta el mercado, 1907," *Ciencia* 2.3 (1975): 134; Mota Acosta, *Los cocolos*, 31.

11 Bryan, "La cuestión obrera," 61; Harry Hoetink, " 'Escasez' laboral e inmigración en la República Dominicana, 1875–1930," in *Santo Domingo y el Caribe: Ensayos sobre cultura y sociedad* (Santo Domingo: Fundación Cultural Dominicana, 1994), 108; Aviva Chomsky, "Laborers and Smallholders in Costa Rica's Mining Communities, 1900–1940," in *Identity and Struggle at the Margins of the Nation-State*, ed. Aldo Lauria-Santiago and Aviva Chomsky (Durham: Duke University Press, 1998), 170–73; J. del Castillo, "Las inmigraciones," 205–7; Cruz Méndez, *Cultura e identidad*, 120, 122–25; Mota Acosta, *Los cocolos*, 35, 43; Mir, "Carta anti-prólogo," vii–viii.

12 Inoa, *Los árabes*, 46, 51; "Lo de Macorís," *Nuevo Réjimen* (27 Mar. 1901); "Acta de la sesión ordinaria del día 27 de enero de 1905," *Boletín* 16.237 (20 Mar. 1905); Francisco M. Veloz, *La Misericordia y sus contornos (1894–1916)* (Santo Domingo: Editora Arte y Cine, 1967), 130; AGN, AytoSPdM, bundle "nuevo" 5551, doc. 81, 2 May 1897; bundle "nuevo" 5563, doc. 230, 23 Feb. 1914; bundle 5559, doc. 609, 21 Aug. 1913; "Acta de la sesión ordinaria del día 2 de julio de 1901," *Boletín* 6.169 (30 Sept. 1901); "República Dominicana: Ayuntamiento de Santo Domingo," *Gaceta* 25.1903 (24 June 1908); "El Poder Ejecutivo," *Gaceta* 25.1862 (1 Feb. 1908), and *Gaceta* 25.1902 (20 June 1908).

13 For a sampling of transactions with the government, see AGN, AytoSPdM, bundle 5534, doc. 333, 17 June 1906; bundle 5559, doc. 748, 20 Oct. 1913; AytoStoDgo, bundle "nuevo" 3842, 19 June 1915; "Francisco Henríquez y Carvajal, Presidente de la República," *Gaceta* 32.2755 (22 Nov. 1916), and *Gaceta* 32.2745 (18 Oct. 1916); "El Poder Ejecutivo," *Gaceta* 25.1860 (25 Jan. 1908), and *Gaceta* 25.1889 (6 May 1908). Humberto García Muñiz, "The South Porto Rico Sugar Company" (Ph.D. diss., Columbia University, 1997), makes reference to the close ties between both islands' populations. For references to trouble with the authorities, see AGN, AytoSPdM, bundle "nuevo" 5563, doc. 483, 20 June 1914; bundle 5516, doc. 167, 7 July 1904; and AGN, AlcStoDgo, bundle 1, 3 Mar. 1893.

14 Frank Moya Pons, *Manual de historia dominicana*, 9th ed. (Santo Domingo: Caribbean Publishers, 1992), 453; "Consecuencias de una ley," *Eco* 72 (8 Oct. 1880); A. Arredondo Miura, "Primer repique," *Nuevo Réjimen* (27 Sept. 1899); "Los terrenos y sus precios," *Renacimiento* 1.12 (15 Aug. 1915).

15 C. T. Wayo, "Cosas," *Eco* 71 (1 Oct. 1880); "Remitidos—a C. T. Wayo I.A.B." and "Cosas," *Eco* 72 (8 Oct. 1880); "Basta! [*sic*]," *Eco* 73 (15 Oct. 1880).

16 X [pseud.], "Campaña odiosa," *Nuevo Réjimen* (21 Apr. 1901); R. J. Castillo, "Espina y aguijones," *Nuevo Réjimen* (28 July 1901); Imparcial [pseud.], "Nuestra opinión," *Nuevo Réjimen* (25 Aug 1901).

17 "Correspondencia del interior," *Eco* 688 (13 Aug. 1892); "Sueltos," *Eco* 662 (13 Feb. 1892); Bass, *Reciprocidad*, 5–6; "Es deber," *Eco* 663 (20 Feb. 1892).

18 María Elena Muñoz, *Las relaciones domínico-haitianas: Geopolítica y migración* (Santo Domingo: Editora Alfa y Omega, 1995), 116–19; Inoa, *Azúcar*, 165.

19 "El objetivo político de los haitainos y cuál deberá ser el nuestro," *Eco* 683 (9 July 1892); "No estamos de acuerdo, y nos defendemos," *Eco* 692 (10 Sept. 1892).

20 Miguel A. Garrido, "Juan Pablo Duarte," *Cuna* 3.3 (20 July 1913); "El objetivo político," *Eco* 683 (9 July 1892); "Correspondencia," *Eco* 670 (9 Apr. 1892); Hostos, "Quisqueya," *Eco* 701 (19 Nov. 1892).

21 "Dominicanos y haitianos," *Eco* 700 (12 Nov. 1892); Rafael Abreu Licariac, "Al insulto, el desprecio," *Eco* 701 (19 Nov. 1892).

22 Pedro San Miguel, *La isla imaginada: Historia, identidad y utopía en La Española* (San Juan and Santo Domingo: Editorial Isla Negra and Ediciones La Trinitaria, 1997), 83; Lauren Derby, "Haitians, Magic, and Money: Raza and Society in the Haitian-Dominican Borderlands, 1900 to 1937," *Comparative Studies in Society and History* 36.3 (July 1994): 488–526; Ernesto Sagás, *Race and Politics in the Dominican Republic* (Gainesville: University Press of Florida, 2000), 40; "Ferrocarril de Enriquillo a Barahona," *La Producción Nacional* 1.1 (1 Feb. 1901); Américo Lugo, *A punto largo* (Santo Domingo: Imp. La Cuna de América, 1901), 213.

23 "Dominicanos y haitianos," *Eco* 700 (12 Nov. 1892); Rafael Abreu Licariac, "Al insulto, el desprecio," *Eco* 701 (19 Nov. 1892).

24 The discussion that follows can be found in its entirety in "Dominicanos y haitianos," *Eco* 700 (12 Nov. 1892); Abreu Licariac, "Al insulto," *Eco* 701 (19 Nov. 1892); "No estamos de acuerdo, y nos defendemos"; and "Muy bien hecho," *Eco* 702 (26 Nov. 1892).

25 "Semblanzas—Juan Pablo Duarte," *Blanco y Negro* 1 (16 May 1909); Pedro Francisco Bonó, "De política" (draft, written after 1880, never published), in Rodríguez Demorizi, *Hostos en Santo Domingo*, 1:248.

26 Ramón Antonio Veras, *Inmigración, haitianos, esclavitud* (Santo Domingo: Ediciones de Taller, 1983), 91; Meindert Fennema and Troetje Loewenthal, *La construcción de la raza y nación en la República Dominicana* (Santo Domingo: Editora Universitaria UASD, 1987), 10; Roberto Cassá, "El racismo en la ideología de la clase dominante dominicana," *Ciencia* 3.1 (1976): 75; Raymundo González, "Peña Batlle y su concepto histórico de la nación dominicana," *Ecos* 2.3 (1994): 36–40. The quote is in Franklyn J. Franco [Franklin J. Franco Pichardo], *Cultura, política e ideología* (Santo Domingo: Editora Nacional, 1974), 50. "Nationalism" is in quotation marks because the author does not believe that anti-Haitianism is an authentic manifestation of Dominicanness.

27 Bryan, "La cuestión obrera," 70; San Miguel, *La isla imaginada*, 68; Franco, *Cultura, política*, 61; Franklin J. Franco Pichardo, *Santo Domingo: Cultura, política e ideología* (Santo Domingo: Sociedad Editorial Dominicana, SA, 1997), 74–75; Sagás, *Race and Politics*, 28–29, 32–33, 119; Inoa, *Azúcar*, 148–49.

28 Arthur J. Burks, *El país de las familias multicolores*, trans. Gustavo Amigó, S.J. (1932; reprint, Santo Domingo: Sociedad Dominicana de Bibliófilos, 1990), 42; Franco Pichardo, *Santo Domingo*, 109; Inoa, *Azúcar*, 156.

29 Franco Pichardo, *Santo Domingo*, 95; San Miguel, *La isla imaginada*, 67–68, 76–80.

30 Franklin J. Franco Pichardo, *Sobre racismo y antihaitianismo (y otros ensayos)* (Santo Domingo: Impresora Vidal, 1997), 70.

31 Muñoz, *Las relaciones*, 39.

32 Inoa, *Azúcar*, 157.

33 Franco Pichardo, *Santo Domingo*, 48, 99, and *Sobre racismo*, 166; Lugo, *A punto largo*, 213–14; Veras, *Inmigración, haitianos*, 96.

34 Inoa, *Azúcar*, 142–45, 158–59; Franco Pichardo, *Cultura, política*, 50.

35 See Aline Helg, *Our Rightful Share: The Afro-Cuban Struggle for Equality, 1886–1912* (Chapel Hill: University of North Carolina Press, 1995); Alejandro de la Fuente, *A Nation for All: Race, Inequality, and Politics in Twentieth-Century Cuba* (Chapel Hill: University of North Carolina Press, 2001); and Louis A. Pérez Jr., *On Becoming Cuban: Identity, Nationality, and Culture* (New York: Ecco Press, HarperCollins, 1999).

36 Sagás, *Race and Politics*, 18, 21, 120. Others who share this view are David Howard, *Coloring the Nation: Race and Ethnicity in the Dominican Republic* (Oxford and Boulder: Signal Books and Lynne Rienner, 2001), 40; Senaida Jansen and Cecilia Millán, *Género, trabajo y etnia en los bateyes dominicanos* (Santo Domingo: Instituto Tecnológico de Santo Domingo, Programa Estudios de la Mujer, 1991), 24; Josefina Zaiter, "La identidad como fenómeno psico-social," *Ciencia y Sociedad* 12.4 (1987): 497; Conferencia Dominicana de Religiosos (CONDOR), "Documentos: Cultura e identidad nacional," *Estudios Sociales* 18.62 (1985): 64; and Carlos Dore Cabral, "La inmigración haitiana y el componente racista de la cultura dominicana (Apuntes para una crítica a 'La isla al revés')," *Ciencia y Sociedad* 10.1 (1985): 62.

37 Cassá, "El racismo," 67; Franco Pichardo, *Santo Domingo*, 81; Carlos Esteban Deive, *Identidad y racismo en la República Dominicana* (Santo Domingo: Ayuntamiento del Distrito Nacional, Junta Municipal de Cultura, 1999), 11, 32–34, 37, 44. Dominicans, of course, were not alone in suffering from these anxieties. See Ernesto Sagás, "El anti-haitianismo en la República Dominicana: Pasado y presente de una ideología dominante," in *Los problemas raciales en la República Dominicana y el Caribe: Seminario celebrado durante los días 30 y 31 de mayo de 1997 por la Comisión Municipal para la Conmemoración del V Centenario de la Ciudad de Santo Domingo* (Santo Domingo: Ayuntamiento del Distrito Nacional, 1998), 136.

38 Nancy Leys Stepan, *The Hour of Eugenics* (Ithaca: Cornell University Press, 1991), 106, 137–38, 168; Ann Stoler, *Sexual Affronts and Racial Frontiers in Tensions of Empire* (Los Angeles: University of California Press, 1997), 199; Carol A. Smith, "The Symbolics of Blood: Mestizaje in the Americas," *Identities* 3.4 (1997): 503–4; Richard Graham, ed., *The Idea of Race in Latin America* (Austin: University of Texas Press, 1990), 1, 3; Helen I. Safa, "Introduction," *Latin American Perspectives* 25.3 (1998): 3–15.

39 Fennema and Loewenthal, *La construcción de la raza*, 26, 29; Howard, *Coloring the Nation*, 154; Silvio Torres Saillant, "The Tribulations of Blackness: Stages in Dominican Racial Identity," *Latin American Perspectives* 25.3 (1998): 126–47; Sagás, *Race and Politics*, 35, 37, and "El anti-haitianismo," 135; Deive, *Identidad y racismo*, 40, 43; Carlos Dore Cabral, "Reflexiones sobre la identidad cultural del Caribe: El caso dominicano," *Casa de las Américas* 118 (1985): 79. The apt turn of phrase regarding Spain and Africa comes from Pérez, *On Becoming Cuban*, 90.

40 Joaquin Ma. Bobea, "Parentela," *Mireya* 2.44 (23 June 1912); Pedro Francisco Bonó, "Apuntes sobre las clases trabajadoras dominicanas," *La Voz de Santiago*, 23 Oct. 1881,

in *Papeles de Pedro F. Bonó: Para la historia de las ideas políticas en Santo Domingo*, ed. Rodríguez Demorizi (Barcelona: Gráficas M. Pareja, 1980), 219; Hugo Tolentino Dipp, "La raza y la cultura en la idea de lo nacional de Américo Lugo," *¡Ahora!* 239 (10 June 1968): 64; González, "Peña Batlle," 13; Lillian Guerra, *Popular Expression and National Identity in Puerto Rico: The Struggle for Self, Community and Nation* (Gainesville: University of Florida Press, 1998), 214, 216. The genial expression of the paradox between Negrophobia and racial oppression is in Torres Saillant, "Tribulations," 4.

41 For a Dominican sampling, see Dore Cabral, "Reflexiones," 75; Conferencia Dominicana de Religiosos (CONDOR), "Documentos," 62–63; Cruz Méndez, *Cultura e identidad*, ii–iii; and J. del Castillo, "Las inmigraciones," 171. Alexander S. Dawson, "From Models for the Nation to Model Citizens: Indigenismo and the 'Revindication' of the Mexican Indian, 1920–40," *Journal of Latin American Studies* 30 (1998): 292, provides the Mexican variant. For Peru, see Marisol de la Cadena, *Indigenous Mestizos: The Politics of Race and Culture in Cuzco, Peru, 1919–1991* (Durham: Duke University Press, 2000), 265, and "The Political Tensions of Representations and Misrepresentations: Intellectuals and Mestizas in Cuzco (1919–1990)," *Journal of Latin American Anthropology* 2.1 (1996): 122–23.

42 Peter Wade, *Race and Ethnicity in Latin America* (London: Pluto Press, 1997), 15, 16–17, 19–21; Torres Saillant, "Tribulations," 12; Cassá, "El racismo," 73; Sagás, *Race and Politics*, 119.

43 De la Cadena, *Indigenous Mestizos*, 4 (citing Gilroy and Stolcke), 26, 140–41, and "Political Tensions," 114; Sarah Radcliffe and Sallie Westwood, *Remaking the Nation: Place, Identity and Politics in Latin America* (London: Routledge, 1996), 49; Howard, *Coloring the Nation*, 155–56.

44 De la Cadena, *Indigenous Mestizos*, 265; Stepan, *Hour of Eugenics*, 151.

CHAPTER 4

1 Antonia García, *La mujer: Lo que es y lo que debe ser el feminismo: Mi modo de pensar sobre el divorcio* (Santo Domingo: Imp. Moderna de J. Gneco y Co., 1913), 16, 18; Valentina Peguero, "Participación de la mujer en la historia dominicana," *Eme Eme* 10.58 (1982): 34, 36; Marivi Arregui, "Trayectoria del feminismo en la República Dominicana," *Ciencia y Sociedad* 13.1 (1988): 9–10; AGN, AytoSPdM, bundle "nuevo" 5551, doc. 8, 7 Jan. 1897. An excellent picture of this moment in Dominican history from the perspective of a woman is Julia Alvarez, *In the Name of Salomé: A Novel* (Chapel Hill: Algonquin Books, 1999), a fictionalized account of Salomé Ureña's life. See Partha Chatterjee, *The Nation and Its Fragments: Colonial and Postcolonial Histories* (Princeton: Princeton University Press, 1993), especially the chapters entitled "The Nation and Its Women" and "Women and the Nation" for the comparative perspective.

2 As noted in the introduction, note 7, men of letters and men of state, if not one and the same, traversed similar territory in Dominican high society.

3 Henry de Forge, trans., "Dionisia," *Blanco y Negro* 4.173 (14 Jan. 1912); J. J. Bobea, "Noctívagos," *Mireya* 1.8 (11 Dec. 1910). Another man-falls-in-love-with-fiancée's-cousin story can be found in Toriko [pseud.], "Del pasado (imitación)," *Blanco y Negro* 4.178 (18 Feb. 1912).

4 Arístides García Gómez, "Mi retrato," *Cuna* 1.12 (21 June 1903); Porfirio Herrera, "¿Te acuerdas?" *Mireya* 2.44 (23 June 1912); Froilán Turcios, "Mujeres y versos,"

Mireya 2.43 (9 June 1912); "Sección para las damas: Sobre el amor," *Renacimiento* 1.9 (1 July 1915); Manuel Díaz Rodríguez, "Morisca," *Mireya* 1.21 (25 June 1911); Germán Ornes, "Novias," *Renacimiento* 1.12 (15 Aug. 1915).

5 Catulle Mendes, "El amante de su mujer," *Blanco y Negro* 1.37 (30 May 1909).

6 Guillermo Egea Mier, "Cóleras de hembra," *Cuna* 1.24 (13 Sept. 1903); Catulle Mendes, "La penitente," *Blanco y Negro* 1.[issue no. missing] (2 May 1909); "Origen de los pasquines," *Renacimiento* 1.14 (15 Sept. 1915).

7 Adolfo Gustavo Mejía, "El esperado," *Cuna* 3.15 (20 Oct. 1913); Luis A. Abreu, "Alma yankee," *Cuna* 3.16 (27 Oct. 1913); U. Heureaux, "La venganza del maquinista," *Cuna* 1.16 (19 July 1903); "Mentiras de la luna," *Cuna* 1.9 (31 May 1903).

8 José R. López, "Nepotismo," *Cuna* 1.16 (19 July 1903); Vicente Diez de Tejada, "Ostras," *Blanco y Negro* 4.184 (1 Mar. 1912).

9 Camilo Millan, "Una tragedia," *Cuna* 1.12 (21 June 1903); José R. López, "La novelesca," and C. Armando Rodríguez, "Un favor de amiga," *Cuna* 1.9 (31 May 1903); Fabio Fiallo, "Fémina," *Cuna* 1.8 (24 May 1903).

10 "Correspondencia del exterior," *Eco* 683 (9 July 1892).

11 San Graal, "El origen de las mariposas," *Blanco y Negro* 4.185 (7 Apr. 1912); Emilia Pardo Bazán, "El viajero," *Cuna* 1.18 (2 Aug. 1903); "El odio ciego," *Renacimiento* 1.13 (1 Sept. 1915); Arturo B. Pellerano Castro, "Final de un drama," *Cuna* 1.11 (13 June 1903).

12 Emilio Ferraz Revenga, "La princesa 'sin lágrimas,' " *Blanco y Negro* 4.172 (7 Jan. 1912).

13 "Como fue hecha la primer [*sic*] mujer," *Renacimiento* 1.4 (7 Apr. 1915).

14 Ulises Heureaux, "Margarita de Ruyssac," *Mireya* 1.1 (4 Sept. 1910).

15 Olga [pseud.], "Ensayo," *Nuevo Réjimen* (6 Jan. 1901); A. de Lamartine, "Heroismo," *Renacimiento* 1.7 (26 May 1915).

16 Luis Rodríguez-Embil, "Cartas a mujeres—soledad," *Cuna* 1.8 (24 May 1903); Arturo Logroño, "El alma de Ahmed," *Mireya* 1.7 (27 Nov. 1910).

17 [Title missing], *Blanco y Negro* [vol. no. missing].39 (1909); "Tragedia pasional," *Blanco y Negro* 4.180 (2 Mar. 1912).

18 Mauricio Montegut, "El cuadro de Teresa," *Nuevo Réjimen* (16 Jan. 1901).

19 "Píldoras tocolójicas," *Eco* 57 (18 June 1880); "Gacetillas," *Eco* 684 (16 July 1892); "Vida femenil: Receta para desarrollar el busto," *Renacimiento* 1.6 (7 May 1915); "Para las damas," *Renacimiento* 1.18 (15 Nov. 1915); "Las ligas," *Eco* 681 (25 June 1892); "Los vestidos estrechos," *Renacimiento* 1.13 (1 Sept. 1915).

20 Mac'SOBIA [Rodolfo D. Cambiaso], "Sobre la educación de la mujer," *La Miscelánea: Revista Trisemanal* 1.1 (25 Sept. 1907); "Sección para las damas: Su talento," *Renacimiento* 1.9 (1 July 1915); "Vida femenil: El carácter de la mujer," *Renacimiento* 1.6 (7 May 1915); Teodoro Roosevelt, "El hogar," *Renacimiento* 1.13 (1 Sept. 1915). For the American perspective, see Paula Baker, "The Domestication of Politics: Women and American Political Society, 1780–1920," *American Historical Review* 89.2 (1984): 620–47; Stuart Ewen and Elizabeth Ewen, *Channels of Desire: Mass Images and the Shaping of American Consciousness* (New York: McGraw-Hill, 1982); Lois Banner, *American Beauty* (New York: Random House, 1983); Alice Kessler-Harris, *In Pursuit of Equity: Women, Men, and the Quest for Economic Citizenship in Twentieth Century America* (New York: Oxford University Press, 2001); and Evelyn Nakano Glenn, *Unequal Freedom: How Race and Gender Shaped American Citizenship and Labor* (Cambridge: Harvard University Press, 2002).

21   "Condición de la mujer," *Renacimiento* 1.9 (1 July 1915); José R. López, "La divorciada—monólogo," *Cuna* 1.2 (8 Mar. 1903); García, *La mujer*, 32–33, 42–43.

22   "Sección internacional—La enseñanza oficial extranjera," *Revista Escolar* 1.3 (31 Oct. 1910); "¿Qué haremos con nuestras hijas?" *Renacimiento* 1.16 (15 Oct. 1915); Anita López Pehna de Senior, "Colón," *Cuna* 3.11 (22 Sept. 1913); Jacinto Benavente, "La mujer y el periodismo," *Renacimiento* 1.13 (1 Sept. 1915).

23   "Las que no deben casarse," *Eco* 34 (5 Jan. 1880), and *Eco* 35 (10 Jan. 1880); "Por esos mundos: Contra la bigamia," *Renacimiento* 1.8 (12 June 1915); "Mandamientos," *Eco* 34 (5 Jan. 1880).

24   "Correspondencias del exterior," *Eco* 685 (23 July 1892); "Las mujeres tendrán bigotes," *Renacimiento* 1.18 (15 Nov. 1915). A similar preoccupation is registered all over Latin America. See Francine Masiello, "Gender, Dress, and Market: The Commerce of Citizenship in Latin America," in *Sex and Sexuality in Latin America*, ed. Donna J. Guy and Daniel Balderston (New York: New York University Press, 1997), especially 224–25.

25   "La carretera a Macorís," *Renacimiento* 1.1 (7 Feb. 1915); "Organicemos," *Eco* 465 (13 Oct. 1888).

26   "Ornato Público: La Plaza de Catedral," *Eco* 59 (2 July 1880); "Parques, jardines y árboles ornamentales," *Revista de Agricultura* (July 1909), 265–72; Santiago Pérez Argemi, "El árbol," *Revista de Agricultura* 7.6 (Sept. 1911).

27   "Labores de mujer," *Renacimiento* 1.12 (15 Aug. 1915). Mercedes Amiama, for example, asked the *ayuntamiento* to exempt the Club de Damas (Ladies' Club) from paying the entertainment tax in the national theater. Years later, she requested tax exemption for some toys imported from Germany, to be distributed to the best students in her kindergarten class; see "Acta de la sesión ordinaria del día 18 de abril de 1905," *Boletín* 16.242 (5 July 1905); and "Sesión del día 10 de junio de 1913," *Boletín* 23.462 (23 July 1913). For other "feminine" activities, see "Acta de la sesión ordinaria del día 3 de marzo de 1905," *Boletín* 16.240 (31 May 1905); AGN, AytoStoDgo, bundle "nuevo" 2842, 12 Nov. 1915; "Conversaciones dominicales," *Eco* 701 (19 Nov. 1892); "Correspondencia del interior," *Eco* 699 (5 Nov. 1892); AGN, AytoStoDgo, bundle "nuevo" 2842, [n.d.] 1915; and "Conversaciones dominicales," *Eco* 701 (19 Nov. 1892). The Trinidad connection can be found in Rhoda E. Reddock, *Women, Labor, and Politics in Trinidad and Tobago: A History* (Kingston: Ian Randle, 1994), 56–57.

28   Bernardo Vega, *Los primeros turistas en Santo Domingo*, selección, prólogo y notas de Bernardo Vega (Santo Domingo: Fundación Cultura Dominicana, 1991), 173–74; García, *La mujer*, 10–11; Arthur J. Burks, *El país de las familias multicolores*, trans. Gustavo Amigó, S.J. (1932; reprint, Santo Domingo: Sociedad Dominicana de Bibliófilos, 1990), xx, 32; Otto Schoenrich, *Santo Domingo: Un país con futuro* (1918; reprint, Santo Domingo: Editora de Santo Domingo, 1977), 152–53; Randolph Keim, *Santo Domingo, pinceladas y apuntes de un viaje* (1870; Santo Domingo: Editora Santo Domingo, 1978), 249.

29   Karin Alejandra Rosemblatt, "Charity, Rights, and Entitlement: Gender, Labor, and Welfare in Early-Twentieth-Century Chile," *Hispanic American Historical Review* 81.3–4 (2001): 565; Elizabeth Dore, "One Step Forward, Two Steps Back: Gender and the State in the Long Nineteenth Century," in *Hidden Histories of Gender and the State in Latin America*, ed. Elizabeth Dore and Maxine Molyneux (Durham: Duke University Press, 2000), 26, 43, 45, 67, 70; Maxine Molyneux, "Twentieth-Century State Formations in Latin America," ibid.; Carmen Imbert Brugal, "Las mujeres en la sociedad:

Marco jurídico," *Ciencia y Sociedad* 7.1 (1982): 52; M. de J. Camarena P., "Reformas constitucionales," *Cuna* 3.22 (14 Dec. 1913); Víctor José Castellanos E., "Aporte jurídico a la integración de la dominicanidad," *Eme Eme* 13.78 (1985): 88–89. The quote about the reliance of modernity on the restricted integration of women to civic life appears in Molyneux, "Twentieth-Century State Formations," 67.

30 AGN, AytoSPdM, bundle 5559, doc. 127, 14 Feb. 1913; doc. 713, 6 Oct. 1913; doc. 742, 16 Oct. 1913; bundle 5526, doc. 165, 8 July 1904; "Acta de la sesión ordinaria del día 15 de diciembre de 1905," *Boletín* 16.256 (20 Apr. 1906).

31 The ideas in this and the following paragraph flow out of comparative and theoretical readings on gender, ethnicity, and national identity. See Floya Anthias and Nira Yuval-Davis, "Introduction," in *Woman—Nation—State*, ed. Yuval-Davis and Anthias (London: Macmillan, 1989), 7; Michiel Baud, "Constitutionally White: The Forging of a National Identity in the Dominican Republic," in *Ethnicity in the Caribbean: Essays in Honor of Harry Hoetink*, ed. Gert Oostendie (London: Macmillan Education Ltd., 1996), 145; Daiva Stasiulis and Nira Yuval-Davis, "Introduction: Beyond Dichotomies—Gender, Race, Ethnicity and Class in Settler Colonies," in *Unsettling Settler Societies: Articulations of Gender, Race, Ethnicity and Class*, ed. Stasiulis and Yuval-Davis, Sage Series on Race and Ethnic Relations, no. 11 (London: Sage Publications, 1995), 19; Francine Masiello, "Women, State, and Family in Latin American Literature of the 1920s," in *Women, Culture, and Politics in Latin America: Seminar on Feminism and Culture in Latin America*, ed. Emilie Bergmann et al. (Berkeley: University of California Press, 1990), 31, 34; Valentine M. Moghadam, "Introduction: Women and Identity Politics in Theoretical and Comparative Perspective," in *Identity Politics and Women: Cultural Reassertions and Feminisms in International Perspective*, ed. Moghadam (Boulder: Westview Press, 1994), 18; and Brackette F. Williams, "Introduction: Mannish Women and Gender after the Act," in *Women Out of Place: The Gender of Agency and the Race of Nationality*, ed. Williams (New York: Routledge, 1996), 8–9. Baud explains mid-twentieth-century visions of Dominicanness as a denial of the social consequences of modernization. I disagree in that I hold that it is precisely ambivalence toward modernization in the late nineteenth and early twentieth centuries that is the moving force behind shaping Dominicanness.

32 "Investidura de maestros en un día de la patria," *Renacimiento* 1.19 (1 Dec. 1915); Apolinar Perdomo, "Divagaciones—A la patria," *Cuna* 1.12 (21 June 1903); Arturo Logroño, "Palabras," *Blanco y Negro* 4.180 (3 Mar. 1912); Masiello, "Gender, Dress, and Market," 231.

33 These ideas are collected from Linda K. Kerber, *Women of the Republic: Intellect and Ideology in Revolutionary America* (New York: W. W. Norton, 1986); Bruce Burgett, *Sentimental Bodies: Sex, Gender, and Citizenship in the Early Republic* (Princeton: Princeton University Press, 1998); Baud, "Constitutionally White"; Andrew Parker, Mary Russo, Doris Sommer, and Patricia Yaeger, eds., *Nationalisms and Sexualities* (London: Routledge, 1992); and Carol A. Smith, "Race/Class/Gender Ideology in Guatemala: Modern and Anti-Modern Forms," in Williams, *Women Out of Place*. The Trinidad reference is in Reddock, *Women, Labor, and Politics*, 120.

34 Doris Sommer, "Foundational Fictions: When History Was Romance in Latin America," *Salmagundi/Saratoga Springs* 82–83 (1989): 111–41, and *One Master for Another: Populism as Patriarchal Rhetoric in Dominican Novels* (New York: University Press of America, 1983), ix–49.

1 David Vincent Trotman, *Crime in Trinidad: Conflict and Control in a Plantation Society, 1838–1900* (Knoxville: University of Tennessee Press, 1986), 7, 244.

2 AGN, AytoStoDgo, bundle "nuevo" 2837, [various dates] 1909, bundle "nuevo" 2830, doc. 12, 11 July 1887; bundle "nuevo" 2833, doc. 8, [n.d.] 1890; "Relación de las multas impuestas durante el mes que termina con la fecha [last day of the month]," *Boletín* 16.239 (20 May 1905) and 16.244 (27 Aug. 1905); AGN, AytoSPdM, bundle "nuevo" 5563, docs. 132, 170, 215, 235, 278, 297, 334, 362, 383, 403, 406, 423, 440, 452, 474, 478, 535, 561, 575, 587, 602, 614, 629, 634, 644, 688, 702, 724, 747, 766, 779, 801, 820, 839, [various dates] 1914, and bundle "nuevo" 5534, docs. 314, 325, 332, 342, 384, 365, 510, [various dates] 1906. My method of calculation is most inexact—oftentimes there are no statistics for some weeks out of the month, or for some months altogether. Equally unreliable is the proportion of males to females, since some listings contain only an initial as a first name.

3 Juan I. Jiménez Grullón, *Sociología política dominicana, 1844–1966*, 2nd ed., vol. 2 (1898–1924) (Santo Domingo: Editora Alfa y Omega, 1978), 213; Trotman, *Crime in Trinidad*, 7.

4 Trotman, *Crime in Trinidad*, 214. As I argue below, the conflation of race and class was a commonplace in the Dominican Republic in this period, as it is today.

5 Sueann Caulfield, "The History of Gender in the Historiography of Latin America," *Hispanic American Historical Review* 81.3–4 (2001): 480.

6 AGN, AytoStoDgo, bundle "nuevo" 3289, "Actas de las sesiones del Honorable Ayuntamiento de la Común de San Carlos," 3 Apr. 1906; "Por la verdad," *Eco* 674 (7 May 1892); Pedro Francisco Bonó, "Opiniones de un dominicano," *El Eco del Pueblo*, 13 Jan. 1884, in *Papeles de Pedro F. Bonó: Para la historia de las ideas políticas en Santo Domingo*, ed. Emilio Rodríguez Demorizi (Barcelona: Gráficas M. Pareja, 1980), 288–89.

7 Untitled, *Blanco y Negro* 1.[3?] (9 May 1909); "El jornal y el costo de la vida," *Renacimiento* 1.5 (22 Apr. 1915).

8 Karin Alejandra Rosemblatt, "Charity, Rights, and Entitlement: Gender, Labor, and Welfare in Early-Twentieth-Century Chile," *Hispanic American Historical Review* 81.3–4 (2001): 563, 570.

9 Enrique Deschamps, "Costumbres nacionales," *Renacimiento* 1.12 (15 Aug. 1915). The quote comes from Enrique Deschamps, *La República Dominicana: Directorio y guía general* (Santiago de los Caballeros: Vda. de J. Cunill, Barcelona, n.d., ca. 1906–11), 273.

10 AGN, AytoSPdM, bundle "nuevo" 5563, doc. 673, 24 Oct. 1914; bundle "nuevo" 5594, "Relación de las patentes despachadas, por este municipio durante el primer trimestre del año de 1888"; Randolph Keim, *Santo Domingo, pinceladas y apuntes de un viaje* (1870; Santo Domingo: Editora Santo Domingo, 1978), 12; "Acta de la sesión ordinaria del día 16 de diciembre de 1902" and "Acta de la sesión ordinaria del día 9 de diciembre de 1902," *Boletín* 13.199 (16 Jan. 1903); "Acta de la sesión ordinaria del día 19 de mayo de 1905," *Boletín* 16.243 (27 July 1905); "Acta de la sesión del día 4 de junio de 1909," *Boletín* 19.371 (22 June 1909); "Acta de la sesión ordinaria del día 20 de enero de 1899," *Boletín* 6.129 (6 Apr. 1899); advertisement, *Eco* 454 (21 July 1888); Secretaría de Estado de Fomento y Obras Públicas, *Reseña de la República Dominicana*

(Santo Domingo: Imp. La Cuna de América, 1906); "Acta de la sesión del 11 de noviembre de 1913," *Boletín* 23.470 (15 Dec. 1913); Arthur J. Burks, *El país de las familias multicolores*, trans. Gustavo Amigó, S.J. (1932; reprint, Santo Domingo: Sociedad Dominicana de Bibliófilos, 1990), 60, 140–42.

11 "Relación de las personas que en el presente mes de Setiembre han sido asistidas por el Médico Municipal que suscribe," *Boletín* 19.380 (15 Oct. 1909). The total number of persons assisted was 137, of whom 108 were women and children. Fifteen women did not list their occupation.

12 Aida Bonnelly de Díaz, *Retablo de costumbres dominicanas* (Santiago: PUCAMAYMA, 1991), 24–25; Francisco M. Veloz, *La Misericordia y sus contornos (1894–1916)* (Santo Domingo: Editora Arte y Cine, 1967), 229.

13 Bonnelly de Díaz, *Retablo*, 82–83.

14 Federico Bermúdez, "Del lavadero," *Cuna* 4.26 (15 Oct. 1915).

15 F. E. Moscoso Puello, *Navarijo* (Ciudad Trujillo: Editora Montalvo, 1956), 92; Bonnelly de Díaz, *Retablo*, 86; Keim, *Santo Domingo, pinceladas*, 12; "Acta de la sesión ordinaria del día 16 de diciembre de 1902" and "Acta de la sesión ordinaria del día 9 de diciembre de 1902," *Boletín* 13.199 (16 Jan. 1903).

16 "Listado de negocios que deben comprar autorización para operar," *Boletín* 19.352 (5 Jan. 1909).

17 "Acta de la sesión ordinaria del día 20 de enero de 1899," *Boletín* 6.129 (6 Apr. 1899); "Nueva empresa," *Eco* 672 (23 Apr. 1892); "Estado demostrativo de las operaciones verificadas en la tesorería del ayuntamiento de Santo Domingo durante el mes de marzo de 1908," *Boletín* 19.354 (20 Jan. 1909); Burks, *El país*, 140–42.

18 AGN, AlcStoDgo, bundle 1, 24 May, 9 June, 14 Nov. 1897.

19 The conflicting social objectives of Liberalism are covered in Lara Putnam, *The Company They Kept: Migrants and the Politics of Gender in Caribbean Costa Rica, 1870–1960* (Chapel Hill: University of North Carolina Press, 2002), 86; Eileen Findlay, "Free Love and Domesticity: Sexuality and the Shaping of Working-Class Feminism in Puerto Rico, 1900–1917," in *Identity and Struggle at the Margins of the Nation-State*, ed. Aldo Lauria-Santiago and Aviva Chomsky (Durham: Duke University Press, 1998); and Teresita Martínez-Vergne, *Shaping the Discourse on Space: Charity and Its Wards in Nineteenth-Century San Juan, Puerto Rico* (Austin: University of Texas Press, 1999). The ambivalence of the Santo Domingo town council is evidenced in AGN, AytoStoDgo, bundle "nuevo" 3431, "Acuerdos y resoluciones del ayuntamiento de Santo Domingo," 21 Dec. 1914 and 12 Feb. 1915.

20 AGN, AytoStoDgo, bundle "nuevo" 3321, "Sesión de 13 octubre 1909," 1909; bundle "nuevo" 3431, "Acuerdos y resoluciones del ayuntamiento de Santo Domingo," 4 May 1915; "Reglamento para la comprobación de las enfermedades infecciosas en las prostitutas," *Boletín* 28.549 (15 Apr. 1918).

21 AGN, AytoSPdM, bundle 5559, doc. 481, 1 July 1913; doc. 504, 7 July 1913; and assorted others; bundle "nuevo" 5563, doc. 158, 30 Jan. 1914; doc. 187, 6 Feb. 1914.

22 J. D. Alfonseca Jr., "Moral pública," *Nuevo Réjimen* (26 Nov. 1899); *Informe que el Secretario de Sanidad y Beneficencia presenta al presidente provisional de la República* (Santo Domingo: Imp. de J. R. Vda García, 1923), 31; untitled, *Eco* 693 (17 Sept. 1892); "Documento: Comisaría de Puerto Plata, 9 agosto 1907," *Eme Eme* 8.45 (1979): 115–16; Deschamps, *La República Dominicana*, 283–84.

23 The various "meanings" of prostitution appear in Gail Hershatter, *Dangerous Plea-*

sures: Prostitution and Modernity in Twentieth-Century Shanghai (Berkeley: University of California Press, 1997). Unfortunately, the sources available to me did not permit the rich analysis that others have been able to engage in when studying prostitution. Putnam, *Company They Kept*, especially 80, 98, 110, reaches conclusions that are in line with the Dominican case, although my evidence is sketchy.

24 "Acta de la sesión del día 11 de junio de 1909," *Boletín* 19.374 (30 July 1909); "Acta de la sesión ordinaria del día 13 de enero de 1899," *Boletín* 6.127 (9 Mar. 1899); "Acta de la sesión ordinaria de día 2 de marzo de 1906," *Boletín* 16.261 (12 July 1906); "Sesión del 11 de febrero de 1913," *Boletín* 23.453 (5 Mar. 1913); AGN, AytoSPdM, bundle "nuevo" 5534, doc. 590, 7 Dec. 1906.

25 "Ayuntamiento de Santo Domingo: Presupuesto económico para el año 1909," *Boletín* 19.356 (30 Jan. 1909); "Acta de la sesión del día 4 de junio de 1909," *Boletín* 19.371 (22 June 1909); "Acta de la sesión del día 11 de junio de 1909," *Boletín* 19.374 (30 July 1909); "Acta de la sesión ordinaria del día 13 de enero de 1899," *Boletín* 6.127 (9 Mar. 1899); "Acta de la sesión ordinaria del día 2 de marzo de 1906," *Boletín* 16.261 (12 July 1906); "Acta de la sesión ordinaria del día 19 de mayo de 1905," *Boletín* 16.243 (27 July 1905); AGN, AytoStoDgo, bundle 5516, doc. 273, 21 Oct. 1904; bundle "nuevo" 3289, "Actas de las sesiones del Honorable Ayuntamiento de la Común de San Carlos," 21 Dec. 1906.

26 "Acta de la sesión ordinaria del día 30 de mayo de 1906," *Boletín* 16.271 (9 Oct. 1906); AGN, AytoSPdM, bundle 5516, doc. 122, 23 May 1904; doc. 238, 16 Sept. 1904; doc. 93, 30 Apr. 1904; doc. 34, 4 Mar. 1904; doc. 52, 3 Apr. 1904; doc. 329, 8 Dec. 1904; bundle "nuevo" 5534, doc. 374, 13 July 1906.

27 AGN, AytoSPdM, bundle "nuevo" 5503, doc. 271, 24 Dec. 1893; bundle "nuevo" 5594, [doc. nos. missing], [date missing] Dec. and 24 Dec. 1888; bundle 5516, doc. 212, 22 Aug. 1904; doc. 114, 13 May 1904; bundle "nuevo" 5534, doc. 405, 1 Aug. 1906; doc. 605, 22 Dec. 1906; doc. 609, 28 Dec. 1906.

28 "Acta de la sesión ordinaria del dia 10 de enero de 1905," *Boletín* 16.237 (30 Mar. 1905); AGN, AytoSPdM, bundle 5559, doc. 535, 21 July 1913; doc. 384, 27 May 1913; bundle 5516, doc. 18, 25 Jan. 1904; doc. 148, 20 June 1904; doc. 202, 12 Aug. 1904; doc. 225, 2 Sept. 1904; bundle "nuevo" 5534, doc. 542, 10 Nov. 1906.

29 Roberto Cassá, *Movimiento obrero y lucha socialista en la República Dominicana (orígenes hasta 1960)* (Santo Domingo: Fundación Cultural Dominicana, 1990), 25, 50–51, 68–76.

30 "Acta de la sesión ordinaria del día 7 de mayo de 1901," *Boletín* 6.167 (29 July 1901); "Acta de la sesión ordinaria del día 17 de junio de 1901," *Boletín* 6.168 (5 Sept. 1901); "Sesión del 29 de abril de 1913," *Boletín* 23.457 (22 May 1913); AGN, AytoStoDgo, bundle "nuevo" 3431, "Acuerdos y resoluciones del ayuntamiento de Santo Domingo," 7 May 1915; AGN, AytoSPdM, bundle 5559, doc. 601, 16 Aug. 1913; Ramón Marrero Aristy, *La República Dominicana: Origen y destino del pueblo cristiano más antiguo de América* (Ciudad Trujillo: Editora del Caribe, [1956?]), 63; "Crónica," *Cuna* 4.25 (1 Oct. 1915).

31 Adán Reyes, "El meeting de los obreros (crónica)," *Nuevo Réjimen* (29 Nov. 1899); José María Pérez, "El catolicismo y las clases obreras," *Nuevo Réjimen* (19 May 1901).

32 R. J. Castillo, "La clase obrera," *Nuevo Réjimen* (1 Sept. 1901); "Correspondencia del interior," *Eco* 673 (30 Apr. 1892).

CHAPTER 6

1   AGN, AytoSPdM, bundle 5559, doc. 298, 5 May 1914; bundle "nuevo" 5563, doc. 591, 16 Sept. 1914; "Acta de la sesión del 7 de octubre de 1913," *Boletín* 23.469 (23 Nov. 1913); "Sesión del 21 de febrero de 1913," *Boletín* 23.453 (5 Mar. 1913); "Acta de la sesión del 11 de noviembre de 1913," *Boletín* 23.470 (15 Dec. 1913); "Acta de la sesión ordinaria del día 27 de abril de 1906," *Boletín* 16.269 (5 Sept. 1906). This is very similar to the comments of Lara Putnam regarding the relationship between Limón officials and the city's residents; see *The Company They Kept: Migrants and the Politics of Gender in Caribbean Costa Rica, 1870–1960* (Chapel Hill: University of North Carolina Press, 2002), 162–63. The quote comes from David Vincent Trotman, *Crime in Trinidad: Conflict and Control in a Plantation Society, 1838–1900* (Knoxville: University of Tennessee Press, 1986), 244.

2   Otto Schoenrich, *Santo Domingo: Un país con futuro* (1918; reprint, Santo Domingo: Editora de Santo Domingo, 1977), 177; "Acta de la sesión ordinaria del día 3 de marzo de 1905," *Boletín* 16.240 (31 May 1905); AGN, AytoSPdM, bundle "nuevo" 5534, doc. 433, 3 Sept. 1906; "De Macorís del Este," *Eco* 683 (9 July 1892); "En Macorís del Este," *Eco* 685 (23 June [July] 1892); "La instrucción en Macorís del Este," *Eco* 686 (30 June [July] 1892).

3   "Acta de la sesión ordinaria del día 2 de marzo de 1906," *Boletín* 16.262 (20 July 1906); "Sesión del 21 de Stbre. del 1909," *Boletín* 19.380 (15 Oct. 1909); AGN, AytoSPdM, bundle "nuevo" 5534, doc. 529, 2 Nov. 1906; doc. 531, 5 Nov. 1906; bundle "nuevo" 5503, doc. 134, 13 July 1893; AGN, AlcStoDgo, bundle 42, doc. 18, Adalberto Chapuseaux, 13 Apr. 1909.

4   AGN, AlcStoDgo, bundle 42, doc. 11, Dominga Mañon, 25 Mar. 1909; doc. 13, Santiago Domínguez, 28 Mar. 1909; doc. 14, Santiago Domínguez, 5 Mar. 1910; doc. 17, Dionicio Pieter, 14 Mar. 1910, and Jacinto Matos, 20 Apr. 1910; doc. 30, Eufemia Wilson, 23 Apr. 1910; doc. 31, Eulalia de la Cruz, 30 Apr. 1910; doc. 40, Anita Gross, 17 June 1910; doc. 41, Antonia Arias, 21 June 1910; doc. 56, Estefana Macuñez, 17 Sept. 1910; doc. 57, Julia Mena, 20 Sept. 1910; doc. 59, Celina Pereyra, 1 Nov. 1909; doc. 60, Luisa Marrero, 1 Nov. 1909; doc. 63, Manuel Hernández, 13 Nov. 1909; doc. 64, Amelia Ruiz, 20 Nov. 1909; doc. 65, Amelia Guelix, 15 Oct. 1910, and Juan Pablo Esterlin, 20 Nov. 1910; doc. 68, María Santos, 6 Dec. 1910; doc. 69, Susana Escalante, 16 Dec. 1910.

5   AGN, AlcSPdM, book 45, 18 June 1909, 4 Oct. 1910, 13 Jan. 1911; AGN, AlcStoDgo, bundle 42, doc. 40, 17 June 1910.

6   AGN, AlcStoDgo, bundle 42, doc. 4, Altagracia Dubreil, 26 Apr. 1910; doc. 2, Nicolasa Mañaná, 20 Feb. 1910; doc. 7, Zoila Blanco Vda Perdomo, 15 Apr. 1910; doc. 1, Teodora Isares, 30 Jan. 1910; doc. 4, Enrique Vélez Viales, 13 Dec. 1909.

7   AGN, AlcStoDgo, bundle 1, 15 Feb. 1893, 2 Aug., 10 Aug., 30 Oct. 1897.

8   AGN, AlcStoDgo, bundle 1, [various dates] 1891, 1893–97; bundle 42, doc. 1, L. H. Penn, 8 Jan. 1910; doc. 16, María Alse, 14 Mar. 1910; doc. 19, Flora Nuñez, 23 Apr. 1909; doc. 59, Ana Salcedo, 22 Sept. 1910; AGN, AlcSPdM, book 45, 21 May 1910.

9   AGN, AlcSPdM, book 45, 2 June, 23 June, 17 Oct. 1910; AGN, AlcStoDgo, bundle 42, doc. 12, José Arneman, 27 Mar. 1909.

10   The same dilemma is explored in Harry Hoetink, "Ideología, intelectuales, identi-
     dad: La República Dominicana, 1880–1980," in *Santo Domingo y el Caribe: Ensayos
     sobre cultura y sociedad* (Santo Domingo: Fundación Cultural Dominicana, 1994), 119–
     20; and Pedro San Miguel, *La isla imaginada: Historia, identidad y utopía en La Española*
     (San Juan and Santo Domingo: Editorial Isla Negra and Ediciones La Trinitaria,
     1997), 96.

11   AGN, AlcStoDgo, bundle 1, 11 May, 23 July 1891, 5 Oct. 1896, 24 May, 8 June, 9 June,
     11 Oct., 2 Nov., 19 Nov. 1897.

12   Putnam, *Company They Kept*, 18–19, 143, 150–51, 153, 159–60. David Sabean's notion
     of culture as disputed, as a language of argument, appears on 153. Marisol de la
     Cadena, "The Political Tensions of Representations and Misrepresentations: Intel-
     lectuals and Mestizas in Cuzco (1919–1990)," *Journal of Latin American Anthropology* 2.1
     (1996): 138, suggests that in knowing one's place, in observing social hierarchy, one
     shows respect.

13   These cases are very similar to those in Sarah C. Chambers, *From Subjects to Citizens:
     Honor, Gender, and Politics in Arequipa, Peru, 1780–1854* (University Park: Pennsylvania
     State University Press, 1999).

14   AGN, AlcStoDgo, bundle 1, 16 May, 17 May, 22 June 1893, 29 Aug. 1895, 2 Nov. 1897;
     AGN, AlcSPdM, book 45, 10 June, 10 Aug. 1910.

15   AGN, AlcStoDgo, bundle 1, 8 May, 16 May 1893, 13 Jan. 1896.

16   AGN, AlcStoDgo, bundle 1, 12 Nov. 1896, 1 Sept. 1893, 30 Sept. 1897.

17   Putnam, *Company They Kept*, 12, 144, 154; and De la Cadena, "Political Tensions," 112,
     offer evidence of similar efforts to claim status and to reject sexualization on the basis
     of personal worth. Trotman's explanation for the difference between the ways men
     and women asserted themselves when they felt impotent (men became violent,
     women used obscenity) holds only partially for the Dominican Republic, as shown
     below; see *Crime in Trinidad*, 257.

18   AGN, AlcStoDgo, bundle 1, 12 Apr., 29 May 1893, 22 July 1896, 29 Sept. 1897.

19   AGN, AlcStoDgo, bundle 1, 5 Sept., 13 Sept. 1893, 7 Aug. 1896, 7 Sept., 26 Nov. 1897;
     AGN, AlcSPdM, book 45, 6 June 1910.

20   AGN, AlcStoDgo, bundle 1, 4 Feb., 31 Mar. 1897.

21   AGN, AlcStoDgo, bundle 1, 25 Apr., 4 Sept. 1893, 10 May 1894, 28 May, 9 June,
     5 Oct. 1897.

22   AGN, AlcStoDgo, bundle 42, doc. 22, Lucila Abreu and Manuel Ortiz, 4 Apr. 1910;
     doc. 28, Manuel Ortiz, 16 Apr. 1910.

23   AGN, AlcStoDgo, bundle 1, 4 Feb. 1891, 19 Sept. 1895, 5 Aug. 1897.

24   AGN, AlcStoDgo, bundle 1, 12 Jan., 5 June 1893, 9 Oct. 1895, 11 Feb. 1896.

25   AGN, AlcStoDgo, bundle 1, 17 Apr., 1 May 1893, 26 Aug. 1895, 10 May, 5 Aug.
     1897.

26   AGN, AlcStoDgo, bundle 1, 10 Mar. 1891, 11 May 1894, 4 Nov. 1895, 13 May 1896,
     24 Oct. 1897.

27   Putnam, *Company They Kept*, 11, 140, 165, 167, 174, 182, 184–87, 190, 192–94, 196.

28   AGN, AlcStoDgo, bundle 1, 10 Mar. 1891, 11 May 1894, 4 Nov., 30 Dec. 1895, 13 May,
     12 Oct. 1896, 4 Oct., 24 Oct. 1897.

29   AGN, AlcStoDgo, bundle 1, 16 Jan., 3 June 1893, 7 Aug. 1897.

30   Karin Alejandra Rosemblatt, "Charity, Rights, and Entitlement: Gender, Labor, and

Welfare in Early-Twentieth-Century Chile," *Hispanic American Historical Review* 81.3–4 (2001): 556, 563, 565. Trotman, *Crime in Trinidad*, 214, makes the connection between culture and morality.

CONCLUSION

1   Nancy Leys Stepan, *The Hour of Eugenics* (Ithaca: Cornell University Press, 1991), 151.

BIBLIOGRAPHY

DOCUMENTARY SOURCES

Archivo General de la Nación, Santo Domingo
  Alcaldía de San Pedro de Macorís
  Alcaldía de Santo Domingo
  Ayuntamiento de San Pedro de Macorís
  Ayuntamiento de Santo Domingo

PRINTED PRIMARY SOURCES

Periodicals
  Blanco y Negro
  Boletín Municipal
  Cuna de América
  El Eco de la Opinión
  Gaceta Oficial
  Mireya
  La Miscelánea: Revista Trisemanal
  Nuevo Réjimen
  La Producción Nacional
  Renacimiento
  Revista de Agricultura: Organo del Ministerio
    de Fomento y Obras Públicas
  Revista Escolar

Books, Articles, and Essays

Abad, José Ramón. *La República Dominicana: Reseña general geográfico estadística*. 1888. Reprint, Santo Domingo: Sociedad Dominicana de Bibliófilos, 1993.

Ayuntamiento de la común de Santo Domingo. *Recopilación de resoluciones, ordenanzas, y reglamentos municipales*. Santo Domingo: Imp. de J. R. Vda. García, 1920.

El ayuntamiento de Santo Domingo. N.p., 1909. (Front cover missing.)

Bass, William L. *Reciprocidad: Exposición presentada al gobierno de la República Dominicana por William L. Bass*. Santo Domingo: Imp. La Cuna de América, 1902.

Burks, Arthur J. *El país de las familias multicolores*. Translated by Gustavo Amigó, S.J. 1932. Reprint, Santo Domingo: Sociedad Dominicana de Bibliófilos, 1990.

Cámara de Comercio, Industria, y Agricultura. *Directorio General de San P. de Macorís*. San Pedro de Macorís: Tip. "Cervantes," 1927.

Cambiaso, Rodolfo Domingo. *Bosquejo sobre la historia*. Santo Domingo: Imp. La Cuna de América, 1913.

Castellanos, Rafael C. *Informe acerca de la reforma educacional iniciada por Don Eugenio María de Hostos, presentado al congreso nacional el 10 de junio de 1901, por el representante por Puerto Plata Pbro. Lcdo. Rafael C. Castellanos, Miembro dela comisión de justicia é instrucción pública*. Santo Domingo: Imprenta de García Hermanos, 1901.

Censo de la ciudad de Sto. Dgo. al 20-XI-1908. [Santo Domingo?: El ayuntamiento de Santo Domingo?, 1909?]. Photocopy.

Censo de población y otros datos estadísticos de la ciudad de Santo Domingo. Edición oficial del ayuntamiento. Santo Domingo: Imprenta de García Hermanos, 1893.

Colección de Leyes, Decretos y Resoluciones emanados de los poderes legislativo y ejecutivo de la República Dominicana. Santo Domingo: Imprenta del Listín Diario, 1929.

Del Castillo, Luis C. "Medios adecuados para conservar el desarrollo del Nacionalismo en la República." In *Tópicos nacionales: Trabajo premiado en los juegos florales provenzales de San Pedro de Macorís por el club "Dos de julio."* Santo Domingo: Imp. La Cuna de América, 1920.

Deschamps, Enrique. *La República Dominicana: Directorio y guía general*. Santiago de los Caballeros: Vda. de J. Cunill, Barcelona, n.d., ca. 1906–11.

García, Antonia. *La mujer: Lo que es y lo que debe ser el feminismo: Mi modo de pensar sobre el divorcio*. Santo Domingo: Imp. Moderna de J. Gneco y Co., 1913.

Hazard, Samuel. *Santo Domingo, su pasado y presente*. Santo Domingo: Editora de Santo Domingo, 1974. Originally published as *Santo Domingo, Past and Present; with a Glance at Hayti*. By Samuel Hazard. New York: Harper & Brothers, 1873.

Henríquez y Carvajal, Francisco. *Cayacoa y Cotubanama: Artículos publicados en La Lucha y en El Liberal: La cuestión palpitante, Improvement, Diarias y otros trabajos de actualidad sobre cuestiones políticas y económicas*. Santo Domingo: Publicaciones ONAP, 1985.

Keim, Randolph. *Santo Domingo, pinceladas y apuntes de un viaje*. Santo Domingo: Editora Santo Domingo, 1978. Originally published as *San Domingo: Pen Pictures and Leaves of Travel, Romance and History, from the Portfolio of a Correspondent in the American Tropics*. By DeB. Randolph Keim. Philadelphia: Claxton, Remsen & Haffelfinger, 1870.

Lisoni, Tito V. *La República Dominicana*. Trabajo presentado al IV Congreso Científico (1° Pan-Americano) de Santiago de Chile por Tito V. Lisoni, delegado de la República Dominicana al mencionado Congreso. Santiago de Chile, 25 de diciembre de 1908. Santiago: Imprenta, Litografía y Encuadernación "La Ilustración," 1908.

López, José Ramón. "La caña de azúcar en San Pedro de Macorís, desde el bosque virgen hasta el mercado, 1907." *Ciencia* 2.3 (1975): 125–49.

——. *Censo y catastro de la común de Santo Domingo: Informe que al honorable ayuntamiento presenta el director del censo y castastro de 1919, Sr. José R. López, el 15 de mayo de 1919.* Santo Domingo: Tipografía "El Progreso" Emiliano Espinal, 1919.

——. *Ensayos y artículos.* Biblioteca de Clásicos Dominicanos, vol. 10. Santo Domingo: Ediciones de la Fundación Corripio, 1991.

Lugo, Américo. *A punto largo.* Santo Domingo: Imp. La Cuna de América, 1901.

——. *Historia de Santo Domingo: Desde el 1556 hasta 1608.* Prólogo de Manuel Arturo Peña Batlle. Ciudad Trujillo: Editorial Librería Dominicana, 1952.

Memoria presentada por el Sr. F. Baehr, presidente del ayuntamiento de Santo Doningo [sic], capital de la República, al nuevo personal que regirá en el bienio de 1908 a 1909. Santo Domingo: Impprenta [sic] de J. R. Vda. García, 1908.

Peynado, Francisco J. *Por el establecimiento del gobierno civil en la República Dominicana.* Santo Domingo: Imp. La Cuna de América, Viuda de Roques & Ca., 1913.

Primer censo nacional de República Dominicana, 1920. Santo Domingo: Editora de la Universidad Autónoma de Santo Domingo, 1975.

Rodríguez Demorizi, Emilio, ed. *Hostos en Santo Domingo.* 2 vols. Ciudad Trujillo: Imp. J. R. Vda. García Sucs., 1939.

——. *Papeles de Pedro F. Bonó: Para la historia de las ideas políticas en Santo Domingo.* Barcelona: Gráficas M. Pareja, 1980.

Schoenrich, Otto. *Santo Domingo: Un país con futuro.* 1918. Reprint, Santo Domingo: Editora de Santo Domingo, 1977.

Secretaría de Estado de Fomento y Obras Públicas. *Reseña de la República Dominicana.* Santo Domingo: Imp. La Cuna de América, 1906.

Tejera, Emiliano. *Antología.* Selección, prólogo y notas de Manuel Arturo Peña Batlle. Ciudad Trujillo: Librería Dominicana, 1951.

PRINTED SECONDARY SOURCES

Album del cincuentenario de San Pedro de Macorís, 1882–1932. San Pedro de Macorís: Comité Directivo Pro-Celebración del Cincuentenario del Distrito Marítimo de San Pedro de Macorís, 1933.

Alemar, Luis E. *La ciudad de Santo Domingo (Santo Domingo, Ciudad Trujillo).* N.d. Reprint, Santo Domingo: Editora de Santo Domingo, 1943.

Almandoz, Arturo, ed. *Planning Latin America's Capital Cities, 1850–1950.* London: Routledge, 2002.

Alvarez, Julia. *In the Name of Salomé: A Novel.* Chapel Hill: Algonquin Books, 1999.

Alvarez-Curbelo, Silvia. *Un país del porvenir: El afán de modernidad en Puerto Rico (siglo XIX).* San Juan: Ediciones Callejón, 2001.

Anderson, Benedict. *Imagined Communities: Reflections on the Origin and Spread of Nationalism.* Rev. ed. London: Verso, 1991.

Anthias, Floya, and Nira Yuval-Davis. "Introduction." In *Woman—Nation—State*, edited by Yuval-Davis and Anthias. London: Macmillan, 1989.

Appelbaum, Nancy P., Anne S. Macpherson, and Karin Alejandra Rosemblatt, eds. *Race and Nation in Modern Latin America*. Chapel Hill: University of North Carolina Press, 2003.

Arregui, Marivi. "Trayectoria del feminismo en la República Dominicana." *Ciencia y Sociedad* 13.1 (1988): 9–18.

Arrom, Silvia M., and Servando Ortoll, eds. *Riots in the Cities: Popular Politics and the Urban Poor in Latin America, 1765–1910*. Wilmington, Del.: Scholarly Resources, 1996.

Artiles Gil, Leopoldo. *El nuevo rol de la ciudadanía*. Santo Domingo: Pontificia Universidad Católica Madre y Maestra, Centro Universitario de Estudios Políticos y Sociales, Grupo de Acción por la Democracia, 1996.

Báez López Penha, José Ramón. *Por qué Santo Domingo es así*. Santo Domingo: Banco Nacional de la Vivienda, 1992.

Baker, Paula. "The Domestication of Politics: Women and American Political Society, 1780–1920." *American Historical Review* 89.2 (1984): 620–47.

Banner, Lois. *American Beauty*. New York: Random House, 1983.

Barros, Juanita de. *Order and Place in a Colonial City: Patterns of Struggle and Resistance in Georgetown, British Guiana, 1889–1924*. Montreal: McGill-Queen's University Press, 2002.

Baud, Michiel. "Constitutionally White: The Forging of a National Identity in the Dominican Republic." In *Ethnicity in the Caribbean: Essays in Honor of Harry Hoetink*, edited by Gert Oostendie. London: Macmillan Education Ltd., 1996.

———. "Ideología y campesinado: El pensamiento de José Ramón López." *Estudios Sociales* 19.64 (1986): 63–81.

Behling, Laura L. " 'The Woman at the Wheel': Marketing Ideal Womanhood, 1915–1934." *Journal of American Culture* 20 (1997): 13–30.

Bolland, O. Nigel. "Creolization and Creole Societies: A Cultural Nationalist View of Caribbean Social History." In *Intellectuals in the Twentieth-Century Caribbean*, vol. 1, *Spectre of the New Class: The Commonwealth Caribbean*, edited by Alistair Hennessy. London: Macmillan, 1992.

Bonnelly de Díaz, Aida. *Retablo de costumbres dominicanas*. Santiago: PUCAMAYMA, 1991.

Bosch, Juan. *La mañosa*. 27th ed. Santo Domingo: Editora Alfa y Omega, 2001.

Brea, Ramonina. "La cultura nacional: Encuentros y desencuentros." *Ciencia y Sociedad* 10.1 (1985): 45–53.

———. *Ensayo sobre la formación del estado capitalista en la República Dominicana y Haití*. Santo Domingo: Editora Taller, 1983.

Brusiloff, Carmenchu, and Juan Alfredo Biaggi. *Santo Domingo, llave de las Indias occidentales*. Santo Domingo: Imprenta Vallejo Hnos., n.d.

Bryan, Patrick. "La cuestión obrera en la industria azucarera de la República Dominicana." *Eme Eme* 7.41 (1979): 57–77.

Burgett, Bruce. *Sentimental Bodies: Sex, Gender, and Citizenship in the Early Republic*. Princeton: Princeton University Press, 1998.

Burkhalter, Nancy. "Women's Magazines and the Suffrage Movement: Did They Help or Hinder the Cause?" *Journal of American Culture* 19 (1996): 13–25.

Calder, Bruce. "El azúcar y la sociedad dominicana durante la ocupación americana." *Eme Eme* 12.69 (1983): 99–115.

Cancian, Francesca M., and Steven L. Gordon. "Changing Emotion Norms in Marriage: Love and Anger in U.S. Women's Magazines since 1900." *Gender & Society* 2 (1988): 308–42.

Carreño Rodríguez, Nelson Ramón. "Una introducción y una conclusión general del estudio sobre la agricultura en República Dominicana de 1875 a 1925." *Eme Eme* 11.62 (1982): 3–24.

Cassá, Roberto. *Historia social y económica de la República Dominicana.* Vol. 2. Santo Domingo: Editora Alfa y Omega, 1992.

——. *Movimiento obrero y lucha socialista en la República Dominicana (orígenes hasta 1960).* Santo Domingo: Fundación Cultural Dominicana, 1990.

——. "El racismo en la ideología de la clase dominante dominicana." *Ciencia* 3.1 (1976): 61–85.

Cassá, Roberto, and Genaro Rodríguez. "Algunos procesos formativos de la identidad nacional dominicana." *Estudios Sociales* 25.88 (1992): 67–98.

Castellanos E., Víctor José. "Aporte jurídico a la integración de la dominicanidad." *Eme Eme* 13.78 (1985): 69–107.

Caulfield, Sueann. "The History of Gender in the Historiography of Latin America." *Hispanic American Historical Review* 81.3–4 (2001): 451–90.

Cela, Jorge, Isis Duarte, and Carmen Julia Gómez. *Población, crecimiento urbano y barrios marginados en Santo Domingo.* Santo Domingo: Fundación Friedrich Ebert, 1988.

Céspedes, Diógenes. "El efecto Rodó: Nacionalismo idealista vs. nacionalismo práctico: Los intelectuales antes y bajo Trujillo." In *Los orígenes de la ideología trujillista,* edited by Céspedes. Santo Domingo: Colección de la Biblioteca Nacional Pedro Henríquez Ureña, 2002.

——. *Salomé Ureña y Hostos.* Santo Domingo: Biblioteca Nacional Pedro Henríquez Ureña, 2002.

Cestero, Tulio M. *La sangre: Una vida bajo la tiranía.* 2nd ed. Ciudad Trujillo: Librería Dominicana, 1955.

Chambers, Sarah C. *From Subjects to Citizens: Honor, Gender, and Politics in Arequipa, Peru, 1780–1854.* University Park: Pennsylvania State University Press, 1999.

Chatterjee, Partha. *Nationalist Thought and the Colonial World: A Derivative Discourse?* Minneapolis: University of Minnesota Press, 1986.

——. *The Nation and Its Fragments: Colonial and Postcolonial Histories.* Princeton: Princeton University Press, 1993.

Chomsky, Aviva. "Laborers and Smallholders in Costa Rica's Mining Communities, 1900–1940." In *Identity and Struggle at the Margins of the Nation-State,* edited by Aldo Lauria-Santiago and Aviva Chomsky. Durham: Duke University Press, 1998.

Conferencia Dominicana de Religiosos (CONDOR). "Documentos: Cultura e identidad nacional." *Estudios Sociales* 18.62 (1985): 61–73.

Cruz Méndez, Manuel. *Cultura e identidad dominicana: Una visión histórico-antropológica.* Santo Domingo: Editora Universitaria UASD, 1998.

Damirón, Rafael. *Revolución.* Ciudad Trujillo: Editora Alfa y Omega, 1942.

David, León. "La ciudad de Santo Domingo en algunos escritores de principios de siglo."

In *La ciudad de Santo Domingo en la literatura: Ponencias presentadas ante el primer foro de la literatura sobre la ciudad de Santo Domingo, 25 al 26 de octubre de 1996*. Comisión Municipal para la Conmemoración del V Centenario de la ciudad de Santo Domingo. Santo Domingo: Ayuntamiento del Distrito Nacional, 1997.

Dawson, Alexander S. "From Models for the Nation to Model Citizens: Indigenismo and the 'Revindication' of the Mexican Indian, 1920–40." *Journal of Latin American Studies* 30 (1998): 279–308.

Deive, Carlos Esteban. "La herencia africana en la cultura dominicana actual." In *Ensayos sobre cultura dominicana*, edited by Bernardo Vega, Carlos Dobal, Carlos Esteban Deive, Ruben Silié, José del Castillo, and Frank Moya Pons. 4th ed. Santo Domingo: Fundación Cultural Dominicana, Museo del Hombre Dominicano, 1996.

———. *Identidad y racismo en la República Dominicana*. Santo Domingo: Ayuntamiento del Distrito Nacional, Junta Municipal de Cultura, 1999.

De la Cadena, Marisol. *Indigenous Mestizos: The Politics of Race and Culture in Cuzco, Peru, 1919–1991*. Durham: Duke University Press, 2000.

———. "The Political Tensions of Representations and Misrepresentations: Intellectuals and Mestizas in Cuzco (1919–1990)." *Journal of Latin American Anthropology* 2.1 (1996): 112–47.

De la Fuente, Alejandro. *A Nation for All: Race, Inequality, and Politics in Twentieth-Century Cuba*. Chapel Hill: University of North Carolina Press, 2001.

———. "Negros electores: Desigualidad y políticas raciales en Cuba, 1900–1930." In *La nación soñada: Cuba, Puerto Rico y Filipinas ante el 98*. Actas del Congreso Internacional celebrado en Aranjuez del 24 al 28 de abril de 1995. Aranjuez: Doce Calles, 1995.

———. "Race, National Discourse, and Politics in Cuba: An Overview." *Latin American Perspectives* 25.3 (1998): 43–69.

Del Castillo, José. "Azúcar y braceros: Historia de un problema." *Eme Eme* 10.58 (1982): 3–19.

———. "Consuelo: Biografía de un pequeño gigante." *Inazúcar* 6.31 (1981): 33–38.

———. "Las emigraciones y su aporte a la cultura dominicana (finales del siglo XIX y principios del XX)." *Eme Eme* 8.45 (1979): 3–43.

———. *La inmigración de braceros azucareros en la República dominicana, 1900–1930*. Santo Domingo: Cuadernos del Centro Dominicano de Investigaciones Antropológicas, UASD, no. 7, 1978.

———. "Las inmigraciones y su aporte a la cultura dominicana (finales del siglo XIX y principios del XX)." In *Ensayos sobre cultura dominicana*, edited by Bernardo Vega, Carlos Dobal, Carlos Esteban Deive, Ruben Silié, José del Castillo, and Frank Moya Pons. 4th ed. Santo Domingo: Fundación Cultural Dominicana, Museo del Hombre Dominicano, 1996.

De los Santos, Danilo. "El Cibao y la sociedad nacional: Un enfoque parcial de las manifestaciones culturales entre 1840–1900." *Eme Eme* 10.56 (1981): 3–30.

———. "Reflexiones sobre la identidad nacional y cultural de los dominicanos." *Eme Eme* 8.47 (1980): 3–16.

Derby, Lauren. "Haitians, Magic, and Money: Raza and Society in the Haitian-

Dominican Borderlands, 1900 to 1937." *Comparative Studies in Society and History* 36.3 (July 1994): 488–526.

Dobal, Carlos. "Hispanidad y dominicanidad." *Eme Eme* 12.71 (1984): 89–97.

"Documento: Comisaría de Puerto Plata, 9 agosto 1907." *Eme Eme* 8.45 (1979): 115–16.

Domínguez, Jaime de Jesús. *La dictadura de Heureaux*. Santo Domingo: Editorial Universitaria, 1986.

———. *Historia dominicana*. Santo Domingo: Editorial abc, 2001.

———. *La sociedad dominicana a principios del siglo XX*. Santo Domingo: Colección Sesquicentenario de la Independencia Nacional, 1994.

Dore, Elizabeth "One Step Forward, Two Steps Back: Gender and the State in the Long Nineteenth Century." In *Hidden Histories of Gender and the State in Latin America*, edited by Elizabeth Dore and Maxine Molyneux. Durham: Duke University Press, 2000.

Dore Cabral, Carlos. "La inmigración haitiana y el componente racista de la cultura dominicana (Apuntes para una crítica a 'La isla al revés')." *Ciencia y Sociedad* 10.1 (1985): 61–69.

———. "Reflexiones sobre la identidad cultural del Caribe: El caso dominicano." *Casa de las Américas* 118 (1985): 75–79.

Doughan, David T. J. "Periodicals by, for, and about women in Britain." *Women's Studies International Forum* 10 (1987): 261–73.

Duany, Jorge. *The Puerto Rican Nation on the Move: Identities on the Island and in the United States*. Chapel Hill: University of North Carolina Press, 2002.

Escalante Gonzalbo, Fernando. *Ciudadanos imaginarios: Memorial de los afanes y desventuras de la virtud y apología del vicio triunfante en la República Mexicana—Tratado de moral pública*. Mexico City: El Colegio de México, Centro de Estudios Sociológicos, 1992.

"Escritores dominicanos." <http://www.escritores dominicanos.com/narradores.html>.

Ewen, Stuart, and Elizabeth Ewen. *Channels of Desire: Mass Images and the Shaping of American Consciousness*. New York: McGraw-Hill, 1982.

Fennema, Meindert, and Troetje Loewenthal. *La construcción de la raza y nación en la República Dominicana*. Santo Domingo: Editora Universitaria UASD, 1987.

Fernández Sosa, Miriam. "Construyendo la nación: Proyectos e ideologías en Cuba, 1899–1909." In *La nación soñada: Cuba, Puerto Rico y Filipinas ante el 98*. Actas del Congreso Internacional celebrado en Aranjuez del 24 al 28 de abril de 1995. Aranjuez: Doce Calles, 1995.

Ferrer, Ada. *Insurgent Cuba: Race, Nation, and Revolution, 1868–1898*. Chapel Hill: University of North Carolina Press, 1999.

Findlay, Eileen. "Free Love and Domesticity: Sexuality and the Shaping of Working-Class Feminism in Puerto Rico, 1900–1917." In *Identity and Struggle at the Margins of the Nation-State*, edited by Aldo Lauria-Santiago and Aviva Chomsky. Durham: Duke University Press, 1998.

Franco, Jean. *Plotting Women: Gender and Representation in Mexico*. New York: Columbia University Press, 1989.

Franco Pichardo, Franklin J. *Cultura, política e ideología*. Santo Domingo: Editora Nacional, 1974.

———. *El pensamiento dominicano, 1780–1940: Contribución a su estudio*. Santo Domingo: Editora Universitaria UASD, 2001.

———. *Santo Domingo: Cultura, política e ideología*. Santo Domingo: Sociedad Editorial Dominicana, SA, 1997.

———. *Sobre racismo y antihaitianismo (y otros ensayos)*. Santo Domingo: Impresora Vidal, 1997.

Gadsden, Gloria Y. "The Male Voice in Women's Magazines." *Gender Issues* 18 (2000): 49–58.

García Canclini, Néstor. *Imaginarios urbanos*. Buenos Aires: Editorial Universitaria de Buenos Aires, 1997.

García Muñiz, Humberto. "The South Porto Rico Sugar Company." Ph.D. diss., Columbia University, 1997.

Gellner, Ernest. *Nations and Nationalism*. Ithaca: Cornell University Press, 1983.

Gómez Alfau, Luis Emilio. *Ayer o el Santo Domingo de hace 50 años*. Ciudad Trujillo: Pol Hermanos, 1944.

González, Raymundo. *Bonó, un intelectual de los pobres*. Santo Domingo: Editora Buho, 1994.

———. "Ideología del progreso y campesinado en la República Dominicana en el siglo XIX." *Ecos* 1.2 (1993): 25–43.

———. "Peña Batlle y su concepto histórico de la nación dominicana." *Ecos* 2.3 (1994): 11–54.

González, Raymundo, et al., eds. *Política, identidad y pensamiento social en la República Dominicana (siglos XIX y XX)*. Madrid: Ediciones Doce Calles, Academia de Ciencias Dominicana, 1999.

González Echevarría, Roberto. *Myth and Archive: A Theory of Latin American Narrative*. Cambridge: Cambridge University Press, 1990.

Graham, Richard, ed. *The Idea of Race in Latin America*. Austin: University of Texas Press, 1990.

Grandin, Greg. *The Blood of Guatemala: A History of Race and Nation*. Durham: Duke University Press, 2000.

Guerra, Lillian. *Popular Expression and National Identity in Puerto Rico: The Struggle for Self, Community and Nation*. Gainesville: University Press of Florida, 1998.

Gutiérrez, Natividad. *Nationalist Myths and Ethnic Identities: Indigenous Intellectuals and the Mexican State*. Lincoln: University of Nebraska Press, 1999.

Hahner, June E. "The Nineteenth-Century Feminist Press and Women's Rights in Brazil." In *Latin American Women: Historical Perspectives*, edited by Asunción Lavrin. Westport, Conn.: Greenwood Press, 1978.

Hardoy, Jorge E., Richard M. Morse, and Richard P. Schaedel, eds. *Ensayos histórico-sociales sobre la urbanización en América Latina*. Buenos Aires: SIAP, 1968.

Hartlyn, Jonathan. *The Struggle for Democratic Politics in the Dominican Republic*. Chapel Hill: University of North Carolina Press, 1998.

Helg, Aline. *Our Rightful Share: The Afro-Cuban Struggle for Equality, 1886–1912*. Chapel Hill: University of North Carolina Press, 1995.

Herdeck, Donald E., ed. *Spanish Language Literature from the Caribbean*. Vol. 4 of *Caribbean Writers: A Bio-Bibliographical-Critical Encyclopedia*. Washington, D.C.: Three Continents Press, 1979.

Hershatter, Gail. *Dangerous Pleasures: Prostitution and Modernity in Twentieth-Century Shanghai*. Berkeley: University of California Press, 1997.

Hobsbawm, E. J. *Nations and Nationalism since 1780: Programme, Myth, Reality*. Cambridge: Cambridge University Press, 1990.

Hoetink, Harry. *The Dominican People, 1850–1900: Notes for a Historical Sociology*. Translated by Stephen K. Ault. Baltimore: Johns Hopkins University Press, 1982.

———. *Santo Domingo y el Caribe: Ensayos sobre cultura y sociedad*. Santo Domingo: Fundación Cultural Dominicana, 1994.

Howard, David. *Coloring the Nation: Race and Ethnicity in the Dominican Republic*. Oxford and Boulder: Signal Books and Lynne Rienner, 2001.

Hungría Morell, José Joaquín. "Influencia de algunos factores geográfico-históricos en la integración de la dominicanidad." *Eme Eme* 14.79 (1985): 39–47.

Imbert Brugal, Carmen. "Las mujeres en la sociedad: Marco jurídico." *Ciencia y Sociedad* 7.1 (1982): 50–60.

Inchaústegui, Arístides. *Altar de la Patria*. Edición conmemorativa con motivo de la inauguración del conjunto monumental Altar de la Patria. Santo Domingo: N.p., 1976.

Informe que el Secretario de Sanidad y Beneficencia presenta al presidente provisional de la República. Santo Domingo: Imp. de J. R. Vda García, 1923.

Inoa, Orlando. *Los árabes en Santo Domingo*. Santo Domingo: Editora Amigo del Hogar, 1991.

———. *Azúcar: Arabes, cocolos y haitianos*. Santo Domingo: Editora Cole y FLACSO, 1999.

———. *Estado y campesinos al inicio de la era de Trujillo*. Santo Domingo: Librería La Trinitaria, 1994.

Jansen, Senaida, and Cecilia Millán. *Género, trabajo y etnia en los bateyes dominicanos*. Santo Domingo: Instituto Tecnológico de Santo Domingo, Programa Estudios de la Mujer, 1991.

Jiménez, Ramón Emilio. *Savia dominicana*. Santiago: Editorial El Diario, n.d.

Jiménez Grullón, Juan I. *Sociología política dominicana, 1844–1966*. 2nd ed. Vol. 2 (1898–1924). Santo Domingo: Editora Alfa y Omega, 1978.

Johns, Michael. *The City of Mexico in the Age of Díaz*. Austin: University of Texas Press, 1997.

Joseph, Gilbert M., and Mark D. Szuchman, eds. *I Saw a City Invincible: Urban Portraits of Latin America*. Wilmington, Del.: SR Books, 1996.

Kerber, Linda K. *Women of the Republic: Intellect and Ideology in Revolutionary America*. New York: W. W. Norton, 1986.

Kessler-Harris, Alice. *In Pursuit of Equity: Women, Men, and the Quest for Economic Citizenship in Twentieth Century America*. New York: Oxford University Press, 2001.

Knight, Alan. "Racism, Revolution, and *Indigenismo*." In *The Idea of Race in Latin America*, edited by Richard Graham. Austin: University of Texas Press, 1990.

Kramer, Lloyd. "Historical Narratives and the Meaning of Nationalism." *Journal of the History of Ideas* 58 (1997): 525–45.

———. *Nationalism: Political Cultures in Europe and America, 1775–1865*. New York: Twayne, 1998.

Lesser, Jeffrey. *Welcoming the Undesirables: Brazil and the Jewish Question*. Berkeley: University of California Press, 1995.

Lizardi Pollock, Jorge L. "Disciplina popular y orden espacial: Una aproximación teórica." *Historia y Sociedad* 11 (1999): 114–38.

———. "Espacio, memoria y ciudadanías: La arquitectura y la representación de las identidades nacionales en la Ciudad de México, 1863–1910." Ph.D. diss., University of Puerto Rico, 2002.

Lozano, Wilfredo. *La dominación imperialista en la República Dominicana, 1900–1930: Estudio de la primera ocupación norteamericana de Santo Domingo*. Santo Domingo: Editora de la Universidad Autónoma de Santo Domingo, 1976.

Mallon, Florencia E. *Peasant and Nation: The Making of Postcolonial Mexico and Peru*. Los Angeles: University of California Press, 1995.

———. "The Promise and Dilemma of Subaltern Studies: Perspectives from Latin American History." *American Historical Review* 99.5 (1994): 1491–1515.

Marrero Aristy, Ramón. *La República Dominicana: Origen y destino del pueblo cristiano más antiguo de América*. Ciudad Trujillo: Editora del Caribe, [1956?].

Marte, Roberto. *Estadísticas y documentos históricos sobre Santo Domingo: 1805–1890*. N.p., n.d.

Martínez Echazábal, Lourdes. "Mestizaje and the Discourse of National / Cultural Identity in Latin America, 1845–1959." *Latin American Perspectives* 25.3 (1998): 21–42.

Martínez-Vergne, Teresita. *Shaping the Discourse on Space: Charity and Its Wards in Nineteenth-Century San Juan, Puerto Rico*. Austin: University of Texas Press, 1999.

Masiello, Francine. "Gender, Dress, and Market: The Commerce of Citizenship in Latin America." In *Sex and Sexuality in Latin America*, edited by Donna J. Guy and Daniel Balderston. New York: New York University Press, 1997.

———. "Women, State, and Family in Latin American Literature of the 1920s." In *Women, Culture, and Politics in Latin America: Seminar on Feminism and Culture in Latin America*, edited by Emilie Bergmann, Janet Greenberg, Gwen Kirkpatrick, Francine Masiello, Francesca Miller, Marta Morello-Frosch, Kathleen Newman, and Mary Louise Pratt. Berkeley: University of California Press, 1990.

Mateo, Andrés L. *Mito y cultura en la era de Trujillo*. Santo Domingo: Librería La Trinitaria e Instituto del Libro, 1993.

McCrone, David. *The Sociology of Nationalism: Tomorrow's Ancestors*. New York: Routledge, 1998.

Meade, Teresa A. *"Civilizing" Rio: Reform and Resistance in a Brazilian City, 1889–1930*. University Park: Pennsylvania State University Press, 1997.

Mejía, Luis F. *De Lilís a Trujillo: Historia contemporánea de la República Dominicana*. Santo Domingo: Editora de Santo Domingo, Sociedad Dominicana de Bibliófilos, 1993.

Mendelson, Johanna. "The Feminine Press: The View of Women in the Colonial Journals of Spanish America, 1790–1810." In *Latin American Women: Historical Perspectives*, edited by Asunción Lavrin. Westport, Conn.: Greenwood Press, 1978.

Miller, Nicola. *In the Shadow of the State: Intellectuals and the Quest for National Identity in Twentieth-Century Spanish America*. London: Verso, 1999.

Minault, Gail. "Urdu Women's Magazines in the Early Twentieth Century." *Manushi* 48 (1988): 2–9.

Moghadam, Valentine M. "Introduction: Women and Identity Politics in Theoretical and Comparative Perspective." In *Identity Politics and Women: Cultural Reassertions and Feminisms in International Perspective*, edited by Moghadam. Boulder: Westview Press, 1994.

Molyneux, Maxine. "Twentieth-Century State Formations in Latin America." In *Hidden Histories of Gender and the State in Latin America*, edited by Elizabeth Dore and Maxine Molyneux. Durham: Duke University Press, 2000.

Moraña, Mabel. "Ilustración y delirio en la construcción nacional, o las fronteras de *La Ciudad Letrada*." *Latin American Literary Review* 25.50 (1997): 31–45.

Morse, Richard M., and Jorge E. Hardoy, eds. *Rethinking the Latin American City*. Baltimore: Johns Hopkins University Press, 1992.

Moscoso Puello, F. E. *Navarijo*. Ciudad Trujillo: Editora Montalvo, 1956.

Mota Acosta, Julio César. *Los cocolos en Santo Domingo: Carta anti-prólogo de Pedro Mir*. Santo Domingo: Editorial La Gaviota, 1977.

Moya Pons, Frank. "Dominican Republic." In *Latin American Urbanization: Historical Profiles of Major Cities*, edited by Gerald Michael Greenfield. Westport, Conn.: Greenwood Press, 1994.

———. *Manual de historia dominicana*. 9th ed. Santo Domingo: Caribbean Publishers, 1992.

———. "Modernización y cambios en la República Dominicana." In *Ensayos sobre cultura dominicana*, edited by Bernardo Vega, Carlos Dobal, Carlos Esteban Deive, Ruben Silié, José del Castillo, and Frank Moya Pons. 4th ed. Santo Domingo: Fundación Cultural Dominicana, Museo del Hombre Dominicano, 1996.

———. *El pasado dominicano*. Santo Domingo: Fundación J. A. Caro Alvarez, 1986.

Muñoz, María Elena. *Las relaciones domínico-haitianas: Geopolítica y migración*. Santo Domingo: Editora Alfa y Omega, 1995.

Nakano Glenn, Evelyn. *Unequal Freedom: How Race and Gender Shaped American Citizenship and Labor*. Cambridge: Harvard University Press, 2002.

Núñez, Manuel. *El ocaso de la nación dominicana*. Santo Domingo: Editora Alfa y Omega, 1990.

Oviedo, José. "Cultura y nación: La búsqueda de la identidad." *Ciencia y Sociedad* 10.1 (1985): 33–44.

Parker, Andrew, Mary Russo, Doris Sommer, and Patricia Yaeger, eds. *Nationalisms and Sexualities*. London: Routledge, 1992.

Peguero, Valentina. "Participación de la mujer en la historia dominicana." *Eme Eme* 10.58 (1982): 21–49.

Peguero, Valentina, and Danilo de los Santos. *Visión general de la historia dominicana*. Stevens Point, Wisc.: William T. Lawlor Publications, 1989.

Peña, Myrna de. *Desde la zona colonial: La perpetua novedad de su pasado*. Santo Domingo: Banco Central de la República Dominicana, 1996.

Peña Batlle, Manuel Arturo. *Constitución política y reformas constitucionales, 1844–1942.* 3rd ed. 2 vols. Santo Domingo: Publicaciones ONAP, 1995.

Peralta, Freddy. "La sociedad dominicana vista por Pedro Francisco Bonó." *Eme Eme* 5.29 (1977): 13–54.

Pérez, Louis A., Jr. *On Becoming Cuban: Identity, Nationality, and Culture.* New York: Ecco Press, HarperCollins, 1999.

Pineo, Ronn, and James A. Baer, eds. *Cities of Hope: People, Protests, and Progress in Urbanizing Latin America, 1870–1930.* Boulder, Colo.: Westview Press, 1998.

"Presidencia de la República Dominicana." <http://www.presidencia.gov.do/ingles/juridica/constituciondominicana.htm>.

Putnam, Lara. *The Company They Kept: Migrants and the Politics of Gender in Caribbean Costa Rica, 1870–1960.* Chapel Hill: University of North Carolina Press, 2002.

Radcliffe, Sarah, and Sallie Westwood. *Remaking the Nation: Place, Identity and Politics in Latin America.* London: Routledge, 1996.

Rama, Angel. *The Lettered City.* Translated by John Charles Chasteen. Durham: Duke University Press, 1996.

Ramón, Armando de. "Suburbios y arrabales en un área metropolitana: El caso de Santiago de Chile, 1872–1932." In *Ensayos histórico-sociales sobre la urbanización en América Latina,* edited by Jorge E. Hardoy, Richard M. Morse, and Richard P. Schaedel. Buenos Aires: SIAP, 1968.

Ramos, Julio. *Divergent Modernities: Culture and Politics in Nineteenth-Century Latin America.* Durham: Duke University Press, 2001.

Reddock, Rhoda E. *Women, Labor, and Politics in Trinidad and Tobago: A History.* Kingston: Ian Randle, 1994.

Rodgers, Daniel T. *Atlantic Crossings: Social Politics in a Progressive Age.* Cambridge: The Belknap Press of Harvard University Press, 1998.

Rodríguez, Ileana, ed. *The Latin American Subaltern Studies Reader.* Durham: Duke University Press, 2001.

Romero, José Luis. *Latinoamérica: Las ciudades y las ideas.* Mexico City: Siglo Veintiuno, 1976.

Rosemblatt, Karin Alejandra. "Charity, Rights, and Entitlement: Gender, Labor, and Welfare in Early-Twentieth-Century Chile." *Hispanic American Historical Review* 81.3–4 (2001): 555–86.

Sáez, S.J., José Luis. *Apuntes para la historia de la cultura dominicana.* Santo Domingo: Centro Juan Montalvo, S.J., 1997.

Safa, Helen I. "Introduction." *Latin American Perspectives* 25.3 (1998): 3–15.

Sagás, Ernesto. "El anti-haitianismo en la República Dominicana: Pasado y presente de una ideología dominante." In *Los problemas raciales en la República Dominicana y el Caribe: Seminario celebrado durante los días 30 y 31 de mayo de 1997 por la Comisión Municipal para la Conmemoración del V Centenario de la Ciudad de Santo Domingo.* Comisión Municipal para la Conmemoración del V Centenario de la Fundación de la Ciudad de Santo Domingo. Santo Domingo: Ayuntamiento del Distrito Nacional, 1998.

———. *Race and Politics in the Dominican Republic.* Gainesville: University Press of Florida, 2000.

San Miguel, Pedro. "La ciudadanía de Calibán: Poder y discursiva campesinista en la República Dominicana durante la era de Trujillo." *Revista Mexicana del Caribe* 4.8 (1999): 6–30.

———. "Discurso racial e identidad nacional en la República Dominicana." *Op. Cit.* 7 (1992): 69–120.

———. "Intelectuales, sociedad y poder en las Antillas hispanohablantes." *Revista Mexicana del Caribe* 6.11 (2001): 243–59.

———. *La isla imaginada: Historia, identidad y utopía en La Española.* San Juan and Santo Domingo: Editorial Isla Negra and Ediciones La Trinitaria, 1997.

———. *El pasado relegado.* Santo Domingo: La Trinitaria, 1999.

Seminar on Women and Culture in Latin America. "Toward a History of Women's Periodicals in Latin America: Introduction." In *Women, Culture, and Politics in Latin America,* edited by Emilie Bergmann, Janet Greenberg, Gwen Kirkpatrick, Francine Masiello, Francesca Miller, Marta Morello-Frosch, Kathleen Newman, Mary Louise Pratt. Berkeley: University of California Press, 1990.

Smith, Carol A. "Race/Class/Gender Ideology in Guatemala: Modern and Anti-Modern Forms." In *Women Out of Place: The Gender of Agency and the Race of Nationality,* edited by Brackette F. Williams. New York: Routledge, 1996.

———. "The Symbolics of Blood: Mestizaje in the Americas." *Identities* 3.4 (1997): 495–521.

Sommer, Doris. "Foundational Fictions: When History Was Romance in Latin America." *Salmagundi/Saratoga Springs* 82–83 (1989): 111–41.

———. *One Master for Another: Populism as Patriarchal Rhetoric in Dominican Novels.* New York: University Press of America, 1983.

Spivak, Gayatri Chakravorty. "Subaltern Studies: Deconstructing Historiography." In *Writings in South Asian History and Society: Subaltern Studies IV,* edited by Ranajit Guha. Delhi: Oxford University Press, 1985.

Stasiulis, Daiva, and Nira Yuval-Davis. "Introduction: Beyond Dichotomies—Gender, Race, Ethnicity and Class in Settler Colonies." In *Unsettling Settler Societies: Articulations of Gender, Race, Ethnicity and Class,* edited by Stasiulis and Yuval-Davis. Sage Series on Race and Ethnic Relations, no. 11. London: Sage Publications, 1995.

Stepan, Nancy Leys. *The Hour of Eugenics.* Ithaca: Cornell University Press, 1991.

Stoler, Ann. *Sexual Affronts and Racial Frontiers in Tensions of Empire.* Los Angeles: University of California Press, 1997.

Tellerías, Jesús. "Algunos aspectos teóricos-metodológicos del problema de la identidad cultural a propósito de la dominicanidad." *Eme Eme* 14.79 (1985): 105–19.

Thurner, Mark. *From Two Republics to One Divided: Contradictions of Postcolonial Nationmaking in Andean Peru.* Durham: Duke University Press, 1997.

Tinkler, Penny. *Constructing Girlhood: Popular Magazines for Girls Growing Up in England, 1920–1950.* London: Taylor and Francis, 1995.

Tolentino Dipp, Hugo. "La raza y la cultura en la idea de lo nacional de Américo Lugo." *¡Ahora!* 239 (10 June 1968): 22–23, 64–66.

Torres Saillant, Silvio. "The Tribulations of Blackness: Stages in Dominican Racial Identity." *Latin American Perspectives* 25.3 (1998): 126–47.

Troncoso Sánchez, Pedro. *Evolución de la idea nacional.* Santo Domingo: Museo del Hombre Dominicano, 1974.

Trotman, David Vincent. *Crime in Trinidad: Conflict and Control in a Plantation Society, 1838–1900.* Knoxville: University of Tennessee Press, 1986.

Turits, Richard Lee. *Foundations of Despotism: Peasants, the Trujillo Regime, and Modernity in Dominican History.* Stanford: Stanford University Press, 2003.

Veeser, Cyrus. *A World Safe for Capitalism: Dollar Diplomacy and America's Rise to Global Power.* New York: Columbia University Press, 2002.

Vega, Bernardo. *Los primeros turistas en Santo Domingo.* Selección, prólogo y notas de Bernardo Vega. Santo Domingo: Fundación Cultura Dominicana, 1991.

Veloz, Francisco M. *La Misericordia y sus contornos (1894–1916).* Santo Domingo: Editora Arte y Cine, 1967.

Veras, Ramón Antonio. *Inmigración, haitianos, esclavitud.* Santo Domingo: Ediciones de Taller, 1983.

Wade, Peter. *Race and Ethnicity in Latin America.* London: Pluto Press, 1997.

Williams, Brackette F. "Introduction: Mannish Women and Gender after the Act." In *Women Out of Place: The Gender of Agency and the Race of Nationality,* edited by Williams. New York: Routledge, 1996.

Zaiter, Josefina. "La identidad como fenómeno psico-social." *Ciencia y Sociedad* 12.4 (1987): 488–99.

Zuckerman, Mary Ellen. *A History of Popular Women's Magazines in the United States, 1792–1995.* Westport, Conn.: Greenwood Press, 1998.

INDEX

British West Indies. *See* West Indies

Brito, Feliz, 158

Brito, Gregorio, 143

Bryan, Patrick, 89

Businesses, 32, 70, 135, 141; cart driving, 143–44; cemetery work, 142, 143; classification of, 137, 143; protecting their interests, 143–44

Cabelón, Matías, 164

Cabral, Agustina, 161

Cáceres, Ramón, 5, 11, 46, 47, 91, 128

Cadena, Marisol de la, 103, 131

Calder, Bruce, 42

Camarena, Sirbano, 152

Cambiaso, Rodolfo Domingo, 15–16

Cambiaso vda. de Sturla, Luisa, 160

Canary Islands, 84, 85

"Cartas a Evelina" (Letters to Evelina) (Moscoso Puello), 5

Cassá, Roberto, 11, 18, 41, 144, 177–78 (n. 10), 178 (n. 13)

Castell, Juan, 142, 143

Castillo, José del, 88

Castillo, Rafael Justino, 4, 33, 54, 92

Castro, Marcos de, 160

Catholic Church, 7, 18, 87, 118, 145

Caudillismo, 11, 179 (n. 21)

Centro Español, San Pedro de Macorís, 22

Chachas (women domestic servants), 134

Chatterjee, Partha, 106

Chile, 131, 166

Chiquet, Margarita, 66

Cholera, 68

Cibao region, and Dominicanness, xiii, 176 (n. 2), 181 (n. 43)

Ciprián, León, 158

Círculo Católico de Obreros (Catholic Circle of Workers), 145

Citizenship: defined, according to constitutions, 55–56; and education, place of in, 57; and force, as only perceived way for change, 35–36; ideals of, 56–58;

ideas of, following Heureaux administration, 13, 15–16, 33–34; of immigrants, 90–91; and modernization, 33–40; and political liberty, 39, 46; and popular enfranchisement, 46–47, 50, 55–56, 57, 58–59, 189 (n. 12); voting rights, 55–56; of women, 56, 105, 123, 125, 166; of working people, 55, 79–80, 146, 147–48, 155, 165–66; and working people's property ownership, 57, 149–55, 189 (n. 10). *See also* Nationalism; Nation-building; Political system

Civilización o muerte (civilization or death), 7

Civil service, 36

Club de Artesanos (Artisans' Club), 145

Club Unión, Santo Domingo, 71, 72–73

Cockfights, 74, 78

Cocoa production, 86

Cocolos (West Indian sugar industry workers), 9, 86–87, 88, 93; British consul defense of, 89; character traits, 89–90; prejudice against, 87

Coen, Anita, 152

Colón, Elías, 163

Colonialism: and anti-Haitianism, 98; as cause of poor character of Dominicans, 28, 29

Columbus, Christopher, 21

Communal lands (*terrenos comuneros*), 8, 30, 31, 45, 96; after U.S. invasion, 171. *See also* Private property, issue of

Concha, Arquímedes, 158

Consuelo sugar mill, 43, 63, 88

Conucos (cultivated plots), 41

Corpus Christi festival, 147–48

Costa Rica: migrant problems in, 23, 89; physical violence in, 164; and women, 159, 206 (n. 17); and working people, 156

Creas, Benito, 160

Crianza libre. See Livestock, free-range

Crime: *escándalo* (scandal/insults), 128, 155–62; fraud cases, 154; prostitution not regarded as, 138; statistics, 128; theft, reports of, 152, 154

Cuba, 5, 8, 171; fiscal management, 184 (n. 19); migrants from, 86, 90; migration from Dominican Republic to, 93; nation-building in, 19, 20; and race, 100, 102; rural archetype of, 21, 170

Cueva, Altagracia (Talinga), 156

Curaçao, 61, 86, 91

Dancing: *bailes de cueros* (drumming dances), 77, 131; and *escándalo* (scandal/insults), 156; *plenas* (African-derived dances), 77; at wakes, 130

Derby, Lauren, xiii

Deschamps, Enrique, 71, 131–33

Diablos de la Marina, 63

Díaz, Porfirio, 10

Díaz Rodríguez, Manuel, 107

Diesch, José, 163

Dilson, Ana Maria, 157

Dobal, Carlos, 17

Domínguez, Jaime de Jesús, 53

Dominicanness, 17–20, 22–23; and Cibao region, xiii, 176 (n. 2), 181 (n. 43); defined vs. Haitians, xiii–xiv, 5, 17–18, 23, 28, 95, 96–99, 174 (n. 8), 196 (n. 26); various definitions of, xiii–xvi; and women, 122–25, 201 (n. 31)

Dominican Republic: Cibao region, xiii, 176 (n. 2), 181 (n. 43); constitutions, 36, 185 (n. 27); economic base, 8–10, 30; foreign rule (1844–65), xi, 18; Haiti, American view of compared with, 27; Haiti, armed conflict with, 36, 97; Haiti, comparative development of, 99; Haiti, independence from (1844), xi, 17–18, 97; Haitian rule (1822–44), xv, 30, 94–95, 97, 99–100; Haitian takeover, fears of, 30, 96, 98; historical development of nationhood, 17–20; independence, date of, 68, 97; land surveys of, during U.S. occupation, 31; legitimate nation, fears

of not being, 26–27, 28; map (1873), 12–13; population, 52; and United States, admiration for, 24, 38, 50–51, 185 (n. 31); United States, fears of collaboration with Haiti, 30, 94, 98; and United States, overpowering influence on, xii, xiv, 1–2, 10, 12, 20, 22, 24, 27, 37, 51–52, 171, 179 (n. 19); United States, treatment of vs. Haiti, 99; United States collecting customs duties in, 5, 10, 20, 51; U.S. invasion (1916), 4, 5, 18, 94, 106, 139, 171; U.S. troops, withdrawal from, 32, 171; untenable financial situation, late nineteenth century, 9–10, 19–20. *See also* Modernization; Nationalism; Nation-building; Political system

Dominico-American convention (1907), 10, 20

Drunkenness, 156

Duarte, Juan Pablo, 17, 94–95, 124

Edison, Thomas, 111–12

Education, 2, 22; and agriculture, need for in, 44–45; as antidote to influence of United States, 37; and citizenship, 57; for girls, 3, 60, 106, 118–19; Hostos's ideas regarding system of, 7, 37–38, 57, 92, 102, 106; institutions in San Pedro, 106, 149; institutions in Santo Domingo, 60, 148; as Liberal priority, 3, 4, 7–8, 15, 23–24, 37, 57, 185 (n. 30); local government concern for, 76, 79, 148; newspaper commentary on, 149; secular nature of system, 37–38, 92; working people's involvement in, 148–49

El Seybo, Dominican Republic, 41

Employment, as key to future progress, 38–39, 46, 82–83

Encarnación, Manuela, 154

Enriquillo, Dominican Republic, 96

Enriquillo (Dominican novel), 102, 125

Escalante, Silvestre (Prieto), 164

Escándalo (scandal/insults), 128, 155–62;

Henry, Carolina, 160

Hérard, Charles, 97

Hermodisis, Gabriel, 160

Hershatter, Gail, xvii

Heureaux, Ulises (Lilís), 27, 36; concessions to foreign interests, 91, 106; connecting tyranny of with prostitution, 140; death, xi, 1, 10, 11, 19; dictatorship, 1, 4, 5; fiscal policy, 9, 36, 46, 52, 85; modernizing during administration of, xi, 1, 7, 10–11; political period following assassination of, 10–13, 15–16, 19, 33–36, 47–48, 176 (n. 4); social unrest during administration of, 128, 146

Heureaux, Ulises, Jr., 110, 116

Higüey, Dominican Republic, 41

Hijas de crianza (live-in girl servants as part of family), 134

Hoetink, Harry, 89

Hostos, Eugenio María de, 14, 21, 49; biographical sketch, 4; and education system, 7, 37–38, 57, 92, 102; and Haitian rule, 95; and immigration, 82–83; as Puerto Rican, 4, 92; and race, 100, 102; and small property holding, 42; and sugar industry, critique of, 31, 42, 45; and women's education, 106

Hungría Morell, José Joaquín, xiii

Illiteracy, 28, 57

Immigration and immigrants: citizenship, requests for, 90–91; *cocolos* (West Indian sugar industry workers), 9, 86–87, 88, 93; Cuba, migrants from, 86, 90; and *escándalo* (scandal/insults), 155–56, 158; Europeans wanted for, 15, 45–46, 83–85, 86, 101; exemptions for immigrants, 91; Haitian immigrants, 50, 82, 86, 167–68, 170; laws/decrees relating to, 84–85, 93; from Lesser Antilles, 86, 87, 89; and local government concern for, 79; in main cities, 59, 62, 66, 86, 88; *poblar es gobernar* (to populate is to govern), 45–46, 82–84; political/economic motivations for implementing, 82–87; privilege, impression of for immigrants, 91; and prostitution, 156; Puerto Rico, migrants from, 85, 86, 88, 90, 195 (n. 13); rural migrants in cities, 128–29; sentiment against, 87, 89–93; Spanish, 85, 90; statistics, 88; and sugar industry, 9, 23, 32, 40, 42, 66, 82, 84–85, 88; Swiss, 86; of "Turks" and "Arabs," 86, 90; West Indian migrants, 23, 50, 62, 66, 82, 86–87, 88, 89, 170. *See also* Race

Improvement, La. See San Domingo Improvement Company

Industrial y Comercial, La (store), 70

Ingenio Puerto Rico. *See* Puerto Rico sugar mill

Ingenio Santa Fe. *See* Santa Fe sugar mill

Inoa, Orlando, 89, 93

Instituto de Señoritas (Girls' Institute), 60, 106

Instituto de Señoritas Anacaona Moscoso, 145

Instituto Profesional, 5

Intellectual elite: backgrounds of men of, 2–6; and the city, significance of, 54–55; Club Unión, Santo Domingo, as gathering place for, 71; cultural/political crossover of, 18–19, 107, 176 (n. 7), 198 (n. 2); and dependence on government for employment, 6, 178 (n. 11); in Latin American nation-building, 2–3; as Liberals, 1, 6–8, 10–11, 18–19, 30, 31, 36, 39–40, 48–49; and national character, 18, 20–24, 25–30; and nation-building, xi, xiv, xv, 1–2, 3, 15–16, 169; and the nation's beginnings, 17–20; and peasantry, 22–23, 28, 31, 42, 54, 56, 57, 130; political aspirations of, 10–13, 36; and political liberty, 35, 39, 46–47, 48, 184 (n. 17); and progress, 13, 15–16, 51; and property ownership, 8, 11, 30, 31, 50, 149; and prostitution, 140–41; and race,

cal liberty, 47, 184 (n. 17); and race, 100, 102; subalterns, distrust of, 50

Luperón, Gregorio, 7

Maduro, Alfredo, 158

Mallon, Florencia, xii

Malnourishment, 27–28

Mambre, Isidoro, 91

Marchantas (women vendors), 135

Markets, of Santo Domingo, 68, 74, 136–37

Martí, Enemencio, 161

Martí, José, 5, 58

Masturzi, Antonio, 163

Masturzi, Daniel, 163

Medical care, 133–34, 203 (n. 11); municipal doctors, 77, 132, 134, 139–40, 203 (n. 11); and prostitution, 139–40

Medrano, Anastacia, 151

Medrano, Félix, 151

Melium, Sofia, 151

Mendes, Catulle, 107

Méndez, Wenceslao, 164

Meriño, Fernando A., 7

Mexico, 2, 103

Miller, Nicola, 3

Moca, Dominican Republic, 31

Modernization, 5–6; cities at heart of, 53–54, 55, 61, 76–77, 81; economic obstacles to, 30–33; employment, as key to, 38–39, 46, 82–83; during Heureaux administration, xi, 1, 7, 9, 10–11; and immigration, 45–46, 82–84; national character at odds with, 26; obstacles to, in Liberal view, 30–33, 49–52, 183 (n. 10); political concerns / citizenship, 33–40, 46–49; progress, ideal of, 13, 15–16, 20, 25, 37, 53; and roads / railroads, 31–32, 45. *See also* Sugar industry

Moscoso, Mercedes, 106

Moscoso Puello, Francisco, 5, 34, 100

Mota, Miguel A., 161

Moya Pons, Frank, 18

Mujer: Lo que es y lo que debe ser el feminismo: Mi modo di pensar sobre el divorcio, La (Woman: What feminism is and what it should be: My thoughts on divorce), 118

Municipal doctor. *See* Medical care

Muñoz, María Elena, 89, 93

Napoleonic Code, 123

Nathaniel, Juan, 153

Nationalism: and anti-Haitianism, 97–99, 196 (n. 26); beginnings of, 17–20; and being hardworking, 22, 82–83; and geography, based on, xiii–xiv; "love of country," 19, 22–23; and maleness, 24; national consciousness, xii–xiii, xv, 1–2; processes of, xi–xiii; and race, 15, 17, 18, 21, 23, 29, 82, 97–99, 100–104; and rural archetype, lack of, 21, 23, 170, 181 (n. 43); Spanish roots, xiii, 21–22, 24, 99, 102; and Trujillo, development of under, xiv–xv, xvi, 18, 98, 103, 175 (n. 11). *See also* Citizenship; Dominicanness; National character; Nation-building

National character: American views of, 27; in literature, 28–29; traits, 2, 5, 20–24, 82, 176 (n. 2); pessimistic view of, 18, 25–30

Nation-building: beginnings of, 17–20; debate about, after Heureaux, 13, 15–16; and elite-centered nation-state, xii, 174 (n. 4); Europe vs. Latin America, rise of nation-state, 2–3, 6, 36, 177–78 (n. 10); fears about legitimacy of Dominican Republic, 26–27, 28; intelligentsia as self-proclaimed leaders in, xi, xiv, xv, 1–2, 3, 15–16, 169; and women, roles in, 50, 105, 106, 121, 122–25, 166–67, 170; and working people, involvement in, xv–xvii, 50, 126–27, 146, 147, 166–67

New Jersey and Santo Domingo Brewing Company, 32

Newspapers: business enterprises, commentary on, 32; and education system,

West Indies: immigrants in Costa Rica, 23,
89; migrants from, 9, 50, 62, 66, 82, 86–
87, 88, 89–90, 93, 167–68, 170; sugar
industry workers (*cocolos*), 9, 86–87, 88,
93

Wilson, María, 153

Women: advertisements / advice columns
for, 116–17; bourgeois, as part of nation-
building, 50, 105, 106, 121, 122–25, 170;
and citizenship, 56, 105, 123, 125, 166; in
Costa Rica, 159, 206 (n. 17); cultural
activities, 60, 121–22, 200 (n. 27);
depicted as good wives and mothers,
105, 124; depicted as cold hearted, 112–
13; depicted as independent, 113–14;
depicted as inherently vulgar, 111–12;
depicted as instinctive, 113; depicted as
intertwined with the fatherland, 114,
124; depicted as "known quantities,"
113; depicted as needing to be tamed,
111–12; depicted as stupid, 112; depicted
as temptresses / schemers, 108–10, 115;
depicted as "transparent," 110–11;
depicted as virtuous, 107–8, 114; and
divorce, 118; education for, 3, 60, 106,
118–19; expected roles and values, 20,
27, 106–7, 113, 115–17, 119–21, 122; and
the fatherland, 114, 124; going beyond
ascribed roles, 106, 121–22, 123–24, 125,
166, 200 (n. 27); health and beauty tips
for, 116–17; legal restrictions on, 123;
marginalized, 49, 50, 105, 125, 167; and
Napoleonic Code, 123; misogynist writings on, 119–20; reflections in press on
subordination of, 117–18; representation
in newspapers, 176–77 (n. 8); of San
Pedro de Macorís, 106, 116; stories written for, 114–15, 124; symbolism of, used
for fertile land, 120–21; as teachers, 106,
123, 133; writings, about how to amelio-
rate situations of, 118–19

—working-class, 50, 106, 118; and citizenship, 166–67; as domestic workers, 133–
34; *escándalo* (scandal / insults) against
other women, 159–60; independent,
135, 137–38, 166; insulting men, 158; as
laundresses, 133–35, 136, 141, 166, 167;
as *marchantas* (vendors), 135; and men,
demanding respect from, 162; obscene
language, use of, 156, 159, 206 (n. 17);
occupations, 133–38; and partnering
arrangements, disputes about, 160–62;
physical violence against men, 164–65;
physical violence against women, 165;
prostitutes, 125, 127, 138–41, 156; and
race, 166, 167–68; and respect, demanding from men, 157–58, 159; as shop-
owners, 137–38; violence against, by
men, 164

Working people, 49; businesses, 135, 137–
38, 141, 142–44; and citizenship, 55, 79–
80, 146, 147–48, 155, 165–66; class
awareness, 143–44; common infractions, 129, 130; cultural life, 60, 61, 62–
63, 77, 132–33; and debt repayments,
153–54; *escándalo* (scandal / insults) of,
128, 155–62; *gremios* (guilds), 143, 144–
45; and intelligentsia, xi, 50, 126–27,
131–33, 146, 147, 155, 165–66; literacy,
affecting land ownership, 57, 189 (n. 10);
livestock keeping, 30, 54, 60, 68, 74–75,
79, 129; and local government attempts
to control, 63, 79–81, 128–29; men as
business operators, 135, 137; migrants
from Haiti and West Indies, 18, 20–21,
23, 50, 93, 95–96, 167–68, 170; and
nation-building, involvement in, xv–
xvii, 50, 126–27, 146, 147, 166–67; newspaper commentary on, 127, 130–31,
145–46; occupations, 65, 132, 133–38,
141; organizations to improve conditions
of, 144–46; and partnering arrangements, disputes about, 160–62; physical
violence by, cases brought to court, 162–
65; and political actions, 147–48, 155;
poverty, 130–31; and property, owner-

ship of, 57, 149–55, 189 (n. 10); and property after death, 151–52, 153; protecting their interests, 143–45, 170–71; and race, 128–29, 165–68, 202 (n. 4); as renters, 150–51; and respect, 155–62, 206 (n. 12); showing rural background in behavior, 128–30; and theft, reports of, 152, 154; and urban living conditions, 63, 65, 80; and "virility" of "industrial" work, 131; "vulgar" habits of, 131–33;

wages, 131, 132, 141, 142–43; wakes, 130; in the workplace, 141–46. *See also* San Pedro de Macorís; Santo Domingo; Sugar industry; Women, working-class

Woss y Gil, Alejandro, 7, 11

Yepes, Simona, 152

Zayas, Armando, 163